PRAISE FOR
Social LEADia

"On average, every 60 seconds, 452,000 tweets are sent, 4.1 million YouTube videos are viewed, 70,017 hours of Netflix are watched, 1.8 million Snaps are created, and 46,200 Instagram posts are uploaded, with numbers continuing to accelerate. How are we preparing today's students to not simply survive and be safe, but to lead and thrive in a globally connected society? Casa-Todd does a masterful job addressing the 'Yeah, buts ... ,' while moving the social media conversation from compliance to leadership. *Social LEADia* is a brilliant read and a needed tool for your educator toolkit."

—*Thomas C. Murray, director of innovation, Future Ready Schools*

"In her new book, Jennifer Casa-Todd explores the concept of digital leadership and its place in today's schools and classrooms. Written in an engaging style and rich with real-world examples, Casa-Todd takes us beyond simplistic, outdated, and ineffective narratives around kids' relationships with technology in order to paint a rich portrait of the world we live in and what that means for our children's futures. Using stories from her own practice, Casa-Todd helps us to make the leap from digital citizenship to digital leadership and provides plenty of concrete ideas and tips that we can bring into the classroom in order to help students become engaged and inspiring leaders who will drive change in both the face-to-face and digital worlds."

—*Dr. Alec Couros, professor of educational technology and media,*
Faculty of Education, University of Regina

"*Social LEADia* brings inspiration and a call to action to educators teaching today in the digital age. Through the lens of digital leadership, Jennifer offers direction and positive encouragement for educators seeking ways to support students at all levels to become connected in their roles as digital citizens of the world. Teachers can fill their toolboxes with ready-to-implement ideas offered through student vignettes, scripts for guided conversations, case studies, project examples, and detailed listings of tech tools. Written with intention, purpose, and a passion for championing teachers and students to find, share, and amplify their voices, this is a must-read book for every educator ready to make our world a better place through the sharing of stories and perspectives from our connected classrooms. Bravo!"

—Dr. Jennifer Williams, professor, global program developer,
and connected educator

"Jennifer Casa-Todd makes an impassioned and compelling case for the use of social media in education. *Social LEADia* beautifully juxtaposes students' voices with Jennifer's experienced educator's lens. This should be required reading for all teachers, especially those who want to support their students in creating positive digital footprints."

—Janette Hughes, PhD, Canada research chair, technology and
pedagogy, Faculty of Education,
University of Ontario Institute of Technology

"Jennifer beautifully captures the power of student voice by having students share their stories as connected learners. *Social LEADia* provides readers an inside perspective of students leading this conversation and changing the narrative in regards to what we need to encourage in all classrooms and schools. The focus on the positive highlights the endless possibilities when student voice is amplified."

—Dr. Marialice B.F.X. Curran, founder of Digital Citizenship Institute and
co-founder, Digital Citizenship Summit

"*Social LEADia* connects the dots between the theory of technology/social media and real-life practice. Jennifer Casa-Todd gives real life examples of how to harness the immense power of the digital age to enhance the education of students. I highly recommend this book to anyone who is connected to education."

—Justin Schleider, physical education and health teacher, and
technology integrationist

"The world today that students and kids are growing up in is filled with near ubiquitous access to information. As we've seen, this information, while mostly helpful, can be difficult to navigate without help and the understanding of how to effectively distill the best. Being naturally social, students are receiving much of this information through social media. Jennifer has written an essential handbook for educators to not only help them best position social media in their classrooms but to also guide students as they learn as well. Any educator would benefit from taking her advice and creating an environment where students can think critically but flourish as well. A must-read!"

—Steven Anderson, educational evangelist, speaker, and consultant

"*Social LEADia* is a must-read for any educational leaders in any role, be it district personnel, administrators, teachers, and perhaps students themselves. Our role as educators is to guide and help our learners maximize their potential to impact change. Jennifer Casa-Todd does an excellent job of detailing how we can help them lead by leveraging the power of social media."

—Sarah Thomas, regional technology coordinator and
Edumatch founder

"In an effort to protect students and keep them safe, we often block social media in schools. *Social LEADia* is a must-read for all educators that will change your perspective on the power of social media to empower learners to connect with others, pursue passions, and even change the world. As a mom and an educator, I am so thankful for this book to push my thinking about why we must leverage social media in schools and create an experience that supports kids to become the digital leaders that our world needs them to be."

—Katie Martin, PhD, director of professional learning,
University of San Diego

"In *Social LEADia*, Jennifer Casa-Todd takes a deeper look at both human nature and the nature of technology. The book not only explores how educators can best use digital tools, but why it is critically important today's students learn the power and potential of these tools in order to become both digital and global citizens. *Social LEADia* is a fantastic book for anyone: every educator and anyone curious about the future of social media, digital citizenship, or the intersection of technology and humanity."

—Matt Murrie, founder and chief curiosity curator, What If...?360

Jennifer Casa-Todd

Social LEADia

Moving Students from Digital Citizenship to Digital Leadership

Social LEADia
© 2017 by Jennifer Casa-Todd

This book is available at special discounts when purchased in quantity for use as premiums, promotions, fundraisers, or for educational use. For inquiries and details, contact the publisher at books@daveburgessconsulting.com.

Published by Dave Burgess Consulting, Inc.
San Diego, CA
http://daveburgessconsulting.com

Cover Design by Genesis Kohler
Editing and Interior Design by My Writers' Connection
Chat bubbles created by lbrandify by Freepik
Social media icons, Freepik.com

Library of Congress Control Number: 2017940102
Paperback ISBN: 978-1-946444-11-0
Ebook ISBN: 978-1-946444-12-7

First Printing: June 2017

CONTENTS

Foreword
by George Couros

I will never forget leading a workshop for educators that a significant number of students also attended. We were discussing the ideas of digital citizenship and digital leadership, and one of the adults expressed that these are not things we need to talk about in school. No matter what I said, he countered that social media isn't important in schools. Then one of the students in the room stepped in and said, "Sir, social media is like water. It is everywhere. You can either let us drown or teach us to swim." Not only did his words move me, but the teacher immediately redirected his focus to get into the conversation, not stop it. This was a beautiful reminder that we need to stop telling our students they are the "leaders of tomorrow," when they can obviously change the world today.

I was reminded of this student's words while speaking at a digital leadership event for approximately 2,000 high schoolers. At the beginning of the event, I encouraged them to share any ideas, thoughts, or questions they had during my talk using a specific hashtag or by tweeting me.

Usually, when I do this, I show videos during my presentations, which allows me to check the hashtag and gauge what the audience is feeling and thinking. What I noticed this time, though, was that one tweet expressed how "boring" the talk was, using an expletive in front of the word "boring" that started with the letter "F." Feeling a little squeamish, I went on, showed another video, and then noticed two more tweets that were much worse, this time attacking me directly. As one of the biggest advocates of the power of social media for helping people make a positive change in the world, I have to be honest; at that moment, I thought: *I need to shut this down.*

Then, while I was presenting, I caught myself and thought, "Am I really going to shut this down because of three students out of two thousand? Am I going to let them drown or help them learn to swim?" I had to redirect. Without directly acknowledging the inappropriate comments, and in the context of the talk, I said:

> *Every single one of you in this room can have a major impact on the lives of others, including me. Do you know how I can tell if you've made an impact on me? If I saw you outside of this school, would I cross the street to come talk to you? If I would, you have made an impact on me, and I hope that I can be the person whom you would go out of your way to talk to as well. Let's be that for each other.*

Showing another video, I checked the tweets again. This time, I saw a student say, "I like the way you present your message. It's really entertaining and informative." I immediately stopped everything and asked for the student to stand up, which he did. With a tear in my eye, I said, "You have no idea the impact you just had on me. Thank you." I will never forget that moment, as the other students cheered for him as well. What followed, though, was incredible, because his impact was not only on me, but his peers, too: They started bombarding the hashtag with positive messages to me about what and how I was presenting. They were literally finding anything nice they could think of to say to me—one student even said, "I love your sweater!"

After the presentation, I was overwhelmed by the positivity that they'd shared toward me. Going through the tweets, the first three that I mentioned were "buried" at the bottom of the pile. So much so, in fact, that the teachers from the school had no idea they'd actually happened until I brought them to their attention; they had only seen the compliments. That group of students taught me something that day that I will never forget: *We need to make the positives so loud that the negatives are almost impossible to hear.*

And to think I was so close to shutting down that opportunity for the majority because of a very tiny few. *Do we do this too often in schools?*

This is why I am so happy Jennifer Casa-Todd has written this book. Her perspective as a leader, educator, and parent brings these ideas together in a way that will not only provide answers, but have you asking questions as well. This is extremely important because adults need to be in on these conversations.

Think of all the stuff that we got away with when we were kids that could totally alter a life today. We all made mistakes growing up (and still do), but our kids don't have the same luxury. Many of you didn't post anything inappropriate on Facebook when you were a teenager—not because you thought so deeply about your future, but because Facebook didn't exist (although you might have posted something on a MySpace page). When I talk about this with students, many of them say it's unfair that they're held to a different standard than we were as kids. I tell them, "You are right, it is unfair. But you also have more opportunity than I ever did at your age. What will you do with it?"

In this book, Jennifer shares not only an adult's perspective on how to lead toward a positive narrative, but she also shares powerful examples of young people already doing this, and rather than speak for them, she lets us hear from those students directly. What's more, some of the stories she shares about the transformative power of social media are because of teachers—and some are in spite of them. I know I, personally, would love to be the reason our students make positive choices in these spaces.

Yes, we must be aware of the negative aspects of social media, but we must also take advantage of the positives. As Jennifer will show you, if we are purposeful in how we look at the world and the opportunities that exist, the positives can become the norm for students. For example, when you look at a device in a child's hand, do you see distraction or do you see opportunity? Your answer will determine how you lead.

I am 100 percent confident that Jennifer will push your thinking and guide you in embracing the realities that exist in our world today. This book might make you feel uncomfortable at some points, but dealing with the *messiness* of learning is what helps us grow.

Knowing Jennifer personally, I can assure you she is just as passionate about changing the current perception of social media in education as I am. As parents and educators, we all want the same thing for our kids: something better for them than what we had at their age. Jennifer has written a book with a theme that is far more powerful than "social media is here to stay, so we might as well pay attention." Her words reveal that the opportunities for our children today are better than ever, and she walks you through how to make this a reality in your school.

Introduction

When I first heard veteran teacher and technology administrator Will Richardson say, "I want my children to be found on the Internet by strangers," repeat his statement, and then let it hang ominously in the air, I couldn't help but wonder of its implications.

My "teacher sensors" were tingling. What role could social media play in school—for students? Even though I'd been preaching the benefits of being a connected educator, as a parent, I shifted uncomfortably in my seat. And if I was uncomfortable, how would any teacher be able to effectively communicate a digitally connected reality with parents and educators, who have formed strong opinions about the negative effects of social media?

My own perspective on social media shifted significantly that summer, when my eldest daughter, then fifteen, was asked during a job interview, "What social media networks are you on, and what will I learn about you if I go there?" (I know she was asked this because the interview was via Skype and I was in the other room.) Although I should have expected the question, neither one of us was prepared for it. In retrospect, I'm not sure why. From what I remember, her answer was noncommittal, and, truthfully, I'm pretty sure I stopped listening because that's when I had my *aha* moment.

I realized then that it was partly my fault she didn't have more to say. When she was quite young, she'd asked me if she could have a YouTube channel so she could post her stop-motion animation videos. As a supportive, albeit protective, mom, I said, "Of course—but only if your name isn't on it and you don't record your face." So she created a channel, and it now has more than 80,000 views, but she didn't think to include the channel in her answer because she didn't feel connected to it. A few years later, when we vacationed in Boston, she asked if she could create a travel vlog. I told her I didn't feel comfortable having her face or name online, so she chose not to create one. My younger daughter never even bothered to ask.

I know it sounds like I am an overbearing and overprotective mom, but in reality, I have always supported my kids' passions and dreams, except when it comes to sharing on social media. That's because when I think of social media as a parent, I can't help but be reminded of the terrible stories on the news about sexual predators and cyberbullying. As a result, I have spent a considerable amount of time and energy ensuring my daughters have a neutral to nonexistent digital presence—so much so that I have actually extinguished my eldest daughter's passion, never helping her discover the online world's potential.

So what does this have to do with education?

Although most school districts have really begun incorporating technology into their schools' teaching and learning, few are truly embracing social media and technology to the fullest.

George Couros, a mentor and friend of mine, is the strongest voice I've heard challenging the conventional wisdom regarding social media's role in education. Couros defines digital leadership as "using the vast reach of technology—especially social media—to improve the lives, well-being, and circumstances of others." When I first heard him express this idea, I was wearing my parent hat; to say that this idea resonated with me and the experiences I'd had with my daughter would be an understatement. We need to explore the power and potential of social media in school. Of this, I am certain. Yet at the same time, questions about how to use technology to improve others' lives, well-being, and circumstances—especially as it relates to students—keep me up at night:

- How do we change our position on social media use in school when there seem to be so many barriers to its use?

- What opportunities exist for using social media? How can we provide the appropriate level of guidance? And at what point do we let students navigate these spaces independently?

- What kinds of conversations should we be having about how social media can influence a child's positive online presence? At the district level? At the school level? With parents?

- Is there a new moral imperative to include social media in curriculum, lesson design, and professional learning?

- Is teaching "digital citizenship" even possible without using social media spaces, and should we, at this point, move beyond digital citizenship?

These questions, along with my quest to find their answers, drive me to continue learning and growing. I approach each of the intricacies of this topic from the perspective of a parent, teacher, scholar, and former district leader. I don't have all of the answers; in fact, some days I have more questions than answers. I also realize that for every person who wholeheartedly agrees with what I put forward here, there will be one who disagrees, but I'm okay with that. I think we need to shift our thinking in education—now. So if this book does nothing except start courageous conversations in schools and districts, then I've achieved my goal.

As I watched the 2016 United States presidential election unfold across social media, complete with fake news stories and controversies, I realized just how important it is to embrace digital leadership. So many adults struggled to express their opinions, contradict opinions, and have civilized discourse. Students watched this play out, and some of the older ones even engaged. And it got a little ugly.

At the same time, though, I also discovered something amazing: We have students who are positive and inspiring and remarkable, and these students are leading the way as to how we could and should behave online.

While I would never call myself an "expert" (is anyone ever really an expert, when every day brings new things to learn?), I have talked to numerous educators and students about social media's role in the classroom. I have done much research, written extensively on the topic, and presented my ideas to different audiences, both nationally and internationally. While writing this book, I had the humbling (and inspiring) experience of serving as a panelist at the DigCit Summit in San Francisco, organized and founded by Marialice Curran, PhD, and David Ryan Polgar. I sat in a room filled with educators, policymakers, psychologists, and app developers, as well as students working toward making a change for the positive in social media. In fact, the hashtag for the event was #BeTheDigitalChange. That experience demonstrated to me that, though many of us are moving in the same direction, we still have much work to do. If we are going to challenge the status quo and truly shift from the current fearful, negative narrative surrounding social media and empower students to create a new norm, we need to talk about technology and social media's changing role in district meetings, at policy tables, in staff rooms, and in classrooms.

This book outlines the characteristics of student digital leadership and highlights the amazing students exhibiting these characteristics, and supports educators with examples, strategies, and ideas. It is my hope that, through the implementation of these strategies and ideas, we can create opportunities for digital leadership to complement our existing digital citizenship practices. Rather than providing comprehensive solutions to the issues typically associated with using technology and social media, this book provides an alternative narrative that focuses more on the positive effects that can result from connecting digitally with experts, organizations, and other classrooms.

More importantly, through the student vignettes for each chapter, I am honored to share the voices of seldom-heard students on this topic. Their voices are strong and powerful, their experiences valuable and different from ours. They can teach us. We just need to listen.

Addressing a Few Assumptions

Student digital leadership—using technology and social media to learn and share learning, to promote important causes, and to positively influence others—is anchored in the idea that we can use technology, and especially social media, in the classroom for positive and meaningful learning experiences.

George said this best in a January 2013 blog post titled "Digital Leadership Defined":[1]

> *We really need to push our students to make a change in their world and highlight how social media can give them an opportunity that we never were given as students. Just being "citizens" online is the average; kids already exist online. We should be pushing for much more than this.*

As we dive into the topic, I'll share more about the characteristics of student digital leadership, but before you continue reading, I ask that you stop and check your own biases while I share how I believe using technology and social media can empower our students and teaching practices.

Let's unpack a few assumptions:

'Social media is bad.'

"We can complain because rose bushes have thorns, or rejoice because thorn bushes have roses." This quote, attributed to Alphonse Karr, is the metaphor I sometimes use for social media. Roses are beautiful flowers; the thorns make me mindful to handle them carefully, but they bring me great joy and I continue to buy them for myself and others. Any social media tool can be used to lift someone up or tear them down—it isn't the tool, but the tool's user, that makes the difference. Are we with our students in online spaces, showing them how to interact positively? Are we teaching students how to show empathy and respect and forgiveness both face to face and digitally? We need to be models of positive social media if we want to dispel this assumption. At the end of the day, though, we as humans are often fearful of what we don't understand. In fact, every generation, when faced with technological change at a rapid pace, has experienced the same unease. Plato believed men were doomed because they would no longer remember anything, thanks to writing being introduced to the common people. And in the 1880s, when the telephone was just making its way into households, an article characterized it as the "greatest menace" to society.[2]

In *It's Complicated*, author danah boyd says social media is a collection of "sites and services that emerged during the early 2000s, including social network sites, video-sharing sites, blogging and microblogging platforms, and related tools that allow participants to *create* and *share* their own content."[3] There is nothing negative about this.

Now, this isn't to say students will never encounter negative or uncomfortable situations while using, creating, and sharing content via social media. However, it's better for these encounters to take place in the context of the classroom, so we can help our students deal with them, rather than flounder when they are on their own. Through examples and ideas, I'll show you what to be aware of and mindful about when using these platforms. If we take the right approach and show students how to interact in meaningful, positive ways, the good far outweighs the negative and we can change the trajectory of future generations' social media interactions.

'Digital citizenship programs are sufficient to ensure our students are behaving ethically online.'

I am in no way suggesting you throw away the digital citizenship lessons you've culled or the excellent books out there providing valuable ideas on how to teach digital citizenship. This important topic needs to be at the forefront of everything we do when we integrate technology into our classrooms. It is essential for students to understand the risks of being in online spaces, and it's our responsibility as educators to look after their health and well-being. So there are important lessons we need to explicitly teach.

However, when we teach using a digital leadership framework, we show students how to interact in a way that goes beyond safe, ethical use. We add context and model the skills and appropriate behaviors our students seldom see while navigating these spaces on their own. We show them what is possible.

'We shouldn't use the word *digital*.'

When we teach kindness, empathy, respect, inclusion, and leadership—among other important character values—we need to consider the whole person and not distinguish between online and offline personas. That said, you may be wondering why I'm not just using the terms "citizenship" and "leadership"—why include "digital" at all? Although I believe we shouldn't separate the two personas, as a society, I don't think we are necessarily there yet, simply because too many people still think of the online world as completely separate. In his essay, "Digital Dualism versus Augmented Reality," sociologist and social media theorist Nathan Jurgenson argues against this "digital dualism," or looking at the digital and physical worlds as separate entities. Instead, he says, "the digital and physical are increasingly meshed."[4]

For most of our students, the digital realm has always coexisted with the analog world, so they don't know anything different. But when we, as adults, talk about our culture or community, we rarely bring Instagram into the discussion as a form of community. We will talk about kindness and empathy, but then we shift to conversations about cyberbullying as if kindness and empathy can't exist online. I have met incredibly nice children in person who are not very nice children on Twitter, and so, too, have I met people who are just as personable, passionate, thoughtful, and generous in their face-to-face interactions as they are online. So, yes, for now, we need to continue to use the terms "digital leadership" and "digital citizen" until we can use the online and offline terms synonymously.

Also, for the purposes of this book, I use the term "digital" to refer to "student leadership." This book is designed to guide teachers and administrators in understanding how technology and social media can help students be more positive, leverage leadership, and change—positions that haven't been widely embraced yet. While one could argue leadership is not

> At the heart of student digital leadership is providing opportunities for empathy and desiring to make others' lives better and more positive, either online or offline.

necessarily something that everyone can (or needs to) strive to achieve, I think for some students, especially shy ones, online spaces can provide avenues for leadership that they could never achieve in a classroom setting.

As I curated the stories in this book, one thing became apparent to me rather quickly: In every example and idea, the online interactions either began with a spark in the classroom itself or as a virtual provocation or experience, which served to strengthen the collaboration and connectedness within the classroom. At the heart of student digital leadership is providing opportunities for empathy and desiring to make others' lives better and more positive, either online or offline.

'Social media is a distraction not necessary for a student's future.'

In an April 2016 article, Hootsuite CEO Ryan Holmes said using social media effectively is "the most important digital skill for tomorrow's CEOs."[5] He also refers to a "social media gap," which is further supported by William Ward, PhD, a former professor of social media at Syracuse University, who said, "Students using digital and social media professionally in an integrated and strategic way have an advantage. [They're] getting better jobs and better internships."[6]

The fact is, students are good at connecting with people they already know, but they don't quite understand how to network professionally. As a result, businesses are having to train their employees how to use social media effectively. Thus, developing a positive online presence and knowing how different social networks work are must-have skills for graduates entering the work force.

'Technology, I get, but social media is not useful to my curriculum or to education in general.'

You may think social media is only about what Justin Bieber or other celebrities are up to, or perhaps as a useful way to get last night's sports highlights, but businesses and news outlets as well as politicians, historians, scientists, authors, and academics use social media to connect with their peers and share thoughts and ideas. Social media isn't just for the Kardashians.

Imagine how much more meaningful your lesson about *The Outsiders* could become if the author, S.E. Hinton, were to comment on your tweet (she's done this), or how much more powerful the issue of water scarcity could be if your students were to connect, via social media platforms, with a young Kenyan who invented a water filtration system (this has happened, too). Social media allows students to explore and compare and contrast in a whole new way: For example, how does what politicians are saying in their social media posts using a specific hashtag compare to what they are saying on the nightly news? Or how could social media help our students understand how children in other countries celebrate birthdays or experience winter?

When we approach social media from a digital leadership perspective, we're showing students that social media isn't just about entertainment, selfies, or communicating with their friends; it can also be a powerful platform for them to understand the world and share their learning in ways impossible with a textbook. Equally important, social media complements and amplifies the learning students are already doing by providing resources and an audience beyond the classroom.

'Not everyone has digital access or uses social media and not all parents are comfortable.'

Despite the fact that many students, at increasingly younger ages, are using social media,[7] I know the reality is that some don't yet have access to this world. I'm mindful of this, and so you'll find that most of the examples and ideas I put forth are framed around guided opportunities for students to work with a class social media account, allowing everyone to participate fully without ever compromising their dignity. Having said that, it is very important to be aware of digital inequity and try to ensure every student has access to the online world whenever and however possible. A digital divide only further marginalizes students.

Throughout the book, you'll notice that I provide examples of how to approach situations where parents aren't quite comfortable with their students using social media. I've presented the positive power of technology and social media to numerous parent groups over the years, and in my experience, parents genuinely don't know what it is they are saying "no" to. They simply need reassurance that a teacher's approach ensures their students' best interests and safety are always considered. So, when I show them the transformational potential of technology and social media, many of them change their minds. Even the American Pediatric Society recommends that parents be a "child's mentor" when it comes to media, which "means teaching them how to use it as a tool to create, connect, and learn."[8] As we know, educators often spend more time with children than parents do, and so we need to assume this mentorship role as well.

In other cases, I've found an intergenerational divide within families, with parents not fully understanding the tools their children are using. By incorporating social media into the classroom, we can invite parents to join the learning process and actually become empowered to use social media with their children. When parents understand these tools and their capabilities, they welcome the use of social media. When we take a digital leadership position at the outset, we create positive learning outcomes and change conversations.

Social Media All Day, Every Day

As you make your way through this book, I'll offer examples and ideas for how to use social media in a guided, thoughtful manner. Now, in no way am I advocating for social media to be used every day or numerous times a day: Balance and moderation are extremely important. The biggest problem is that policies banning cell phones or that block social media in the classroom prohibit opportunities to bring its practice and use into the learning context at all. Imagine if each teacher were to have a child engage in a powerful, positive learning experience using social media just once a year, every year that child were in school. Doing so would provide children with a better understanding of how to use social media in a more productive way. This is a far better approach than simply saying they can't use social media at all.

'Using social media in the classroom will further students' dependence on it.'

It is an all-too-common narrative told by both parents and teachers that students are "addicted" to their phones. The thing is, though, by not allowing students to use social media, we aren't actually solving the issue—we're just avoiding it. In *It's Complicated*, danah boyd's research into the networked lives of teenagers, leads her to assert that what we call "addiction" is more of a dependence on staying connected with friends, which students use social media as a tool to do.[9] Apart from dependence, the fact that students don't know how or when it's important to give someone their full attention is also an often-raised problem. Having a cell phone in class, complete with the urges to check their status or friends' posts, provides an exceptional opportunity to teach students self-regulation and to actually unpack and discuss these behaviors as they occur, rather than out of context, which has little to no effect. But more importantly, when we begin this work before students begin to develop these behaviors, we actually have a chance at making a change.

'Not everyone needs to change the world.'

This generation, often called "Generation Z," is made up of kids who have never lived in a world without smartphones. According to innovation consultant Jeremy Finch, they believe "the weight of saving the world and fixing our past mistakes [is] on their small shoulders."[10] In fact, many teachers have said to me, "My students are going to change the world."

And yet I am mindful of a sentiment expressed by Dean Shareski, author of *Embracing a Culture of Joy*, in a December 2014 blog post:

> Not every kid needs to change the world. Not every kid will invent something that changes lives. For some of our students, simply finding some peace and confidence to survive another day is enough. For others, building a life and a family is a worthy goal. I worry about kids uninterested in these sentiments. I don't think it's always because they're apathetic or immature. I think for some, this is not how they see their lives unfolding. Asking and expecting them to change the world can be overwhelming and perhaps even deflating.[11]

I wholeheartedly agree with Dean's assertion here, and I think it's an important one to keep in mind as we work with students. However, I wrote this book to encourage educators to show students the world beyond their schools and communities. To show students how they can learn and then share their learning, and along the way, possibly even discover their passions. In no way is my goal to put pressure on students (or teachers) to change the entire world in one fell swoop. Rather, this book is an invitation to change one person's world at a time, through their actions or gifts. Using technology to expose students to a variety of experiences, ideas, and people is what twenty-first-century learning should look like.

Perhaps not everyone can change the world, but everyone can make a positive influence in their world and in the lives of those around them.

This Is Messy

I want you to know right now that I don't present the ideas in this book to you from a rose-colored-glasses-do-this-and-everything-will-be-right-with-the-world perspective. That would be irresponsible.

I have been profoundly influenced by danah boyd's book, *It's Complicated* (I actually wish I could have borrowed that title for my own book), in which she explores how gray the topics of technology and social media are when we consider them from an analog perspective, or that of an outsider's (adult's) perspective. This is why I bring students' voices into the discussion. Those student voices are important for teachers to hear. Most of us were not born into a world of technology. We talked to friends on the telephone. We met at the park and played outside all day. And while we often romanticize this as the best thing ever, we forget to consider how many amazing opportunities technology has afforded us. Only when we include the voices of students at every level can we truly understand the roles technology and social media can play in education.

And so ...

I think eleven-year-old Ishita Katyal said it best in her TED-Ed Talk, "When I Grow Up": "I believe age is just a number. I believe anyone is capable of great actions and can touch the lives of others, regardless of his or her age."[12]

I consider myself a curator almost as much as a writer. I have collected the stories and experiences of a variety of educators and students I know with whom I have had the privilege to work either online or in person. These are teachers who are playing in social media spaces and using them to teach, connect, and engage students in learning opportunities that allow them to act. These teachers understand that whether we choose to ignore it or embrace it, social media is a powerful tool. They know students can have a voice and can positively and actively contribute to society, and they believe their students can change the world—because they've empowered them to believe that.

As famed personal-development author and speaker Wayne Dyer, PhD, says, "If you change the way you look at things, the things you look at change." If you are one of these educators at the forefront of the movement to empower students to use social media, then I hope this book provides a tangible point of reference to continue your work. As a result, I hope you will share your own stories using the hashtag #SocialLEADia[13] so that we may all learn from you as well.

You may not think social media has a role in education, or you may be somewhat skeptical about the role it could play. I hope this book helps you see how we can empower students to use social media and technology differently—not just because I said so, but because the ideas presented, as well as the stories from other teachers and students, inspire you to embrace digital leadership.

Chapter 1 Notes

1. George Couros, "Digital Leadership Defined," *The Principal of Change,* January 7, 2013, georgecouros.ca/blog/archives/3584.

2. "True Stuff: The Menace of Telephones," *Wondermark*, December 30, 2010, wondermark.com/true-stuff-telephone-menace.

3. boyd, danah. *It's Complicated: The Social Lives of Networked Teens*, New Haven: Yale University Press: 2014, pg. 6 (emphasis added).

4. Jurgenson, Nathan, "Digital Dualism versus Augmented Reality," *The Society Pages: Cyborgology*, February 21, 2011, thesocietypages.org/cyborgology/2011/02/24/digital-dualism-versus-augmented-reality.

5. Holmes, Ryan, "The Most Important Digital Skill for Tomorrow's CEOs," *The We Forum*, April 20, 2016, weforum.org/agenda/2016/04/the-most-important-digital-skill-for-tomorrows-ceos.

6. Holmes, Ryan, "The 5 Social Media Skills Millennials Lack," *Fortune. com,* March 28, 2014, fortune.com/2014/03/28/5-social-media-skills-millennials-lack.

7. "Kids Not Equipped for Coming of Digital Age at Nine," *Nominet*, February 6, 2014, nominet.uk/kids-not-equipped-for-coming-of-digital-age.

8. "American Academy of Pediatrics Announces New Recommendations for Children's Media Use," *American Academy of Pediatrics*, October 21, 2016, aap.org/en-us/about-the-aap/aap-press-room/pages/american-academy-of-pediatrics-announces-new-recommendations-for-childrens-media-use.aspx.

9. boyd, danah. *It's Complicated: The Social Lives of Networked Teens*, New Haven: Yale University Press: 2014, Chapter 3.

10. Finch, Jeremy, "What Is Generation Z and What Does It Want?" *Fast Company*, May 14, 2015, fastcoexist.com/3045317/what-is-generation-z-and-what-does-it-want.

11. Shareski, Dean, "The Problem with Exemplars," *Ideas and Thoughts*, December 2014, ideasandthoughts.org/2014/12/03/the-problem-with-exemplars.

12. Katyal, Ishita, "Before When I Grow Up," YouTube, June 9, 2016, youtube.com/watch?v=1JzgJFccUyw&feature=youtu.be.

13. To do this, simply include #SocialLEADia in your tweet when you're sharing on Twitter or Instagram.

SECTION I

WHY DIGITAL LEADERSHIP MATTERS

Digital Leadership:
We Need a New Direction

I never realized the impact that your voice can have on others, but once I began observing the number of people that listened to me, I felt empowered as a student.

—*Aliyah Ali, twelfth grade*

A situation I was involved with at a southern Ontario school convinced me that digital leadership is crucial. A few individuals began anonymously targeting several of the school's teachers and students using a now-defunct social networking app, Yik Yak. The app, intended for users age eighteen or older, worked like this: When someone made a comment, other users could "upvote" it (the equivalent of "likes" on Facebook) or "downvote" it. Once a comment received five downvotes, it disappeared.

Although some students did downvote a few of the negative comments made against the targeted teachers and students, making them disappear within minutes, many of the comments received several upvotes. Since users (at the time) weren't required to sign up for this particular app, the anonymity made it difficult for the school's administrators, including Principal Richard Maurice, to identify the culprits behind the mean attacks. This was a simple case of a few students utilizing the power of anonymity to be extremely rude and hurtful, while bystanders allowed this to happen or encouraged it by not being a part of the solution.

Understandably, the teachers and administrators wanted the school's IT department to shut it down. In this instance, so did I. So while Yik Yak and IT worked on creating a "geofence" around the school's geographical coordinates (blocking at the district level would not necessarily have helped the situation), the school's administrators made guidance and chaplaincy aware of the situation, as it was clear some students would need support.

Additionally, the principal, who truly values student voice, called for an assembly of the President's Council (student representatives from each of the school's councils), where he asked the students what they thought should be done. Students engaged in genuine dialogue about resolving this problem while the principal moderated. It was a fascinating discussion. It was also interesting to hear their thoughts on so many issues, including the debatable impact of IT shutting down access to the site on the school's network. Much of the behavior was happening under the radar of the teachers and, with the site blocked, many students had simply switched to using their own phones with their own data. What was clear was that the students at the assembly really wanted to be part of the solution, and their opinions and ideas were so much more nuanced than you might think.

In the end, the students came up with an action plan:

1. Flag inappropriate comments and posts made by unidentified users. (This would let Yik Yak know abuse was happening.)

2. Post on the app in more positive ways, ensuring anyone who was targeted would find support or compliments. The students would encourage their councils' members to do so as well.

3. Speak to their classmates in person about the situation.

At the surface level, you might feel like you can stop reading this book right now: This incident is precisely why districts ban and block social media. It is every fear we have materialized.

Or are you seeing what I'm seeing? Some students demonstrated leadership without adults intervening because they knew it was the right thing to do, while the majority of students didn't move to action until adults gave them ownership of the situation. The students were extremely committed to determining what they could do to solve the problem, and in the end, the student leaders created and modeled a positive resolution for their peers and used their actions and voices in online spaces to make a real difference in the lives of their peers. We so seldomly empower students in this way.

Beyond Digital Citizenship

One of the real problems is that digital citizenship, from a typical adult perspective, concerns itself almost exclusively with Internet safety.

I remember talking with a friend whose son had attended a presentation on cyber safety. She said he'd come home and wanted to place duct tape on all of the webcams, because he'd been told webcams were always on and that predators could see inside your house, even when your computer is off. Now, think about this: If the teacher had used a webcam to bring in the guest speaker or connect with a class and then made sure to explicitly point out how and why to turn the webcam off after the video conference, that would have been a much more effective way to present the topic of webcam safety. And though I think safety is paramount, I find looking at the differences in how kids and adults see digital media's potential fascinating. In the 2014 *Children's Rights in the Digital Age* report, for example, an Argentinian youth said, "For me, [technology] unites the world," and an Australian participant said, "It connects us all on another level." Some of the young people surveyed described the role of technology as a way to unite people as well as promote a spirit of peace, equality, tolerance, and friendship. One youth from Colombia talked about the role of digital media in society: "I think technology is a key element regarding the development of a nation."[1]

The report also found that while children can articulate how digital media facilitates their communicative, educational, and informational needs, many have difficulty identifying how it enhances their lives and their rights in more specific terms. By contrast, children can much more easily express the risks and challenges associated with their digital media practices,[2] which makes sense considering that this is what is most explicitly emphasized in school and likely at home as well.

While fear may work temporarily with younger students, as it did with my friend's son, in my experience as a high school teacher and a mother of two teenagers, I can tell you fear tactics have very little effect on the older set. Perhaps this is because many of them have been using technology long enough without ever really encountering too much negative, or maybe it has more to do with the fact that they think adults are just being *extra* (a term some teens I know use to describe extreme or over-the-top behavior). I would rather my students (and children) be *mindful*, not fearful; that they have a regular, healthy skepticism rather than random moments of fear.

I've also found an extremely huge variance in what educators think digital citizenship should look like and how it should be taught. When I was researching digital citizenship for a master's course, I was completely overwhelmed by the different ways people interpret it, as well as the number of definitions available (506,000 came up in a single Google search). Of those 506,000 definitions, Common Sense Media's resonates most: "Digital citizenship is the ability to think critically, behave safely, and participate responsibly in the digital world."[3] Additionally, I like the way the "Digital Citizenship Education in Saskatchewan Schools" document speaks to why it is important:

> Just as schools have played a role in preparing students to be citizens in the traditional sense, educators must now ensure that our children are ready to be active and responsible participants in our increasingly digital society.[4]

While I agree with those definitions and the fact that digital citizenship is essential, there are three main problems with *how* we're implementing it in schools:

1. Teaching digital citizenship as independent of what is expected of face-to-face behavior.

2. Digital citizenship is approached as a discrete unit taught by a homeroom teacher or a media specialist, instead of as an ongoing conversation.

3. Focusing on the negatives: what students *should not* do rather than focusing on digital leadership and what students *can* and *should* do.

Digital leadership goes beyond just being safe and responsible; it brings to light the extent to which students can exemplify really positive actions if they're given the opportunity to do so. And the student digital leaders I've met aren't waiting until they grow up to follow their passions. They are confident, and they are leveraging technology and social media in ways that are creative, inventive, and in many instances are making their communities better.

A perfect example is Joshua Williams who was thirteen when we "met" virtually during an EduMatch Passion Pitch in 2015. He was the keynote speaker that summer, and he spoke with impressive poise and conviction about his organization, Joshua's Heart. What began as a personal quest to help feed the homeless has turned into an incredible not-for-profit foundation with a mission to inspire people and "bring kindness and hope into this world" and, ultimately, stomp out hunger. His belief in helping youth "be the best we can" was beyond inspiring, and he completely held his own as the only teen on a panel of adults.

Joshua's story began before he had even turned five years old when, one Sunday on his way to church, he saw a homeless man on the side of the road. Although he was too young to read the man's sign, Joshua asked his mom about him and began to wonder about homelessness. Joshua's grandmother had just given him a twenty-dollar bill, and he wanted to give it to the man to help him. It was at that moment, he realized everyone can make a difference, big or small, no matter how old or young they are. Joshua became passionate about his cause, so he and his family looked for an organization for him to join, but there really wasn't anything out there for children his age. So, with the help of his mother, Joshua founded Joshua's Heart.

Together, the family began cooking and delivering food for the homeless. It started with five or ten people, and eventually they were helping 100, then 200. Joshua's persistence has paid off: As of July 2016, Joshua's Heart has distributed 1.3 million pounds of food to more than 240,000 individuals through the organization's Backpack Distribution, Food Distribution, and H.O.P.E. Boxes programs, ensuring adults and children who need food receive it.

Joshua uses his blog and social media accounts to promote his non-profit as well as other causes close to his heart. Every time I speak with him online (I'm looking forward to meeting face to face), I am inspired by his positivity and zeal for helping people. He confidently says youth hold the key to changing the world, and I can't help but agree.

He is leading the way by inspiring youth to create chapters in Ohio, Connecticut, and West Palm Beach. His foundation is one of the only agencies in south Florida that accepts volunteers of all age groups; 100+ Youth Board members and 12,500 youth volunteers (called "elves") are actively involved in helping to stomp out hunger.[5]

A few months after we met, Joshua introduced me (via Twitter direct message, no less) to Todd Nesloney, author of *Kids Deserve It!* I was a little

Promote Digital Leadership by Igniting Students' Passions

Passion and learning are at the very core of digital leadership. Teachers, by virtue of the themes and experiences they bring into their classrooms, ignite students' excitement about learning. In some cases, that passion is stomping out hunger, in others, it's saving the environment or reading or changing our idea of school.

As educators, we may not know the impact we have on our students until much later. But we can support students when they demonstrate a passion for a topic or a cause by showing them they can pursue those interests *now and* helping them connect with others who share similar interests or concerns.

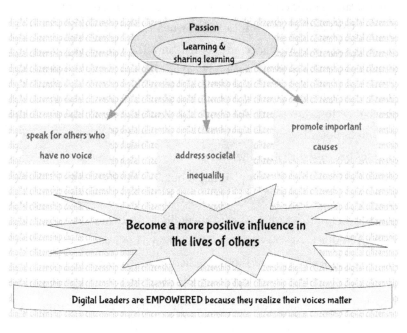

Figure 2.1

surprised. When I asked Joshua what prompted the introduction, he told me Todd was a friend of his, and he thought the two of us should meet. Now, in my role as literacy consultant and teacher-librarian, I often connect educators to other educators who I think might work collaboratively together. However, the fact that Joshua did this made me think about the extent to which he, as a result of his positive experiences and comfort in online spaces, assertively speaks with adults in a way few students have the confidence to do. I like telling Joshua's story because, to me, he embodies the very definition a digital leader, in what he does and how he acts both offline and online. He is positive, hopeful, and completely genuine and inspiring.

When I think of student digital leaders, I also think about Curran Dee, a fourth grader from Connecticut, who, along with his mother, Marialice, created DigCitKids.[6] Whenever Curran and I communicate online, he demonstrates confidence, curiosity, and leadership. He connects with both students and adults with ease. But when I met Curran in person, he was extremely shy. Marialice admits that in a traditional classroom, his teachers never, ever would have said he demonstrates leadership qualities. With this in mind, I invite you to consider how technology and social media, together with digital leadership, provide a voice to those students who might not otherwise ever find their voice in their face-to-face communities because they are different.

When I hear people complaining about, "Kids these days … " I think of Joshua and Curran, as well as Hannah, Timmy, Olivia, Gabe, Braeden, Annie, Yumi, Jin, and Alfred—all student digital leaders whose voices you will hear in this book. As a teacher-librarian in a high school, I've realized that most students are consuming media for productive (and sometimes silly) purposes, while comparatively a few students are using social media to be hurtful. I've also realized that some students need a caring adult to show them what they can do with social media, something that too seldomly happens in schools. So I propose we change that by shifting the conversation from digital citizenship to digital leadership.

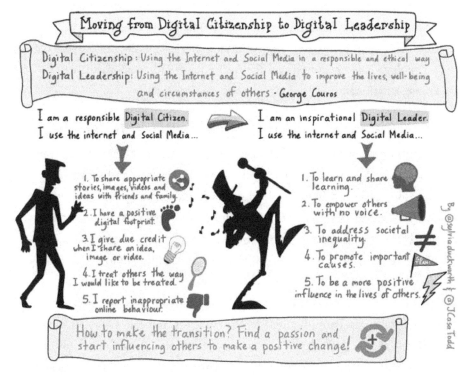

Figure 2.2, Created by Sylvia Duckworth and Jennifer Casa-Todd

Shifting to Digital Leadership

At its core, digital leadership is the belief that students can use "the vast reach of technology (especially the use of social media) to improve the lives, well-being, and circumstances of others."[7]

What I have observed is that students do this by the following:

1. Learning and sharing their learning
2. Empowering others who have no voice
3. Addressing societal inequality
4. Promoting important causes
5. Being a more positive influence in the lives of others

You may be reading this list and saying to yourself, "That's me!" Many educators do all of these things. The question is, though, to what extent are you empowering your students to do this? That's what this book is all about: getting students to connect with people beyond their friends, giving them the tools and the opportunities to pursue a more positive use of technology, and showing them that technology and social media can be transformational.

It begins with learning and sharing learning.

When we embrace digital leadership, we rethink how and why we share on social media and reconsider how our learning and sharing can affect others. Using digital leadership as a framework improves the kinds of opportunities teachers provide their classes, principals provide their schools, and IT and curriculum departments provide their districts. Most of all, we validate the voices of our students and help them to understand the extent to which their voices matter.

More often than not, students understand that technology and social media tools can connect them to their friends and allow them to follow celebrity and entertainment news, but it really doesn't occur to too many of them to use these tools for learning, much less to follow posts from NASA, *National Geographic*, *TIME for Kids*, *The New Yorker*, or the History Channel. That's why it's up to us to show them what learning through social media could look like and listen to the students who have discovered online spaces for learning—and to value that learning in the classroom.

One of the most important aspects of teaching digital leadership is helping students see the potential that lies in learning and in sharing their learning using technology and social media. This can begin with face-to-face opportunities in the classroom and extend beyond, or it may begin with a virtual learning experience that then becomes a powerful propellant for learning even more in the classroom.

And what do students say? When I asked 103 students in sixth through eighth grades (ages eleven to fourteen years old) whether or not they believed social media should be used in school, the majority (nearly 56 percent) said "yes" (Figure 2.3). And, interestingly, when I asked the same students, "Why or why not?" the students who'd used social media in their classroom for learning purposes at least three times in the school year had a more positive attitude toward the potential of social media than the students who never had.

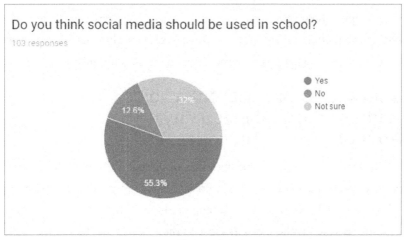

Figure 2.3

Social media can allow students to learn from one another. Many schools already promote in-person, peer-supported learning opportunities with reading buddies and guest speakers. Social media and technology extend those kinds of connections, allowing students to gain greater perspectives and benefit from real-time collaboration. What these opportunities look like varies according to grade level, but creating opportunities for students to learn from others is vital. It is through such interactions that students begin to learn what collaboration looks and sounds like and both offline and online.

The more I ask and observe, though, the more I have come to understand that students are learning and sharing learning on their own, independently of school. When I asked, I discovered that one of the students in my book club has been blogging about the books she has been reading since she was twelve (you will meet Michelle later). In 2013, I was invited to a book launch for two students, Brittany Watson and Nikta Sadati from St. Therese of Lisieux, who had written a novel collaboratively online with coauthor, Blaze Earl from England, through a writing platform called Wattpad. They had never met in person.

We need to take the time to see what and how our students are learning. Imagine how much more meaningful our lessons might be if we incorporated some of the students' own positive online learning experiences into our classrooms to complement our curriculum expectations.

Speak for those without a voice. Address societal inequality. Promote important causes.

Joshua Williams truly believes he can change the world; he already is. In classrooms where educators foster digital leadership, students are taking to social media to address inequity in their local and global communities and to promote causes close to their hearts. In fact, many of the students you will meet throughout your career believe they can—and actually are—collectively making the world a better place.

Standing up for those who need help and promoting important causes aren't new concepts; you may have been doing and teaching students to speak up and reach out for years. We know, as Nelson Mandela has so eloquently stated, that "education is the most powerful weapon which you can use to change the world." As part of our various curricula, we teach about issues such as racial inequality, water scarcity, poverty, homelessness, and the environment. Typically, most of this learning takes place in the form of news articles, videos, and textbooks, with students creating public service announcements (PSAs), posters, and brochures advocating for important causes as the culminating activity. In some schools, students even put on a social justice fair, where their peers come and learn about a variety of highlighted issues. And though this is fantastic, there is so much more students could share and learn if we were to embrace digital leadership.

Students can now exchange ideas from the class discussion and artifacts (posters, PSAs, etc.) they've created with another class; they can begin to see that they aren't the only ones who care about an issue and learn from students who may have a different perspective on it. What's more, connecting with not-for-profit organizations can show them that not only are adults addressing the issues they care about, but that they, too, can voice their ideas and solutions—and be heard. By the time students enter high school, they may be reaching out to local politicians or joining organizations who share their passions for a cause.

School should be where students not only learn about social issues, but where they are empowered to take action to make the world a better place. School should be where we help them see that they, too, can make a difference. When we include opportunities to extend student learning beyond our classrooms' four walls and address some of these issues, we may inspire kids in ways that are surprising to even themselves.

This is digital leadership. With the power of technology and social media, students can learn directly from people affected by the issues they champion. They can actively work toward creating a more just society now, instead of waiting until they are adults to make a difference. ·

Become a positive influence in others' lives.

The way students (and adults) interact through social media has the potential to be life-changing, for better or for worse. Do a quick Google search for "cyberbullying," and countless articles come up with titles such as "8 Ways Kids Are Using Social Media to Bully," "How Kids Are Using Snapchat to Sext and Cyberbully," and "Bullying on Twitter: Researchers Find 15,000 Bully-Related Tweets Sent Daily (STUDY)." And it's true, the way some use social media can leave kids feeling alienated, bullied, or shunned, as in the Yik Yak incident I shared at the beginning of the chapter. But it's also true that the very same medium can empower kids to help their peers feel valued, accepted, and celebrated.

Research suggests it takes six positive comments to counteract one negative,[8] so I believe we need to work together to reinforce the positive. As George Couros wrote in this book's foreword, "We need to make the positives so loud that the negatives are almost impossible to hear."

That's why I love talking about students like Konner Sauve and Jeremiah Anthony,[9] who have demonstrated digital leadership and made the lives of their peers better. Konner secretly created an Instagram account[10] so he could brighten the day of each and every single one of his classmates, by posting something positive about them. It was only at the end of his valedictorian graduation speech that he revealed his identity. Similarly, Jeremiah, a junior in high school, used the @westhighbros Twitter handle to tweet compliments to friends and classmates.

In a blog post titled "More Powerful than You Know," best-selling author Seth Godin argues we all have power. "Cultural power, mostly," he says. "The ability to speak up, to paint a picture of a different way, to share words and images with those that care to hear them."[11] So when we only focus on social media in a "don't do this" kind of way, we miss out on opportunities to promote and highlight the positive that comes with digital leadership.

What if every school community had a Jeremiah or a Konner? What if part of the learning experience at every school included discovering how to make social media a place for positive, empowering interactions and seeking opportunities to make someone's life a little happier? In fact, as you'll see, every one of the students I'll introduce you to has positively influenced others' lives. And very often (although not always), an encouraging adult is cheering on and guiding those students.

Author and founder of Blue Sky School, Shauna Pollock, shares a powerful example of students making a difference in *Creating Classroom Magic*. When one of her students, Molly, was diagnosed with an illness and passed away, her class wanted to do something special to honor their friend. Inspired by the Japanese legend of a thousand paper cranes and knowing how much Molly loved unicorns, Shauna created

#Unicorns4Molly and asked people to share pictures of unicorns. It went viral (meaning it was shared widely and frequently in a short period of time), with notable Canadians, astronaut Chris Hadfield, and even comedian Rick Mercer, participating.

There are so many layers of awesome in this story:

1. Strangers on the Internet lightened the students' grief.

2. The students in Shauna's class were part of the movement and saw the impact it was making on others.

3. The students researched a disease that had affected someone they knew, so they were learning on a much deeper level than they would have previously.

4. A teacher-mentor created a real contextual opportunity to teach kids about technical and digital literacy, online etiquette, positive commenting, and sharing, but the experience went well beyond that.

Shauna's belief in the positive power of social media created a transformational learning experience for everyone. In one of the later chapters, I'll tell you about how I took a similar approach to rally teachers and students so we could support a young girl in our community suffering from a brain tumor.

By embracing digital leadership, we can help our students understand that their words matter, no matter if it's face to face or online. We can't teach one in isolation of the other anymore. When we add social media into the equation, even at a young age, we can send the powerful message to our students that these tools have the potential to make other people's lives brighter.

The Benefits of Digital Leadership

Digital leadership provides a counter-fear narrative. We know many people are afraid of social media—so much so that the fear seems to influence every decision made around the use of the Internet in schools. There is a sense of hesitancy to allow kids to talk to strangers on the Internet, but when students network with professionals, experts, and authors, they not only gain insights into and ideas about careers, but they also come to see their voices as important and adults as less intimidating. If students are exposed to the "right strangers," using a critical and educated lens, they will know what appropriate exchanges and requests from those strangers look like. Of course we need to protect kids, but we also need to ensure that students come to see the value and purpose of professional and academic networking before they leave high school.

The student leaders I've met, both in person and virtually, are confident and assertive—or they become so as a result of their experiences. Aliyah's student vignette (below) is a testament to this. Her teacher, Jamie Reaburn Weir, allowed her students to organize and execute a panel discussion with educators and educational stakeholders through a student-led inquiry project about the future of education.[12] The experience demonstrates the truth that when students are given real opportunities to be heard—not just by their classmates, but by their peers and adults online—they come to understand that their voice matters.

Student Vignette 🔊

As a student entering grade eleven, I was extremely intimidated. Along with all the new and challenging thoughts ahead, what seemed most difficult was my introverted personality. In past English classes, I had always struggled with being anxious while presenting and sharing my ideas with others. I lacked people skills, which resulted in a lack of self-confidence. I was introverted, mainly because I was always concerned about the thoughts of others being superior to mine, which greatly discouraged me from sharing my ideas; therefore, I never saw the potential my voice truly had.

Although at the beginning of the course there weren't many familiar faces, by the end, the class felt like my second family. The class's topics encouraged me to share my ideas during discussions. They were based on the modernization of society and current situations—things I was familiar with and understood. The slowly increasing group sizes we worked in increased my confidence when presenting my thoughts, which made them easier to share. I began to think less and less about what people would think about my ideas. By the end of the class, I had matured tremendously and was able to share my ideas with many authentic audiences.

As a result of the many in-class experiences I had through Google Hangouts with authentic voices in society, such as Desire2Learn (D2L) representatives, a principal in Ottawa, the community manager for Discovery Canada, representatives from my school district, and even from the Ministry of Education, I have had the opportunity to lead in speaking roles, facilitate conversations with diverse audiences, and become a confident speaker.

As I've been reflecting on this course, I've realized that for me to have grown, it was essential that I have my voice heard. When I was younger, I never realized the impact that your voice can have on others, but once I began observing the number of people who listened to me, I felt empowered as a student. Sometimes all it takes is for one person to listen to you to make you believe in yourself. As I noticed my growth throughout the school year, I have now become a leader who can easily connect with others and encourage others to open up and share their ideas. Just as my teacher, Ms. Weir, and my peers were there to listen to my voice, I want to be the one who will listen and support your thinking. After all, as Stephen Covey reminds us, being a good leader means that you listen with the intention to understand, not only to reply.

—*Aliyah Alli, eleventh grade*

In Summary ⬇

- Digital leadership, as defined by George Couros, is using the vast reach of technology and social media to improve the lives and well-being of others. It can take the form of students learning and sharing their learning, standing up for important causes, and being a positive influence in the lives of others.

- We underestimate the positive impact we can have when we share online spaces with students.

- Digital leaders are more confident and assertive, and they know their voices matter.

Discussion Questions ✖

1. Which of the characteristics of digital leadership most resonate with you?

2. Which of your students demonstrate leadership qualities? How can you help to foster those leadership qualities both online and offline and help the other students in your class develop these qualities, as well?

3. What was the last powerful learning experience you had with your students? How might this have looked different if you had taken a digital leadership approach?

Chapter 2 Notes

1. Third, Amanda, et al., "Children's Rights in the Digital Age: A Download from Children around the World," Young and Well Cooperative Research Centre, Melbourne, 2014, pg. 29, unicef.org/publications/files/Childrens_Rights_in_the_Digital_Age_A_Download_from_Children_Around_the_World_FINAL.pdf.

2. ibid.

3. "Introduction to Digital Citizenship," *Common Sense Media*, commonsensemedia.org/educators/training/6-8/introduction-to-digital-citizenship.

4. Couros, A. & K. Hildebrandt, "Digital Citizenship Education in Saskatchewan Schools," 2015, Retrieved from iamstronger.ca/pages/digital-citizenship-education-in-saskatchewan

5. Joshua's Heart Foundation, 2016 Impact Report.

6. The Digital Citizenship Institute, digitalcitizenshipinstitute.com/digcit-kids.

7. George Couros, "Digital Leadership Defined," *The Principal of Change*, January 7, 2013, georgecouros.ca/blog/archives/3584.

8. Zenger, Jack and Joseph Folkman, "The Ideal Praise-to-Criticism Ratio," *Harvard Business Review,* p. 15, March 2013, Retrieved 20 May 2016.

9. I learned about these students from George Couros.

10. Pelletiere, Nicole, "Washington Valedictorian's Secret Instagram Reveals Tear-jerking Thoughts on Classmates," *ABC News*, June 11, 2015, abcnews.go.com/Lifestyle/washington-valedictorians-secret-instagram-reveals-tear-jerking-thoughts/story?id=31689197.

11. Godin, Seth, "More Powerful Than You Know," April 4, 2016, sethgodin.typepad.com/seths_blog/2016/04/more-powerful-than-you-know.html.

12. More info about this project here: edugains.ca/newsite/21stCenturyLearning/innovation_action/buildiing_communities.html.

MEET THE STUDENTS
JOSHUA WILLIAMS

JoshuasHeart.org

 @joshuasheart

 /joshuasheartfoundation

Joshua Williams is a south Florida high school student who discovered his passion for philanthropy when he was just four-and-a-half years old. Fueled by the belief that no child should ever go hungry, Joshua has dedicated the last ten years of his life to helping "stomp out world hunger" through his organization, Joshua's Heart Foundation. He also empowers and engages young people ages two and older to find their passion and purpose—and to then use it for the greater good. He believes that alone we can do something, but together we can move mountains.

Joshua has received numerous awards for his work, and has participated in several documentaries. He is even featured in Foundation for a Better Life's national billboard campaign.

Use Joshua's Story to Inspire Your Students

Check out all of the young people on the Junior Advisory Board and then have your students brainstorm how they, too, can help end hunger.

Did you know that every time you make a purchase on Amazon using the AmazonSmile icon, organizations like Joshua's Heart Foundation receive money? What is AmazonSmile? How are other companies helping to stomp out hunger?

We Can (and Need) to Change the Current Trajectory

I have a radical concept for you, especially those of you who talk negatively about social media: Stop. Really. If you present social media as a positive space, as a place where students can express themselves and connect with professionals and other students, then that's the type of learning you are going to see there.

—Timmy Sullivan, graduate

Timmy Sullivan tells us exactly why we need to change our stance towards social media in school. Timmy's participation in the Burlington High School (BHS) Help Desk, and his experiences in that class, have shaped not only his ideas about the role of social media in a young person's life, but have changed his online behaviors and have led him on a path towards educational reform and advocacy. Led by Jennifer Scheffer, a mobile learning coach in Burlington, Massachusetts, the BHS Help Desk allows students to earn school credit while learning important digital, leadership, and entrepreneurial skills. The BHS Help Desk is open several class periods each day and is a space where parents, students, and teachers can go for help troubleshooting problems they're having with their devices. Part of the course involves the students learning customer-service skills ("I have been assigned this project—what should I use?"); how to conduct themselves as young professionals; important lessons about the ethical and responsible use of technology; how to reach out to experts and app developers; and writing skills through their own blogs.

Last spring, when Marialice Curran shared a blog post titled, "8 Ways Kids Are Using Instagram to Bully," written by Sherri Martin, Curran issued a challenge to students to create a rebuttal. Twelve BHS students contributed eloquently and powerfully to a blog post called, "Students Speak out about Digital Citizenship,"[1] talking about the extent to which using technology was having a positive, rather than negative, influence on them and their school communities.

Caroline Akerly, one of the BHS Help Desk students, said:

> *Having teachers and administrators with a strong online presence encourages students to be conscious of what they are posting. There are very few incidents of social media misuse at our school as a direct result of the involvement of adults in the school community. Several of my teachers and sports captains follow me on Twitter, and I interact with them regularly.*

It is obvious that a program like BHS and a mentor teacher like Jennifer provide a powerful example of what is possible when we stop banning social media and instead participate in these spaces with students.

Educators who embrace a digital leadership stance don't ask, "Should we allow social media in school?"

Instead, they ask:

- "How can we help students understand their own relationship with social media?"

- "How could social media be a useful learning tool to add to my existing toolkit?"

- "How can technology and social media allow me to expand upon my relationships with my class and with the larger community?"

- "How can I harness those relationships' potential to empower my students and to transform our learning experiences?"

Student experiences like Timmy's and Caroline's are rare, simply because most schools don't allow open access to social media, nor do they encourage teachers to be online with their students.

In my experience, one of the greatest barriers holding educators back from embracing digital leadership is the fear of social media. When I ask teachers how they use social media in their classroom (I literally ask every person I meet both face to face and online), they often say their schools and districts are so afraid of social media that there is a "shut everything down" mindset. The decisions often stem from fear—from not understanding what social media is or how it could be a powerful learning tool.

I'd be lying, though, if I said I have never felt the instinct to "shut it down." In the spring of 2016, I tweeted the link to the #OSSLT2016 hashtag, which students created after writing the Ontario Secondary

One of the greatest barriers holding educators back from embracing digital leadership is the fear of social media.

School Literacy Test (a standardized test in Ontario). My eldest daughter and I got a real kick out of the students' very clever posts, including one with a photo of someone swimming featuring the caption, "Booklet 1," and another photo with the same person engulfed by life-threatening waves with the caption, "Booklet 2." Even EQAO (the governing body overseeing the test) responded lightheartedly with Figure 3.1.

Figure 3.1

Then a friend pointed out that there was one extremely inappropriate post in the feed. When I looked, I was mortified because I felt that anyone looking at my Twitter feed would think I was condoning this behavior. The student had basically likened writing the test to a suicide bomber and included a photo. I deleted my tweet.

It's just what we do.

We shut it down.

But then I took a closer look. This was just a tenth-grade kid trying to be funny and not really understanding the full effect of what he was saying. I looked at his Facebook page, which was easy enough to find, and realized from the very innocent profile and posts that this young man had just made a vast error in judgment.

I instinctively contacted him via Twitter. Of course, this could have gone one of two ways: He could have responded maliciously or he could have realized his error and been grateful for the advice.

Here is how the exchange went:

Me: This is never, ever appropriate. Nor is it funny. And this tweet can come back to haunt you in the future.

Student: (Liked, retweeted) Thx

Me: You are welcome. Delete it and think before you post next time. Good luck!

Student: Kk (Deleted the tweet)

If I hadn't been in this space, I never would have been able to help this student. And this experience reminded me why it is so important that we enter these online spaces with our students. And though this exchange was no different from what I would've done if I'd seen someone doing something inappropriate in a mall or on a playground—I am a teacher after all—it was the first time I'd mentored a student I didn't know. His response was one of gratitude; the fact that he "liked" and "retweeted" my comment showed that. Kids make mistakes, and sometimes they just need adults to help along the way.

> *Whilst I understand that they have a "duty of care" to protect young people, developing a true understanding of the power of networks (and, indeed, networks of networks) requires more immersion than they are often currently allowed. How can young people be expected to behave appropriately if they have not been guided through the communication protocols and norms of a given platform? We are setting them up to fail.*[2]

—Doug Belshaw, EdD, *The Essential Elements of Digital Literacies*

How do we set students up to succeed with social media? It's likely that they are accessing their personal social media accounts on their mobile devices until class begins, but then we tell them put their phones away. What if we showed them how to use the technology in their pockets in a learning context or taught them how to use it for good? Now, one could argue this is the parent's role; while that may indeed be true, not every parent in every home has taken up this cause, and we all know that if issues arise at home, they can sometimes enter the classroom. School is a place of learning—not just the learning we are accustomed to from our youth, but current, real-life stuff, and social media is a part of that. We also need to understand that school is most effective when its educators partner with community members and parents. Together, we can educate the whole child.

Consider this: 92 percent of American teens report going online daily, including 24 percent who say they are online "almost constantly,"[3] according to a 2015 Pew Research Center study. And in a survey I sent out via Twitter to Canadian students in June of 2016, eighty-three out of the one hundred respondents in fifth through eighth grades use social media for personal use, with 60 percent of them using it daily.

It is important for us to acknowledge that social media is a new reality, and that it is impacting our lives (and our students' lives) in countless ways. We need to embrace it as a potential learning tool and give our students the knowledge and skills they'll need to survive, thrive, and excel in our connected world.

Defining Social Media

So what exactly is social media?[4] I often find that the districts saying they don't allow social media at all, upon closer look, actually do embrace some platforms that function as social media. The problem lies in how we define the term "social media."

Remember, danah boyd defines social media as the tools and platforms that allow us to *create* and *exchange* content.

Let's pause right here for a minute. Creating and sharing of content is what education is all about. In this vast, connected world, we shouldn't limit our students to creating and sharing content solely for us, when so many opportunities exist for them to share with an authentic, real audience. We must also realize that the vast majority of our students are creating their own content and then exchanging that content when they aren't at school. So, you see, social media already plays an important role in teaching and learning today—just not in the traditional classroom setting.

Scholars speak to the ambiguity around what we're calling social media, however. In the *Encyclopedia of Social Media and Politics*, Kerric Harvey, PhD, an associate professor of media and public affairs at George Washington University, wonders what constitutes social media. Does e-mail count? What about reposting sites where nothing new is added to the actual content but there is opportunity for the sharing of ideas? In her book, Kerric suggests social media can be considered anything that connects people in a large-scale conversation, exploration, and opinion-sharing.[5] I love this nuanced definition.

Blocking Access Does Not Help Anyone

If academics and students have a tough time defining social media, what are the criteria by which districts make decisions about which "social media" sites to block? Technically, any platform or tool which allows a user to share publicly and comment can be considered social media.

Are decisions to block and ban determined by facts (or feelings) firmly anchored in the way we see the world based on our experience? Are they decisions that stem from a couple of isolated negative incidents which shut down opportunities for the majority of students? In a quick, informal survey I conducted on Twitter, only 27 percent of respondents had open access to social media at school (Figure 3.2). Scholar Henry Jenkins, PhD, suggests, "adults are shutting down opportunities that are meaningful for young people out of a moral panic response to technological and cultural change."[6]

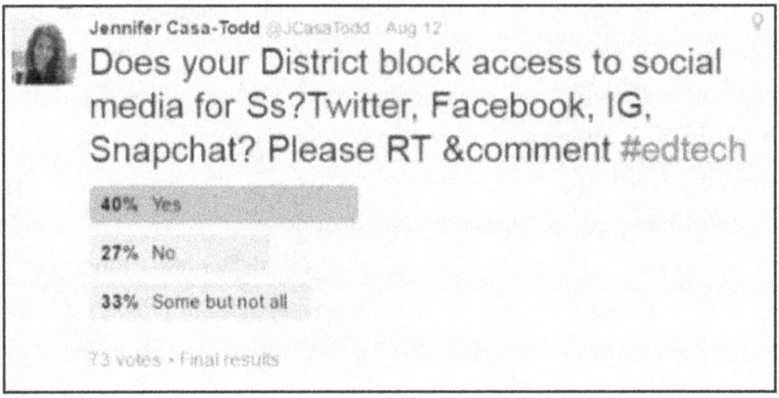

Figure 3.2

Indeed, "moral panic" is a great way of framing the conversation. We worry technology and social media are making our kids obese, socially inept, narcissistic, etc., but the bottom line is that technology and social media don't inherently cause any of this.

Having worked at the district level and sat around tables where we'd extensively debate which tools should or shouldn't be blocked, I understand educators' very real concerns about legal and liability implications that often accompany the decisions to block and ban. However, I don't agree that blocking and banning help.

In fact, we need to stop having the "to ban or not to ban" social media debate; we need to focus instead on how are we teaching our students to be empathetic, kind, and thoughtful citizens of the world, in every aspect of their lives. We need to talk about and discover what teaching with this focus looks like on and offline.

The other really important point to consider is this: Teachers who are truly passionate about engaging their classes *will* find a way to tap into their students' interests; and those interests, rightly or wrongly, will more than likely include social media. We can make blanket district-wide policies and we can block access to websites, but social media exists. Blocking it only provides a false sense of security because when a student (or teacher) wants access, they will find a way. I know because I have always been one of those teachers.

When I taught high school English, I was constantly trying things and pushing the envelope a little to excite my students about literature (today, I would teach English entirely differently, but that's another book). When we studied *The Secret Life of Bees*—which I insisted our department buy to replace some of the more "classic" books—I brought in beekeeping artifacts for students to explore, came dressed in a beekeeper's outfit, and had a honey festival. We had a medieval banquet when we read *Macbeth* and a Roaring Twenties party to celebrate *The Great Gatsby*. The point is, I used every means I could to get my students to love literature in a fun, relevant way (and clearly any excuse to have food and a party).

When I saw that all my students were using Facebook (this was in 2010), I thought, *Why not incorporate the social media platform into my class's study of* Romeo and Juliet? Then it hit me: Students could create Facebook profiles for the story's characters.

Since I'd set up the assignment at home, when I introduced it to the students the next day, I discovered the district had blocked Facebook on our school's computers. My students and I were so disappointed. I knew this assignment would interest them and that it would also give me a real understanding of what my kids knew about the play, more so than I could get through a test.

Confession time: I'm not exactly proud of the solution we came up with. Immediately, a few students said, "Don't worry, Ms. Casa-Todd, we can get on Facebook." And so, every day, a few of my students would circumvent the firewall so we could log onto Facebook and work on our assignment. Together, my students and I determined what the rest of the assignment would look like, including sharing which books, music, and television shows their character would enjoy, and at the very minimum, each character needed to post three status updates and comment on other characters' profiles.

I didn't realize it at the time, but I was putting myself and my school's principal at risk if anything had gone wrong because I was actually working on this with my students in secret, as co-conspirators. But nothing went wrong, and I would have done it again, even knowing the risks. Honestly, they were so into this project that it just didn't end—they continued posting on one another's profiles in character well after the unit was over. They would come in chattering about the posts to the point where it was hard to reel them back in. I was giddy by how excited they were about the play and how much they had obviously understood it based on their conversations.

You could say I was irresponsible, and, strictly speaking, you'd be right—I stood by while my students "broke the rules." Yet in the moment I made the choice to use Facebook, there was a thoughtful combination of critical and creative thinking and my own professional judgment guiding my decisions. I knew the risks but decided to put student engagement first and face the consequences. Even without knowing what it was, I had engaged in digital leadership, believing social media could lead to positive opportunities for my class. I didn't put my students in harm's way; rather, I put my students' interests and needs above "arbitrary" rules based on a fear narrative. Teachers who connect to other educators and use social media in positive ways know this well—isn't it time we show our students?

My daughters often tell me how they or their friends use tools they aren't supposed to (and that are supposedly "blocked") while the teacher isn't looking. I see this every single day as I walk around in my Library Learning Commons. This begs the question: Are we truly protecting students or are we, in fact, deluding ourselves and avoiding the problem because kids are smart and can get around anything if and when they want to?

It could also be argued that not engaging in guided use of social media with our students might actually put them at greater risk. Consider my active role with the student who posted to the #OSSLT hashtag and the extent to which I was able to guide him. This is not just my opinion, but one shared among scholars as well. In their book, *Participatory Cultures in a Networked World*, Henry Jenkins, danah boyd, and Mimi Ito, PhD,

> Real learning isn't simple—it's messy and unpredictable and challenging and wondrous.

say blocking sites "actually perpetuates risk, as it ensures that many kids will be forced to confront online risks on their own." They continue on to say many young people lack opportunities to learn how to use new media tools effectively and appropriately, and "a reliance on blocking sends the message that sites and tools important to students have little to nothing to contribute to intellectual pursuits."[7]

Would life be simpler without smartphones and social media in the classroom? Perhaps, but real learning isn't simple—it's messy and unpredictable and challenging and wondrous. Although we can seemingly control the technology students are bringing into the classroom now, with the Internet of Things becoming a reality, will we soon be asking students to check their Internet-enabled watches, glasses, and shirts at the door before they come into the classroom? Of course not. We need to be proactive now, while we can still see the devices students are using to connect to others.

Both adults and kids currently use social media to connect with friends and family and follow celebrities and/or news outlets, mostly for social purposes and entertainment. What they don't necessarily encounter is the outlet for leadership development that Timmy Sullivan was able to develop through his BHS Help Desk experience. This type of learning opportunity is what many educators, including myself, have come to understand about the amazing potential of social media.

I think of how social media has affected my own teaching practice. I follow educators, organizations, businesspeople, and news outlets, and

I've been learning with and from educators living in Argentina, Norway, Spain, the United Kingdom, Ghana, Australia, and across North America. Simply by virtue of being connected, I know to whom to go for knowledge. I don't have to wait for professional learning opportunities to come to me. I have been able to collaborate with educators in my own district in ways I would never have thought possible ten years ago. I have even helped organize major initiatives, including a book club for George Couros's *The Innovator's Mindset,* and an *Amazing Race* global collaborative project without once being in the same room (and in some cases, the same city) as the other organizers. What's more, I don't have the opportunity or the financial means to travel to every conference, but by using a conference's hashtag, I can often follow the participants' learning and get numerous resources from the comfort of my own home at no cost.

I think it's important that before we begin encouraging our students to become digital leaders, we must first think about how we can be digital leaders as well. Whether you're on Facebook or Instagram and only connect with your family, or if you enjoy having a PLN on Twitter or Voxer, are you modeling positive interactions? Do you learn from others and share your learning in kind? Do you give credit where credit is due? When you see an injustice happening, do you step in with a kind word, an inspirational image, quote, or a direct message? Or do you ignore it, or make flippant and mean comments? Do you solely promote yourself and your own work, or do you praise and celebrate others for their accomplishments?

It's one thing to be critical of social media spaces, and it's another thing to do something to make those spaces better with your own digital leadership. I urge you to select one social media platform and then engage with other educators on it. (I, of course, recommend Twitter—I have a ton of resources to help you get the most out of Twitter on my website.) Follow creators, authors, artists, and scientists. Follow the awesome students you have (and will) meet throughout this book. When you do, you will be simply amazed by the sharing you'll see, the learning you'll do, and the ideas and inspiration you'll get.

Once you experience how powerful, meaningful, and transformational technology and social media connections can be, introducing them into your classroom for students to experience becomes not only desirable, but imperative. When I reflect upon the reasons I sought out a Personal Learning Network on Twitter to begin with, it was to help me be a better teacher and leader. Ultimately, I have come to realize that we need to help students create their own PLNs and make it a priority to empower them to connect, to use their voices beyond their classrooms, to find a community that shares their passions, and to leverage a network. That's what was missing for me before, and that's how I feel I am a better teacher and leader today—because I can awaken my students to the possibilities which we were never afforded.

Tools for Learning, Not Just Playing

The following are a list of the top five social media tools as of January 2017, and examples of how we might rethink their current use as potential classroom tools to foster digital leadership.

Twitter

Twitter is a microblogging tool that allows users to "follow" people, organizations, news outlets, educational institutions, and companies. When I first started my role as a program resource teacher at the district level, my role was to provide professional learning to teachers. Unfortunately, it seemed that I had few opportunities myself to learn and, when I did, it was in isolation (for example, reading an educational book). When I started using Twitter, I discovered that I could engage in book studies, read the blogs by educators from around the world, and learn about educational technology and innovative classroom practices. I felt supported and challenged by strangers who have since become close friends. It's common for people to blame social media for destroying relationships, but through Twitter, I have forged new and unexpected relationships with people. My own positive experiences are part of the reason

I encourage teachers to have a class Twitter account. The connections I've made are certainly a factor in my enthusiasm when talking to students about using Twitter as they begin their digital leadership journey. In fact, most of the students who are featured in this book have a Twitter account, and it has been the primary means of our communication together.

Another reason Twitter is a great tool for public sharing and connection is that communication happens in real time and is fairly ubiquitous in academic, marketing, and cultural circles. As a result, Twitter is a tool that allows teachers to empower their students. For example, Laurie Azzi, a teacher from Ottawa, Ontario, posted a question on behalf of one of her sixth-grade students, Valerie, to Justin Trudeau, Canada's prime minister. His response didn't come in the form of a 140-character tweet—he actually spoke directly to Valerie in a video message (Figure 3.3), creating an empowering experience for her and her peers, as well as all of us who follow either Justin Trudeau or Laurie on Twitter.

Figure 3.3

So many students do not know Twitter can be a powerful tool for learning until a teacher provides them with that opportunity. The younger the students are, the less they have already made up their minds about Twitter's use for entertainment or for posting random thoughts (a current trend I see in the high school where I teach and among the friends of my daughters). Teachers can expand their students' use of Twitter by having conversations about how the platform could be a powerful vehicle for digital leadership. So many of the examples you will read about started with a Twitter connection.

Instagram

According to my daughters, *everyone* has an Instagram account. And though this obviously isn't entirely true (equity and access, as well as cultural differences, affect this), the use of Instagram is indeed prolific: The social media platform reported having 500 million users as of June 2016—and more than 300 million of those users access it daily.[8] Many parents are also using this app to share images with one another. Unlike Twitter, which at the time of writing this book only allowed for 140 characters (excluding images and replies), Instagram is a social media platform without limits that allows you to share images and videos—and their corresponding commentary—publicly or privately from a smartphone. And like Facebook and Twitter, users have a profile and newsfeed, but Instagram also has stickers and "stories," making it an excellent option for digital storytelling.

Cara Lodoen, a high school English teacher in Newmarket, Ontario, started a class Instagram account for her students to share their insights into her course's literature and readings. Students simply pair a photo they have captured with a quote from the work they're studying. Sometimes students choose a quote and then stage a picture, or they will take a picture because it reminds them of a quote from the novel. Cara tells them to keep their eyes open and to be aware of how the world around them reflects a moment or message from the text. As a class, they spend time sharing quotes and posting them on bulletin boards in the class; their focus is diction and rhetorical devices. Then, they post their quote and picture pairing to Instagram. Using their knowledge of the text, images, and quotes, students are then required to comment on one another's posts using their personal Instagram accounts. Of all these components, Cara says she's been most impressed with the students' comments, as they offer her the most insight into whether or not the students understood the literature's ideas and themes. She also found that her students enjoy having a real, authentic audience for their work and that most were already familiar with Instagram when she introduced the project.

At the opposite end of the educational spectrum, kindergarten teachers have also found success using Instagram; however, they focus more on sharing what's happening in their classrooms with parents. For example, Aviva Dunsiger and Maureen Cicinelli, two southern Ontario kindergarten teachers, have been expertly doing just this for many years. They both share color-rich images featuring exploratory materials used for inquiries and students at work or at play. And since their Instagram accounts are public, educators from across the globe can take a peek into what's happening in their classrooms as well. They say they've had very few parents express reluctance to have their kids' images online, but for those who do, the teachers simply take pictures of hands and backs of heads. Like Aviva and Maureen, administrators and teachers the world over are using Instagram to share their schools' and classrooms' stories with parents and educators.

Let's talk about how some students use Instagram for digital leadership. Joshua Williams of Joshua's Heart, for example, uses Instagram to share inspiration or stories of his organization, showcasing how students are helping others or to advertise events. On Instagram, I "met" Khloe Thompson, a nine-year-old who inspires children to lead, and who, together with her great-grandmother, sews "Kare bags" for the homeless. On Instagram she shares her charity work and inspires others to care. Following both of these students (as well as some of the others you will meet through them), is a great way to show your own students what digital leadership looks like.

But there are students who are also doing good in their own way. One of the students at my school, a wonderful student-leader, Isabella Sakitkovski, shared a story about a social "problem" she had encountered: that her peers might potentially go to prom wearing the same dress as someone else. Her solution? She took it upon herself to create an Instagram account where all twelfth-grade girls could post their dresses so there would be no worry about someone wearing the same one. Her account was also an extremely positive place where the girls could offer one another compliments.

Now, we could trivialize this and shake our heads about where today's students' priorities lie, or we could look at it differently. Isabella took what she knew about her peers (they are all on Instagram) and how the social media platform functions, then applied that knowledge to create a solution that could save someone from feeling embarrassed and uncomfortable during an important rite of passage: the senior prom. She isn't changing the lives of others in the local community, yet she created community and focused on a sense of well-being amongst her own peers.

Snapchat

Ever since I read danah boyd's book, *It's Complicated*, I have to say I've been wary of jumping onto every social media tool my students use and then incorporating it into my class. "Many teens get frustrated when adults 'invade' teen-centric spaces, and so," she says, "in an attempt to achieve privacy, some move on to newer sites and apps to avoid parents and other adults."[9] Snapchat, a mobile-messaging app that allows users to capture moments in their lives as a photo or ten-second video, was one of those apps that I didn't necessarily embrace for this reason, but it's also the one I initially feared the most as rumors flew of kids sending nude photos of themselves knowing they would disappear within twenty-four hours.

> Snapchat is on pace to have 217 million users by the end of 2017.

Having said that, as a teacher, I'm always on the lookout for ways I can use my students' interests and skills positively in the context of learning. Despite the fact that I was at first extremely opposed to using Snapchat in the classroom, I readily acknowledge that its filters and ease of use, as well as the fact that nearly every teenager and tween I know within a hundred-mile radius uses it, made resisting it as a possible tool for engaging and empowering my students very hard. (As of June 2016, Snapchat had 150 million daily users, resulting in 10 billion video views per day; according to an article from *Business Insider*, it is on pace for 217 million users by end of 2017.)[10]

So I joined and, since then, I've been amazed by the ways schools and companies are using it to tell stories. Since Tara Martin, a curriculum facilitator in Kansas, shared the "BookSnaps" idea with me, I've started taking pictures of texts and annotating them by adding doodles and using Snapchat's filters and Bitmoji characters.[11] Think of this as an updated (and more fun) way to have students engage in a "close reading" of text. I use it with my students as a way for us to share our thoughts about a reading selection.

But Snapchat is an ideal storytelling tool, so I love the way Dana DiLoreto, a middle school French teacher who taught high school English in summer school, used it. Her students were asked to create a Snapchat video depicting an analysis of a character in *The Great Gatsby* that would give her insights as to how well they understood the characters in the novel. Students, who normally dislike having to attend school in the summer, were engaged by the creativity of the task and really enjoyed editing and creating using a familiar tool. Schools are also using Snapchat to share "stories" with their parents and communities.

Jahmeelah Gamble, a special education educator and consultant from Toronto, used Snapchat to connect with a five-year-old student with autism.[12] Although she was partially nonverbal and her language was limited, Snapchat motivated the young girl to be more expressive with her language because she could use the app's unique filters and lenses to tell her stories. Some students with autism need to repeat things, so with Snapchat, the young girl could create something fun and wonderful, allowing her to have that repetition she desired. As she created stories, Jahmeelah used her personal Snapchat account and saved her student's images and videos to her personal phone's camera roll, never actually sharing the work. And even though Snapchat's minimum age requirement is thirteen, the girl's parents were supportive of Jameelah's using the app with their daughter because they saw how much she was benefiting from it.

Facebook

Although it's primarily known as a social media tool for connecting with family and friends, so many educators and organizations are using Facebook for other reasons that we can't discount it as a powerful tool for fostering digital leadership. In fact, as of February 2017, there were more than 1.86 billion monthly active Facebook users worldwide.[13]

I really took a second look at Facebook's potential for digital leadership when I saw how Brandon Stanton's Humans of New York (HONY) project could inspire students to use Facebook in a similar way. In 2010, when Stanton started HONY, his goal was simply to catalog 10,000 New York residents using photographs, to which he began to add quotes and then stories. Today, his cataloging is featured on HumansofNewYork.com, Twitter, and Instagram, and has led to HONY gaining more than 20 million followers on social media.[14] Besides the fact that reading these stories is a literacy-rich activity, the people Brandon talks to offers us glimpses into their lives.

A student attending Vaughan Secondary, where my husband was vice principal, was inspired by Stanton's project and created "Humans of Vaughan Secondary," featuring my husband in one of the posts[15] (Figure 3.4).

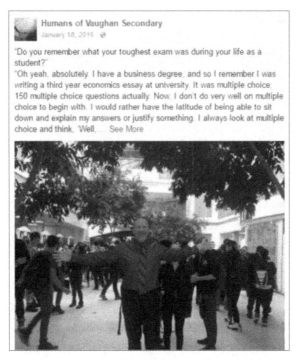

Figure 3.4

I chatted with graduating student Sarika Goel, Humans of Vaughan Secondary's creator, who chose Facebook as the platform since she felt her peers could easily access it and because, she says, Facebook is "the go-to spot for a teenager to unwind and catch up with their social life after completing hours of mind-numbing calculations, research, and essay-writing." My husband helped Sarika gain permission to do the project. A less-flexible administrator would have told her to do it on her own time or dissuade her from using Facebook at all, because Facebook is blocked in their district.

She says:

> *Although this was an independently run project, it certainly would not have taken off as well as it did or receive as much exposure were it not for the ceaseless support of the school staff. From granting the initial consent to create the Facebook page to generously donating their time to allowing me to interview the teachers, support staff, and administrative team, everyone played a key role in the success of this project.*

As a result, Sarika was able to create a legacy for the school. She reflects:

> *Overall, the friendship, inspiration, and wisdom I acquired through this project could not have been found in any textbook, which is why I advise every student to make the most of their years in school by exploring opportunities to build and create themselves outside of the classroom.*

Sarika's HOVS project really challenged me to rethink Facebook as an educational platform. I quickly learned many teachers are part of educational groups on Facebook, but, again—while there is much value and potential there, this tool is rarely encouraged for kids. While Facebook does have privacy problems and creates ads based on your posts, it's actually a great vehicle for discussion, especially since you can create private groups through which students can learn and practice "public" behavior authentically; using a tool they would use in their "real lives". When I taught media studies, I asked students to deconstruct ads; it is equally important that students look at how algorithms affect the ads we see on Facebook.

What's more, there are also so many nonprofits[16] and educational organizations, including TED, National Public Radio, and UNICEF. One of my favorites, DoSomething.org,[17] offers students opportunities for digital leadership by taking part in action campaigns on a variety of topics.

Many of these organizations share valuable information that could be a starting points for students in their academic research, or allow them to think critically about the credibility of information, or to find causes they are passionate about supporting. Students may even be inspired to create their own Facebook page, much like Sarika did with Humans of Vaughan Secondary.

YouTube

My husband finished our entire basement by watching YouTube videos. I've learned how to use every technology tool I utilize to facilitate professional learning via YouTube tutorials, and my older daughter told me she didn't need guitar lessons because she could learn how to play the guitar watching YouTube. And, yet, districts block access to the video-sharing platform, meaning one of the most useful resources available today doesn't exist once students walk inside the school building.

YouTube allows us to upload videos, create playlists, and exchange ideas and feedback through the comments section. And, while, yes, comments can sometimes be very negative, this platform (like every social media tool) relies on the honor system to properly identify explicit content and report inappropriate content. We have more power than we think when we embrace the safety tools to make a change, rather than ignoring the negativity and thinking someone else will take action. YouTube can be such a powerful tool to teach our students how to respond positively to others' creative work. We also need to remember that students may likely stumble upon inappropriate videos as well, so we need to show them how to report these—which can only happen if we are allowed to explore these tools together. If your kids are too young for regular YouTube, KidTube has kid-friendly content and you can use that to help your class create appreciative comments to the videos posted.

But instead of thinking about YouTube solely in terms of consumption, let's instead think about it from a digital leadership perspective. For example, similar to the Humans of Vaughan Secondary example, Chris

> A school or class YouTube account can be a place to showcase events, news, celebrate students, and invite constructive comments and dialogue.

Aviles, the EdTech coach for New Jersey's Fair Haven school district, said "yes" when two students approached him about creating a video news show to celebrate what makes their school great. Despite the fact that the students didn't have any experience or equipment, he supported their ideas and offered them guidance and technology support. Ultimately, though, they had control of the project and could create anything they wanted.

The students recorded the segments with Chris during his prep and lunch breaks, allowing them—as well as the rest of student body—to take control of their school's narrative. This resonated with not only the school community, but also with the community at large. Chris says, "Our school has become a better place to be because two students wanted to make a TV show." *The Bengal Buzz*, as they called it, moved to both YouTube and Twitter, allowing it to have a positive impact beyond their school.[18] Consider how having a school or class YouTube account can be a place to showcase events, news, celebrate students, and invite constructive comments and dialogue.

Another big piece of the YouTube puzzle I think we're ignoring—either intentionally or unintentionally—is that, for so many students, their role models are "YouTubers," or the (mostly young) people sharing their insights about a variety of topics through YouTube videos. Just like my generation wanted to be Wayne Gretzky (a Canadian, eh?), our students are aspiring to be like the successful YouTubers (male and female) who have made their careers by becoming famous on YouTube. And while you may be thinking how stupid that sounds, you can't dismiss the fact that kids are looking up to these people and that important conversations could be had if we were to just ask our students, "How are YouTubers effective role models?" the next time we wanted them to write a supported opinion piece. You may actually be surprised by some of the insights they come up with. Students at my school are happy to share with me the YouTubers they watch regularly, and they are often fun and frivolous, but other times, they're quite educational and interesting. Case in point: I actually didn't know there was such a thing as "booktubers" (young people sharing their passion for the books they're reading) until I asked students about it, but I'm really excited to explore this further with my book club.

I also really like the more civic-minded direction YouTube has taken recently. Hunter Walk, former director of product management at YouTube, spoke to this fact in May 2016, when he wrote on his blog, "My final year at YouTube was spent on a set of activities aimed at extending YouTube's capabilities as an education and activism platform, not just an entertainment vehicle."[19]

In that same vein, Rosanna Rooney, a teacher at my school with whom I was co-planning and co-teaching, transformed her more traditional research lesson into an opportunity to use social media in a positive way. Rather than have students simply research a nonprofit, she instead had them find an organization that they believed strongly in and create a PSA for it using iMovie. The results were uploaded to YouTube and shared with the organizations the students had selected. I'll never forget one student's response when he realized his work would go public: "*Aww*, man, now I have to make it better."

From a digital leadership standpoint, YouTube has the potential to be an incredible tool, in that it can empower students to learn and then share that learning, to speak for the voiceless, and to be a more positive influence in other people's lives. Since its invention, film has been a powerful medium, so the fact that YouTube allows us to create, edit, and easily share content is something to be celebrated, not blocked. It's also an extremely underutilized tool which could be a powerful complement to a digital portfolio (or a digital portfolio in and of itself). Any districts that use G Suite automatically have a YouTube channel. As a result, I've seen some teachers create playlists for their students to watch, but seldomly have I seen a student-run class YouTube account where they can learn the ins and outs of the tool. YouTube can be a wonderful platform for students to curate their interests, to upload their own video creations on a variety of topics, and to curate videos focusing on their career aspirations. So many kids I know have YouTube channels for their personal interests, but never really make the connection between their own personal learning, video creation for school, and their online identity. What's more, when students upload work they're proud of on YouTube, we can remind them the difference between publishing a video as private, unlisted, or public (I say "remind" because a tenth-grade, fifteen-year-old student reminded me that he had been using YouTube since the age of eight!!). Privacy settings can be changed at any time, so a class or school YouTube channel can gradually move from "unlisted" to "public" as comfort with the tool expands. There is also the potential within YouTube to moderate comments or to block comments with certain words contained in them, which would serve to empower their own use of the tool and to keep them safe.[20]

A Digital Leadership Approach Changes Behavior

The most important reason we need to change the current practice when it comes to using social media in the context of digital leadership is that it works. Although there is no empirical evidence yet (this is a topic I am actively pursuing at the graduate level), I continue to be amazed by the positive impact digital leadership is having on teachers and students who embrace it.

Rachel Murat, a New York high school teacher who teaches a digital citizenship course, for example, has used the digital leadership framework in her course. For their final presentations, her students create a digital portfolio whereby they are required to show how they had moved from becoming a responsible digital citizen to being a digital leader over the course of the semester.[21] Former students have shared how they had used a variety of social media platforms to learn and share their learning, to support a cause that is important to them, and to intentionally and positively influence others. I know this because Rachel used Periscope (a live-streaming video platform) to share her students' projects, and I was given a Google Form assessment rubric to provide feedback from my home in Ontario. A few students created and contributed to their school's kindness wall, while others worked on projects and campaigns about cyberbullying and Internet trolls. When I was watching, Stephanie Muggeo was talking about how she was striving to be a more positive influence online. She said, "You don't always have to share your opinions, and especially not if they are negative." Many adults could use that advice! Rachel's students each expressed ways that their perspective on digital leadership had changed during the course of the semester. Every single one of them sincerely thanked Rachel for what they'd learned. Beyond this, her students organized a Digital Citizenship Summit in February of 2017. They planned the logistics, procured speakers (including ten-year-old Curran Dee as a keynote speaker), and set the agenda for the day. One of her students, seventeen-year-old Casey Adrian, talked about how he used social media to become a published author. He also shared his beliefs about the importance of digital leadership:

> We are responsible to help spread the messages. We are responsible to forge new paths. We are using social media, a tool that is so readily available to us and that we understand so well, and we are using it to challenge what people believe. We're using this to change the world.[22]

I know that students in Rachel's class have come away with a very different understanding of how they should and could behave online.

The fact that digital leadership works effectively in changing behavior makes sense when you consider the theory of observational theory in which Albert Bandura, PhD explains that children pay attention to role models and may imitate the behavior they observe.[23] A teacher who embraces digital leadership is modeling positive behaviors. When I look at the Twitter accounts of the students you will meet in this book, I see how their experiences affected their behaviors online and how, in turn, others respond in kind.

Just as Timmy and Caroline believe that having their teacher interact positively with them online had an impact on their behavior, I have also seen this happen in the case of Alfred Lau, a seventh-grade student in Robert Cannone's class. Alfred's experiences in Robert Cannone's sixth-grade class, the previous year and through the various projects he's done, have helped him and his peers understand others' feelings and perspectives. He isn't just acting appropriately online; rather, he seeks to provide hope and inspiration to others. Here is someone who will likely never use social media to be hurtful, and I see this as a direct link to what he's learned in the classroom. His account is atypical to the Twitter accounts of other students his age who have not had similar role-modeling, in that he is assertive and positive and believes that what he posts can inspire others.

Figure 3.5

It is in these early years, when students are beginning to experiment with and play in online spaces, that we have the greatest impact on students, which is why we need to oversee our class accounts and be the ones to hit "send" (so we are following the law); however, the ownership of what is posted needs to belong to our students.

Student Vignette 🔊

When I say "social media," most people, especially parents, scream in fear, "Ah, social media—that's where my kids go and write bad comments about their teachers or post pictures from that party they were at. This is where malicious behavior takes place." But that doesn't have to be the case. I recently wrote a blog post called, "Why Is the Conversation Surrounding Social Media so Negative?" and in it, I document that my experience with social media is unusual, but that it doesn't have to be.

So why is social media abused? What I've found is that the conversation is always negative. "Social media is abused by young people" is the rhetoric that older people are using. So adults come and lecture students by saying, "Don't use social media." "Social media is bad." "Don't do this." And students start to identify social media as a negative place. Once you start lecturing to someone that they can't do something, it motivates them to do that thing and then they start developing these negative schemas of social media. I have a radical concept for you, especially those of you who talk negatively about social media.

Stop.

Really.

If you present social media as a positive space, as a place for students to go to express themselves, as a place to connect *with professionals and with other students, then that's the type of learning you are going to see there.*

So the question is, how do we help students understand their digital tattoo? And the answer to that is by using social media. I frequently interact with my teachers online, and it is encouraged that teachers and students interact with each other, because it makes it a safe learning space for everybody. When students go online and see their teachers there, they are first going to freak out; they are not going to want to interact with them. But, honestly, that's how it has to happen. When students see how their teachers are using social media appropriately to further their learning, connect with others, and build meaningful relationships, that's what students are going to think social media is used for. If everyone changed the way they interacted on social media to reflect a more positive image, then those around them would do the same.

By leveraging social media to work in a way that highlights and reflects my professional and academic endeavors, I have been able to achieve unbelievable milestones in my career, even as an eighteen-year-old! Through my digital involvement, specifically on Twitter, I have been able to share my voice internationally through blogging, webcasts, podcasts, and international speaking engagements; developed a partnership deal with Rosetta Stone Education; been invited to present at the 2016 Digital Citizenship Summit at Twitter's headquarters; and spread my message for educational reform to a receptive audience. I have also been able to connect with high-ranking professionals, including leading innovative public school teachers, educational policymakers, educational corporations, and now social media companies themselves, as a way to pioneer change in public education and promote student voice.

—Timmy Sullivan, graduate

In Summary ⬇

- Social media can be considered anything that connects people in a large-scale conversation, exploration, and opinion-sharing.

- Banning social media does not help anybody, nor does it work effectively.

- Modeling, supporting, and practicing digital leadership using common social media tools shows students how to use these tools to learn and share learning.

- Capitalizing on the tools students are currently using in the context of digital leadership can be a powerful, efficient way to cover curriculum goals and empower students to make a difference in their communities.

Discussion Questions ✂

1. How can districts support teachers as they explore the use of social media in the classroom with students in meaningful, authentic, and guided ways?

2. What are your own experiences with social media in teaching and learning? What is one way you might model and explore digital leadership?

3. What opportunities exist for engaging in critical conversations about which sites to block and which sites should be used for teaching and learning? What creative solutions can you come up with which allow students the opportunity to use social media for digital leadership?

Chapter 3 Notes

1. Scheffer, Jen, "12 Students Speak out about Digital Citizenship," *BHS Help Desk*, March 28, 2016, bhshelpdesk.com/2016/03/28/12-students-speak-out-about-digital-citizenship.

2. Belshaw, Doug, *The Essential Elements of Digital Literacies*, p. 50, 2015, frysklab.nl/wp-content/uploads/2016/10/The-Essential-Elements-of-Digital-Literacies-v1.0.pdf.

3. Lenhart, Amanda, "Teens, Social Media & Technology Overview 2015," April 9, 2015, pewinternet.org/2015/04/09/teens-social-media-technology-2015.

4. Although a plural noun, most people use the singular.

5. Harvey, K. (Ed.), *Encyclopedia of Social Media and Politics* (Vols. 1-3). Thousand Oaks, CA: SAGE Publications Ltd, 2014, doi: 10.4135/9781452244723.

6. Jenkins, H., Itō, M., & Boyd, D. *Participatory Culture in a Networked Era: A Conversation on Youth, Learning, Commerce, and Politics*. Cambridge: Polity Press, 2015.

7. Ibid.

8. "500 Million Views to the World," *Instagram Blog*, June 21, 2016, http://blog.instagram.com/post/146255204757/160621-news.

9. boyd, danah. *It's Complicated: The Social Lives of Networked Teens*. New Haven: Yale University Press: 2014, 59.

10. Snider, Chris, "Social Media Statistics," *Chris Snider Design*, chrissniderdesign.com/blog/resources/social-media-statistics.

11. Martin, Tara M. "#Booksnaps—Snapping for Learning," August 23, 2016, tarammartin.com/booksnaps-snapping-for-learning (Search "#BookSnaps" for ideas).

12. This is the tool that was most used by students at the time of writing this book, but the same idea could be implemented using any digital storytelling tool popular with your class.

13. Fiegerman, Seth, "Facebook Is Closing in on 2 Billion Users," *CNN Tech*, February 1, 2017, money.cnn.com/2017/02/01/technology/facebook-earnings.

14. Stanton, Brandon. *Humans of New York*, humansofnewyork.com/about.

15. Humans of Vaughan Secondary, Facebook, facebook.com/humansofvss.

16. "Top Nonprofits on Facebook," *TopNonprofits*, topnonprofits.com/lists/top-nonprofits-on-facebook.

17. Do Something, Facebook, facebook.com/pg/dosomething.

18. Aviles, Chris, "It's the Little Things," *Teched Up Teacher*, December 18, 2013, techedupteacher.com/its-the-little-things.

19. Walker, Hunt, "It's Hard to Convey the Impact Seeing the Work in Person Has on People," *HunterWalk.com*, May 4, 2016, https://hunterwalk.com/2016/05/04/its-hard-to-convey-the-impact-seeing-the-work-in-person-has-on-people-charity-waters-scott-harrison-on-making-a-difference.

20. I am creating video tutorials to help you learn how to customize your YouTube channel; please visit SocialLEADia.org.

21. Murat, Rachel, "We Have Become Digital Leaders," *All Things Social Studies,* January 29, 2017, spartansocialstudies.blogspot.ca/2017/01/we-have-become-digital-leaders.html.

22. Maine-Endwell High School, "Positively Social," YouTube, March 9, 2017, youtube.com/watch?v=BTMIryyR-nI&t=1s (8:30 - 8:50).

23. McLeod, Saul, "Bandura - Social Learning Theory," *Simply Psychology*, 2011, simplypsychology.org/bandura.html.

TIMMY SULLIVAN

timmysullivan.com

@timmysull1van

/timmysullivanMA

Timmy Sullivan is an eighteen-year-old bilingual international speaker from Burlington, Massachusetts, dedicated to empowering students in public education by giving them a voice. He is a freelance blogger advocating for the adoption of personalized learning in schools and a public speaker for the advancement of digital citizenship in students' lives. Today, he is pursuing a degree in political science and is eager to continue campaigning for students at the legislative level.

Use Timmy's Story to Inspire Your Students

If your school has a technology team, consider having those students reach out and connect with companies to ask questions, propose ideas, and offer suggestions.

If your students are interested in blogging, have them connect with Timmy on Twitter for advice.

Social Media Is a Part of Teaching and Learning Today

I encourage everyone to Google their name and see if that digital footprint truly reflects who they are. If it doesn't, get on social media and change it for the better!

—*Aidan Aird, twelfth grade*

In 2010, I began experimenting with social media in my classroom by starting a creative writing blog for my class using the Blogger platform. I had absolutely no idea what I was doing, but my ninth graders and I learned as we went. Together, we determined what the writing should include, and I very explicitly stated what effective commenting would look like. My students surprised me: They worked on their posts at all hours of the day, and I was impressed with how much they wrote. I was so excited to comment on their posts, and they absolutely amazed me by how much feedback they were giving one another. Simply put, my students were excited to read, write, create, and share. It was at this point that I recognized the extent to which having an audience beyond the teacher could have such a positive impact—and we hadn't even opened the blog up to the world yet. To this day, it's one of the most literacy-rich activities I've ever done, but it was also, at the time, one of the least traditional.

Fast-forward three years, and I was a program resource teacher for literacy and one of the lead learners in a district-wide initiative focused on technology-enabled learning called "21C." Many of my colleagues looked at what I was doing and saw it as two separate job descriptions. In fact, someone actually asked me, "Are you working on literacy today or 21C?" And, certainly, in those early days, I, too, thought the work we were doing to assist teachers using technology in their classrooms operated separately from the literacy support I was providing. I very quickly began to realize, though, that it was actually the same work: multidimensional, multimodal, and very necessary. Thankfully, my coordinator and superintendent supported this modern approach.

We seem to be bound by "tightly framed definitions of literacy that dominate many educational contexts," as Sheffield Hallam University literacy professors Cathy Burnett, EdD, and Guy Merchant, PhD, put it in their 2015 article, "The Challenge of 21st-Century Literacies."[1]

Many of us understand that literacy is nuanced and layered and connected to being able to read and write the world. Whereas yesterday's tools were the results of the printing press and paper and pen, today, technology and social media have increased our ability to communicate exponentially. Because of this, we need to embrace all methods of communicating.

The National Council of Teachers of English's position statement defining twenty-first-century literacies reminds us that literacy changes as society and technology change: "The [twenty-first] century demands that a literate person possess a wide range of abilities and competencies, many literacies. These literacies are multiple, dynamic, and malleable."[2] So, for students to become successful, they need to be proficient in all literacies, not just the traditional ones we're accustomed to or with which we are comfortable.

The Essential Elements of Digital Literacies author Doug Belshaw, EdD, says that in today's world, negotiating online social networks is extremely important. "At the most basic procedural level there is the understanding that, for example, Twitter allows only 140 characters, whereas other social networks do not tend to limit text input," he says. "More conceptual is an understanding of hashtags as 'channels' of communication and how these can be appropriated and re-appropriated by groups and loose networks of individuals."[3] He suggests, however, that we are continuing to evaluate and consider literacy from an analog perspective, never realizing digital technology has created completely different environments for learners.[4]

In that same vein, when he visited our district, George Couros asked us, "If you don't know what a hashtag is, are you considered illiterate today?"

And consider what internationally acclaimed author Margaret Atwood says:

> A lot of people on Twitter are dedicated readers. Twitter is like all of the other short forms that preceded it. It's like the telegram. It's like the smoke signal. It's like writing on the washroom wall. It's like carving your name on a tree. It's a very short form and we use that very short form for very succinct purposes.... It's sort of like haikus [and] prose.5

I continue to think about these expanded notions of literacy as I watch students engage in more reading and writing than any other generation because they text and share to social media. I would add they don't often know how social media can support their learning, nor would they consider the texting (writing and reading) they're doing as a literacy practice either. "We need to help students see that their blogging, texting, and tweeting on social media is real writing," The Writing Project's Rusul Alrubail shares in her *Edutopia* article, "How to Use Social Media to

Strengthen Student Writing."[6] I couldn't agree more, and yet I understand the struggle of parents and educators who can't quite see these as literacy behaviors because they are so contrary to what they have come to learn from their own past school experiences.

My younger daughter Kelsey has taught me much here. She has never, ever been an avid reader. Whenever we'd go to a bookstore, my older daughter and I would leave with armfuls of books, while she would come out with an eraser and a few stickers. Today, as a teenager, she explores her social media feeds' "Discovery" and "Explore" sections and often shares what she's reading and learning with us. It took me a long time to accept that she's engaging in literacy, but she is. In fact, when my husband and I were reading the Sunday morning paper one day and I gave her a "don't you know there is a no-cell-phone-at-the-table rule" disapproving look, she challenged me by saying, "You are reading the paper ... I'm reading too. What's the difference?" *Gulp.* My husband and I looked at each other and realized she was absolutely right.

It is important to know that students might have digital skills (that is, they know what a hashtag is, how to upload images, how to share information) but do not always possess the necessary digital literacies. Belshaw talks about the essential elements of digital literacies as being cultural, cognitive, constructive, communicative, confident, creative, critical, and civic.[7] I took an entire grad course on digital literacies, so while I recognize that it's not so simple, I am convinced we need to at least ask questions about how text and technology interplay and how this will ultimately affect the message. For example, we should be asking students how and why a message is different because it is conveyed as a blog post, a tweet, a news article, or an infographic.

When students learn and share their learning (a key component of digital leadership) using technology and social media, they are engaging in valuable literacy skills. And we can bemoan the fact that kids these days don't know enough about Chaucer or Shakespeare, but if literacy is about reading and writing the world, then we need to remember that the world today is different than the one in which we were educated. In light of that, we need to balance what we perceive to be valuable with what students will need to be active participants of the society into which they will graduate.

Have You Noticed the 'Media' in Social Media?

Traditionally, the media has been accused of being the culprit of any number of negative social outcomes, including "unrealistic body images; modeling; pressure to conform; gender-typed socialization; objectification of the body; internalization of appearance ideals; increased negative affect that results from viewing unrealistic images of the body; social comparisons; interactions with peers, etc."[8] As you can see, this list is quite extensive.

Now, social media is receiving its share of the blame in the form of posts, articles, studies, and musings about the same issues I was tackling twenty years ago in my media studies class and then continued to tackle when I taught English. Perhaps the reason why these messages seem to be a more pressing concern today, though, is because social media amplifies our access to them; although many scholars were just as worried about the impact of television as its use and popularity rose.

In a study examining how social media affects body image, Cleveland State University professor of communication Richard Perloff, PhD, says, "Social media, in Western countries, such as the United States, United Kingdom, and Australia, have infiltrated individuals' lives in ways that was not possible with previous mass media."[9]

I have yet to find a study, though, that makes a significant correlation between narcissism and selfies. Having said that, sharing excessively and posting provocative photos, and then subsequently taking them down if they don't receive enough "likes," has more to do with self-esteem issues that were harder to detect ten years ago, but that now, social media is making far more obvious.

> We have to teach our students to ask critical questions when confronted with a media text.

In a July 2016 blog post titled "'Deficit Comparisons' to 'Abundance Introspection,'" George Couros wrote:

> With Instagram, one thing has changed: the amount we con-sume of one another's edited lives. Young women growing up on Instagram are spending a significant chunk of each day absorbing others' filtered images while they walk through their own realities, unfiltered. In a recent survey conducted by the Girl Scouts, nearly 74 percent of girls agreed that other girls tried to make themselves look "cooler than they are" on social networking sites.[10]

Social media, like all media, is an interplay of purposefully cho-sen audience, text, and production (techniques and conventions) in an attempt to represent a construct of reality. And this applies to all types of media, including "reality" TV, magazine covers, film, news articles, and posters. So we have to teach our students to ask critical questions when confronted with a media text and to always be slightly skeptical of what is being portrayed.

Take, for example, the story of Australian Instagram celebrity Essena O'Neill, who "blew up the Internet" when she swore off social media. This is an especially interesting case study to look at with older students because she openly admits that every picture, every post on her Instagram account, was completely contrived and that she was never truly happy. In an opinion piece titled "Social Media Is Not Real Life, But That's Not the Problem," *The Everygirl's* News and Culture editor, Daryl Lindsey, empha-sizes that the concept of faking a "perfect" life on social media has been around almost as long as social media itself.[11]

What's more, students are using tools independently and being targeted in ways they simply don't understand. Companies have moved their marketing to social media and are now speaking directly to preteens and teens using sophisticated ads guising as posts and stories.

And so, with this in mind, how can we possibly engage our students in media literacy if they aren't allowed to use social media in our classrooms? There is no such thing as "too young" for media literacy, and when we teach students how social media works, we are empowering them to think critically about the messages they are viewing.

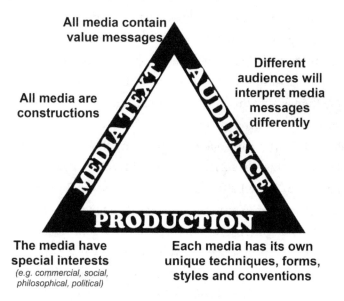

Figure 4.1[12]

Whether we're talking about an advertisement, a Facebook story, or an Instagram photo, we, along with our students, can isolate all of the elements of the media triangle. In that way, we are able to help those kids who may not readily recognize the posts' (albeit by their friends or favorite celebrities) contrived nature so they can gain a clearer sense of what's real and what's fake.

Research suggests media literacy *does* prove effective in combating women's body-image perceptions and that a "multisystem approach is necessary to empower youth and adults" to start to challenge media-propagated images of narrow and harmful idealized bodies. This approach *should include social media*, which is "capable of dramatically expanding the reach of media literacy programs on body image," writes Julie Andsager, PhD, a communications professor at the University of Tennessee, in her 2014 article "Research Directions in Social Media and Body Image."[13] This is especially important when we consider that so many students derive their self-worth from the number of "likes" they receive. Adolescence is a time when youth are particularly susceptible to peer pressure and influence. So using social media in context, and as a point of reference, will go a long way toward helping them. But we have to begin before they develop a deep-rooted sense of what social media "should" be.

My thoughts on this topic have been largely shaped by my professor and mentor, the University of Ontario Institute of Technology's Janette Hughes, PhD, who has done extensive research on the effects of social media in education. In a 2013 study she did with graduate student Laura Morrison, they looked at two ninth-grade classes in Toronto and determined that we need to reshape how students think about the potential of social networking sites at a formative age. Their study identified a "need for educators to incorporate a critical analysis of [social media] and its role in identity development, and to start incorporating [social media] as a tool for raising awareness about critical issues facing adolescents. These include body image, depression, and cyberbullying."[14]

At this point, you may be wondering how on earth you have time to possibly teach one more thing during an already packed day. In Ontario, the English/language arts curriculum is divided into "Oral Communication," "Reading," "Writing," and "Media Studies," meaning a quarter—that's 25 percent—of the course should be dedicated to deconstructing and creating media. The United States' Common Core standards also emphasize media literacy as a necessary skill for students, and like the

Ontario Curriculum, Common Core doesn't designate a list of key texts to study, nor does it specify what a "text" is.

In fact, The Critical Media Project from the University of Southern California Annenberg states:

> A text could be a canonical piece of literature, a painting in the Louvre, a 1970s sitcom, a comic book or a video game. The Common Core does not designate a list of key texts. Rather, in tandem with media literacy education platforms, the Common Core centers on a set of skills that emphasize the importance of interpreting and understanding a myriad of texts.[15]

We can limit the our kids' exposure to social media—and for health reasons, we should; but we may also have to take a look at other, more proactive ways to address the multilayered issues that arise here. We can't solve these problems by blaming our kids' social media use, nor by banning it, but, rather, through educating and having conversations with them.

Julie Andsager, PhD, a professor of media says:

> [S]ocial media shouldn't just be a part of the conversation, it can be a part of the solution; not just because of the potential of widespread messaging, but because when students actually create using technology and social media, they are learning about the interplay of text, production, and audience which will serve to help them to become critical of the media they consume.[16]

We need to rethink how we're teaching media and remember that all media, including "social" media, is a construct of reality. We need to show our students how to discover the true nature of this edited version of reality and help them become creators of media.

Rethinking the Selfie: A Selfie Center

What if we approached selfies differently beginning at a young age? Nine-year-old Olivia Van Ledtje (who you will meet later) and her mother,

Cynthia Merrill, do just that. They contend that selfies can "create a land-scape of understanding and reflection."[17] So they advocate students from pre-kindergarten through fifth grade use a "Selfie Center" as a means to enrich their literacy.

When students take photos of themselves, then use those images to reflect on their learning, they are highlighting their own strengths as readers. The focus shifts from the selfie itself toward metacognition, fostering independence, and reading. "A selfie becomes a powerful tool for building understanding about how we view ourselves and how we are viewed by others," Cynthia says.

Students take turns using an iPad or other video-recording tool and capture themselves and their reflections on independent reading, which they then upload to a class account and share on Twitter using the hashtag #selfiecenter. Depending on the learner's readiness, a Selfie Center can either be a guided or independent experience, but eventually the goal should be for it to become an activity the student does individually.[18] I've already seen classroom teachers who are taking Olivia's lead and having their students create and share their own reading selfies!

"Fake" News

Almost every day during the 2016 US presidential campaign, mis-leading pictures, headlines, and false news stories were making the rounds on social media. *BuzzFeed News* even suggested that more people were engaged with these stories than legitimate stories between August and the November election day.[19]

During those months, most evenings, my family would share exam-ples of things we'd seen that day around the dinner table, and my youngest daughter, especially, would ask us if what she was reading was true. I wish I could say that most families sit together and have these conversations, but the fact of the matter is, my daughter was born into a middle-class white family with two teachers for parents. This alone gives her inher-ent advantages over her peers. Only when the educational system begins including these conversations in classrooms will her peers have similar learning opportunities.

A November 2016 Stanford University research study of 7,804 students found that "students have trouble judging the credibility of information online."[20] The study looked at middle school to college-age students and tested how effectively they could determine which sites were reliable and which ones were sponsored. Of the middle school students studied, more than 80 percent believed an advertisement with the words "sponsored content" written on it was a real, credible news story.

We can only begin to address this problem by approaching social media as a tool for learning. Even as an adult, I have to apply critical thinking and constructive skepticism to what I see in my social media feeds, so I think bringing this into the classroom, particularly to our work with older students, is a necessary and worthwhile endeavor.

Figure 4.2

Here's an example from the winter of 2016. I was drawn to the Twitter account of Bana Alabed, a seven-year-old girl, and her mother (Figure 4.2). I was intrigued by Bana and her tragic circumstances, living in Aleppo, Syria, during a time of war and destruction. I never questioned the account's authenticity—after all, I'd been reading about amazing children from around the world who were promoting important causes and sharing them on Twitter and other social media outlets. So, in my mind, it wasn't beyond reason that her mother was moderating her account. And, yet, as I read through some of the comments, many adults were accusing the account of being fake; for a brief moment, I began to doubt Bana's credibility.

How do you know if something is real or fake?

This is the process I went through:

1. Is the account verified? (Yes, there was a blue check mark beside the user's name to indicate Twitter had verified her account.)

2. Are the posts plausible and realistic? (It's plausible that she would speak English and that she would have access to technology, as I have met many educators from around the world who have these privileges.)

3. If I do a "reverse image search" on Google images, will I find the pictures featured in other sources?[21] (No, in this case the images I found were only connected to this young girl.)

4. If I do a Google search for this account, do legitimate news sources come up? (Yes, specifically an article from the BBC, "Meet the Seven-Year-Old Girl Tweeting from Aleppo."[22])

For those who dismissed Bana as fake, they missed out on both an opportunity to gain insight into what is happening in real time in the world and an incredible provocation for an inquiry project. Here was an example of a young girl who asked her mother to tweet for her because she "genuinely wanted the world to hear her voice."[23]

To help my colleagues and my students more easily identify fake websites, I use a template called "SOURCE" (Figure 4.3).[24] We could also use this template to look at Bana's Twitter account.

S	How is the source **Sponsored**?
O	Does it contain **Opinions** or *Facts*?
U	What is the **Underlying Bias**? What assumptions are being made?
R	How **Reputable** is the source and/or organization?
C	How **Current** is the source?
E	Is the author a known **Expert**? (i.e., credentials can be verified by various sources)?[25]

Figure 4.3

There are different variations of this such as CRAAP[26] and SMELL[27] which similarly ask students to think critically about what they are reading and viewing and which are equally easy to remember.

Misleading News

Another issue is misleading news. One day, my children came home and said, "Mom, the Great Barrier Reef is dead. You guys killed it, and now there won't be any fish as of 2050." I responded with, "Wow, where did you get that information?" They said, "It's trending[28] on Twitter." So, of course, I asked them to show me, and although it was trending during the school day, it certainly wasn't when we looked together. When they proceeded to delve into the topic further (our rule of thumb is three credible sources), they admitted they hadn't checked other sources.

Here's what really happened: A journalist posted an ironic piece warning readers about the impact of climate change, and people on Twitter misread it (or rather they skimmed it rather than actually reading it). I thought it was an incredible opportunity to learn, so I tweeted about it (Figure 4.4).

> **Jennifer Casa-Todd**
> @JCasaTodd
>
> My teens insisted that Great Barrier Reef died today. Led to great talk about news media, hyperbole, hoaxes & environment #literacy
>
> **Seacology** @seacology
> No, the #GreatBarrierReef isn't "dead." But it is in serious trouble.
> huffingtonpost.com/entry/scientis...

Figure 4.4

Teachers responded to me, sharing that they'd used my experience as a springboard for discussions in their classes. An English teacher might look at the original piece's persuasive language, including its use of hyperbole as a stylistic technique. A geography or science teacher might investigate the facts and myths surrounding global warming's effects on the Great Barrier Reef, and students are naturally interested because they are very keen to notice when learning is connected to what they perceive as "real life." Teachers who couldn't access Twitter missed out on an incredible teaching opportunity.

When we begin with social media "news," we are providing students with important skills to learn how to ensure they are looking critically at what is being shared; for the same reason, I often let my students begin with Wikipedia. When I taught high school English, many moons ago, my curriculum told me I had to have my students write for a variety of purposes, using a variety of forms, for a variety of audiences, so I would always ask them to write some form of review. When I met an executive from Yelp while visiting San Francisco, we had a great conversation about the prevalence of fake reviews, and he told me his company has a security team in place that sifts through all of the posts to find fake ones. I had no idea this was even a career, and it made me think about how when I was teaching English, there were so few opportunities to leverage an authentic audience. At best, I had students to submit editorial comments to our local newspaper, but the ease with which students can now write for real audiences in real time through social media is absolutely incredible.

Today, I could have my students write for authentic audiences online, including Yelp, TripAdvisor, Amazon, Rotten Tomatoes, and Goodreads (all of which can technically be considered social media). They could use the criteria we establish together in class for what makes an "effective" review, but also hunt for fake reviews to discuss together. I could never have fathomed this could be done so easily.

Now, don't get me wrong: I'm not saying we should abandon great literature—I wholeheartedly believe stories, poetry, and drama are essential to our humanity. However, we also need to make time to help our students use technology and social media to think critically about the media they consume.

As you plan your lessons, consider whether or not you're providing your students with a balance of what they will need and what you think they need. I want students to be the ones asking questions before blindly liking or sharing something. Now, more than ever, we need to help our students navigate the myriad of fake websites and news sources so they can become digital leaders. Students can share this learning with others, perhaps younger students in their area or at their school; contact news outlets; or even become journalists for a local paper (physical or online). I truly believe this is the generation that holds the power to change this unfortunate and dangerous trend of misleading news.

Distraction

Students are distracted by their phones—they are far more interested in what Sally and Johnny are doing at lunch than the War of 1812, and they would rather play a game than work on a school assignment. Guaranteed. But I can't admonish them too harshly: When I was a teenager, I was easily more interested in boys than what any of my teachers were lecturing on; and even today, I have to admit, I would rather see what my PLN is sharing on Twitter than listen to someone regurgitate information at a workshop or meeting.

That's why we need to rethink our natural response to distractions and help students (and adults) develop self-regulatory skills so they can exercise "deliberate media mindfulness," as Howard Rheingold, a social media scholar and University of California Berkeley lecturer puts it.[29] That is, students (and perhaps adults too) need to be made aware of their use of media and the extent to which it is distracting them.

In his 2010 article, "Attention, and Other 21st-Century Social Media Literacies," Howard discusses five "social media literacies":[30]

1. **Attention**: The ability to identify when focused attention is required and to recognize when multitasking is beneficial.

2. **Participation**: More than consumers, participants actively participate—knowing when and how to participate is important.

3. **Collaboration**: Participants can achieve more by working together than they can working alone.

4. **Network awareness**: An understanding of social and technical networks.

5. **Critical consumption**: Identifying trustworthiness of the author or text.

We have already touched (or will touch) on many of these literacies, but for our intents and purposes right now, I want to focus on "attention," which, as Howard says, is "of particular importance both in the classroom and in life." We need to have conversations about how companies (including news outlets) try to get our attention on social media, how we try to get one another's attention, as well as reflect upon how their own divided attention is helping them or hurting them.

I remember reading about "flow," a theory created by education and psychologist Mihály Csíkszentmihályi, PhD, to describe the psychological state whereby you are so involved in an activity that you lose track of time and everything else. I then started thinking about the connection between flow and cell phone distraction and dependence.

In one of his studies, Mihály gave teachers and students pagers. When the pager went off, both groups recorded exactly what they were doing and thinking. This particular lesson was on the history of China. The teachers' thoughts and recordings had everything to do with Genghis Khan and the Great Wall of China. The students' responses had absolutely nothing to do with China at all—it was actually quite the opposite: Twenty-five out of the twenty-seven students were thinking about being hungry, sleepy, and what their dates were doing. The two students who did reference China were thinking about a Chinese restaurant they'd visited. There was no mention of the content the teacher had talked about. As a result, Mihály concluded students don't engage with content in the same way teachers do. "People will seek out flow anyway," he says. "If they can't find it in school, they will find it somewhere else."[31]

Today, I'd argue that "somewhere else" is the smart phone, which offers a whole world of connections, entertainment, and interests—and it just happens to be in students' pockets. So how do we help our students learn to use their phones when it's appropriate if we don't first help them recognize when they're turning to their phones as a distraction? (This also begs a whole other question about instructional practices, which is again an entirely different book.)

Although Mihály's study had nothing to do with cell phones or social media, I think adding these twenty-first-century components would make for a great social experiment or thesis. Increasingly, research is suggesting that multitasking isn't necessarily good for our brains. I wonder to what extent we recognize how our multitasking behaviors affect our performance. However, in a more practical context, I think it would be an excellent way to reinforce self-regulation, a skill that would serve everyone well to learn in our connected world.

In Ontario, we actually assess students' self-regulation, which includes their ability to set their own individual goals and then monitor their progress toward achieving them; critically assess and reflect on their strengths, needs, and interests; and identify learning opportunities, choices, and strategies that will help them reach their personal needs and goals.[32] If I knew all my students had cell phones (remember, equity), I would have students log (perhaps on their devices) exactly what they were doing when they checked their phones; then after about a week, I would have them reflect, identify any patterns they notice, and create a goal for themselves, which we could revisit later on. In a math class, they could graph their findings; in an English or language arts class, they could write about them; and in any class, it would make for a very interesting discussion.

As a teacher-librarian, I don't have my own class per se, so the line I use most often when I'm walking around the library is, "Is your device helping you or distracting you?" This starts a dialogue with the student because it presumes positive intentions. When a device is helping them, the student will more than likely show me what they're working on (and I've learned so much as a result of this approach). Because here's a reality: Adults often assume kids are distracted when, in actual fact, they may be looking up information, adding information to their calendar, or taking notes. Often, a student, when asked in the inquisitive way I inquire, will acknowledge their device is distracting them, and immediately put it in their bag. I don't "make" them do this, nor do I use an accusatory tone that suggests I already know the answer. Instead, it's an invitation that often leads to a conversation where I share my own struggles with distractions, offer some of the strategies I use for managing them, and invite other students to talk about what they do.

> "Is your device helping you or distracting you?"

Having these conversations empowers students to take responsibility for their own actions, while also allowing them to practice honing these skills. When we collaborate with students and determine clear expectations for using their devices, and then we hold them accountable for these behaviors, we're teaching them far more than we would be if we had a blanket "no cell phone use" policy. Thus, when I co-teach with teachers where cell-phone distraction is an ongoing concern, we explicitly make self-regulation a learning goal we assess. We ask students to set a goal for themselves, and check back with them at the end of the period to reflect upon how they achieved their goal.[33]

I don't just struggle with distraction as a teacher, but as a mother as well. We have no-device dinners, because when I'm talking to my children, they need to give me their full attention, and bedtime means no cell phones in their rooms. While I am very cognizant of helping my own kids moderate their technology use, I realize other parents don't have these same rules. And while we can ban cell phones in classrooms to address this issue, we risk not helping a whole generation of kids understand how to strike a healthy balance.

However, on this flip side of this argument, as we have seen in the previous chapter, students only know social media to be a distraction, a form of entertainment, because the typical classroom rarely uses it in the context of teaching and learning. Furthermore, when we use digital leadership as a framework for technology and social media use, we know students can, in fact, become advocates for these same issues and address them with their peers, if we educate them and empower them to take action.

Teaching Digital Leadership *and* Twenty-First-Century Competencies

We are almost two decades into the twenty-first century, and it seems as if only now are we gradually beginning to understand the extent to which we can improve our current education system so it can better help students develop the skills they'll need to succeed—and thrive.

In an age where students' names are the subject of Internet searches before receiving a college or university acceptance letter or given the stamp of approval for a summer job, let alone a career, it is essential that we provide our students opportunities in the school environment to inter-act positively in online spaces. The younger the better.

In his article, "From Robot-Proof: How Colleges Can Keep People Relevant in the Workplace," Northeastern University President Joseph Aoun, PhD, speaks to the possibilities that exist for us in this age:

> *The robot age invites people to be not drones, servants, or vag-abonds, but creators. Technology will free us to ask questions that have never been posed, to envision beauty never before unveiled in the mind's eye. To achieve this, though, we'll need to educate people very differently.*[34]

To me, part of what it means to "educate people very differently" is to see technology and social media as opportunities for our students to think crit-ically about what's going on in their communities and actively try to make the world around them a better place. In this same vein lies the importance of collaboration and how it's evolving to require an increasingly sophis-ticated set of competencies. As Harvard's Graduate School of Education professor, Chris Dede, EdD, says, "In addition to collaborating face to face with colleagues across a conference table, [twenty-first-century] workers increasingly accomplish tasks through mediated interactions with peers halfway across the world whom they may never meet face to face."[35] He goes on to explain that students need to graduate with tools that will enable them to successfully collaborate online as well as offline.

By promoting digital leadership and providing opportunities for stu-dents to connect with experts, organizations, and causes, we're allowing them to develop and hone the skills they'll need to handle new workplace realities. We're also challenging them to listen thoughtfully and formulate their ideas orally. Too often, we fear obstacles like technology not working or needing to work around time zone issues, but overcoming them allows students to participate in real-life creative problem-solving.

Entrepreneurial Skills and Career Readiness

When we talk about the skills students need to be successful in today's world, most literature references entrepreneurship, or "the process of creating and implementing innovative ideas to address economic opportunities or social problems, whether that is through enterprise creation, improved product development, or a new mode of organization."[36]

In their 2014 white paper, "New Pedagogies for Deep Learning," educational reform advocates Michael Fullan and Geoff Scott say entrepreneurship is connected to "creativity," which they define as "having an 'entrepreneurial eye' for economic and social opportunities, asking the right questions to generate novel ideas, and demonstrating leadership to pursue those ideas into practice."[37] However, they also add that today's entrepreneurialism is "not just about making money but also being able to identify and resolve complex personal and societal challenges locally and globally."

This definitely applies to digital leadership. I am so impressed by how many of the students I am meeting are already taking advantage of social media to simultaneously address social problems and capitalize on economic opportunities. For example, if you take a look at eleven-year-old Nyeeam Hudson's Twitter account,[38] you can't help but notice how inspiring and positive his tweets are; he's building upon this presence by authoring a book, *We Are All Kings*, which encourages "young males around the world to believe in themselves as kings of greatness."[39] He is also traveling the world as a motivational speaker encouraging other students. But Nyeeam isn't alone—Timmy Sullivan received a company sponsorship that allowed him to travel to the Digital Citizenship Summit, and Yumi Lee has built a thriving baking business—and she isn't even in high school yet! What's more, ten-year-old Calramon Mabalot, of San Diego, California, not only built a 3D printer, but then used it to create a prosthetic hand for his teacher.[40] Today, his business, Brother Robot, offers a variety of 3D printing services. Their connections and exposure via social media are leading them to make money.

How do you feel about students cashing in using their social media presence? Are you upset that we're suddenly in a society where everything is being monetized? Or are you wondering, as I am, to what extent we're aware of this shift? Are we helping our students understand that kids their age are earning money for being inventive and creative? It really comes down to rethinking what we know.

While these questions may make us uncomfortable, they're part of a larger conversation we need to have about how social media is providing opportunities to those students who may (or may not) be headed toward an academic, post-secondary path but who are really creative and inventive. I believe that we can't possibly teach a careers course today without encouraging students to think about their social media presence. I'm thankful to have been fortunate to have the opportunity to bring in these necessary conversations to our Careers Studies courses at my current school.

Earlier in the book, I shared the question my daughter fielded during a Skype interview for a summer job: "What social media networks are you on, and what will I learn about you if I go there?" When we consider how ubiquitous technology and social media are, of course it makes sense to ask kids about their social media presence. Increasingly, though, many employers and admissions counselors aren't formally admitting to this, instead opting to do Google searches about students before accepting them into their college or university or approving their job application. And I realize this may be disheartening because it is an added stressor, but it has also increasingly become a new reality. Sadly, there are stories circulating about kids creating fake online personas to ensure they have a positive presence online, while others are "scrubbing" their social media and online identities so the bad stuff doesn't get seen, which, unfortunately, is as suspect as not having an online presence at all. *Does this bother you as much as it bothers me?*

What's more, every time we communicate in public online spaces, we leave traces or "footprints." These footprints can be "passive"

> How can we still "be ourselves" on social media while crafting a "Brand of Me" to use in our career planning?

(unintentional) or they can be "active" (actively created).[41] Do students understand that every time they communicate online, they are contributing to their digital footprint and that once something is posted, it continues to exist? This is why some people refer to these footprints as a "digital tattoo," suggesting a more permanent and purposeful mark. Whichever term you use, though, we need to make sure our students know "the more you spend time on social networking websites, the larger your digital footprint will be," as TechTerms.com author Per Christensson puts it.[42]

Monster's director of digital communications and social media, Patrick Gillooly, wrote in a 2016 *New York Times* article: "Your social media presence—and, really, your whole digital footprint—is no longer just an extension of your résumé. It's as important as your résumé. Social media use is now a standard of the hiring process, and there's little chance of going back."[43]

In the spring of 2016, a friend of mine chose to go into business for herself and was made to learn social media: Facebook, Instagram, and Snapchat. Our students know how to use the tools, but have no knowledge of networking or leveraging the tools for their future and we have done little to assist them. So, understanding this, in the Careers Studies lesson[44] I teach, I focus on what I believe to be a crucial question: How can we (as high school students) "be ourselves" on social media while crafting a "Brand of Me" to use in our career planning?

In this lesson, students do Google searches of themselves, think about what their current social media presence says about them, then think about how this conflicts with (or complements) who they really are—their interests, their personality, their passions, and their career aspirations. During the lesson, we unpack what it means to create an intentionally positive online presence. We need to address the idea that some students think it's wise to have a completely sanitized personal digital presence. I ask them if they think that having a nonexistent, private account, or sanitized presence would be as suspect to employers or admissions officers as having a negative one. By the time students are in high school, these conversations are not only important, but necessary. The lesson culminates in students looking at various student-created About.Me profiles, Twitter accounts, and YouTube Channels in order to make strides to create their own positive online presence.

I don't love the idea of kids (or adults) branding themselves (we are people, not products); however, I do really like the way Jason Shaffer—who teaches a mandatory personal branding and digital communication course at North Broward Prep in Florida—defines the foundations of personal branding: "Identify your passions, stick to your moral code, focus on your goals, and tell your personal story through a variety of social platforms."[45]

Every student should have the opportunity to develop an online identity that highlights their accomplishments and interests beyond the academic. The fact is that some schools, like North Broward Prep and my own school, are already doing this, and some parents are also helping their children to stand out on social media, while others have no idea where to begin. This can happen for every student, however, if we develop an attitude of mind which includes digital leadership.

The more we talk about it, the more we get our own students thinking about it. For example, after talking with one student in my book club about the advantages and disadvantages of creating a Goodreads account, he sent me this note:

Hi, Ms. Casa-Todd,

As I was thinking about our book club meeting today, I thought of an idea we could try to do for the Innovation Team.

Maybe we could make a guide on how people can make more professional social media accounts and we could go through things like finding a profile picture and stuff like that. Students know how to make accounts to connect with friends, but making accounts to connect with schools or employers isn't really a known skill.

There are definitely articles already on this topic, but making our own exclusive post might be cool and beneficial.

Not sure if the idea will work out, but it's something to think about as for the direction of the Innovation Team.

Have a good evening,

Ali Bashar

Of course I supported Ali and his idea.

A student I've learned a great deal from about these necessary conversations is Aidan Aird, a seventeen-year-old from Markham, Ontario, who I found on Twitter during my ongoing quest in search of digital leaders. His website, *Developing Innovations*, impressed me, and I loved the fact that he'd created a not-for-profit organization of the same name to advocate and inspire youth to get involved in science, technology, engineering, and math (STEM). When I was working on a blog post discussing digital leadership, I reached out to him, and you can imagine my surprise when I discovered he was a student in my own district. So when we hosted an Edcamp in November 2015, I invited Aidan to speak to our educators. Aidan shared with us how he uses his website, Facebook, and Instagram to promote students; his passion for social media; how it's had such a positive effect in his life; and the role he believes it should play in school.

Further, Aidan said that because of the connections he's made through Twitter, he has had a number of opportunities open up to him, including receiving a nomination for the Association of Fundraising Professionals'

Greater Toronto Chapter's 2016 Youth Philanthropist of the Year.[46] What I love about Aidan is that he promotes other students rather than himself, but that by doing so, he is still cultivating a positive online presence for himself. Think for a moment about how countercultural this is right now, but also how important it is to emphasize and model, so this can change.

Aidan is living proof that if students focus their social media posts on learning, sharing their learning, making a positive impact, sharing their passion, and addressing societal inequality, then their digital presence will be nothing short of positive—they'll never have to sanitize or prune it. Almost as important is the fact that if and when students ever do make a minor error in judgment (they are kids, after all), the good stuff will generally supersede the not-so-good stuff.

The purpose of school is to open our students' eyes to new learning and new possibilities, so it's a shame that many educators don't look at technology and social media with the same lens as they would any other important invention or discovery that's transforming the way we do things. We need to reflect on how we currently view social media instruction in school, rethink ways to embrace it, and use it in purposeful and positive ways so we can inspire our students to do the same.

Combating the New Digital Divide

In her field research, sociologist Annette Lareau, PhD, reinforces what many of us have known for a while: "[M]iddle-class parents have cultural knowledge and social networks that they can leverage to improve their child's educational experiences. The working-class parents do not. This differential access to cultural and social capital creates inequalities in children's educational experiences and, ultimately, educational success."[47] In this case, she was talking about face-to-face social networks; however, I'd argue that in today's world, these social networks include connections via social media and that the advantages are more further-reaching than ever.

Many of the student leaders embodying the characteristics of digital leadership have an adult who encourages them, often outside an

> If we don't provide opportunities in all schools for all students to become digital leaders, we'll have students at an additional disadvantage.

educational setting. For example, Curran, who makes a compelling argument for why he should be able to use technology in school, has found his greatest cheerleader in his mother, Marialice, a scholar, connected educator, and advocate for student voice and digital citizenship. This is also true for young Yumi Lee. In fact, during her speech at a TEDx event in Ontario, Canada, she cited her dad, Royan—an educator and blogger who also presented a TED Talk that day—several times as her inspiration and mentor. Hannah Alper's father is well connected on social media and her mom supports her and co-moderates her account. The fact is, most young people demonstrating digital leadership, in the way it is defined here, are doing so because of, or in collaboration with, supportive parents or a caring adult. Now, this isn't to take away from the awesomeness of these kids, who are truly inspiring role models for their peers, but the fact that adults are supporting them has certainly given me pause.

I know that out of the thirty students in any one of my classes, less than half have solid family support. Few sit down at a dinner table with their families each night, and some have so many other issues to contend with that creating a website that explores their passions, developing a positive online presence, or improving someone else's life in person or through technology or social media is completely inconsequential. I am gravely concerned that if we don't provide opportunities in all schools for all students to become digital leaders, we'll have students at an additional disadvantage, especially if they don't have digital access at home. In fact, I would be in good company if I were to suggest that this might be the new digital divide. In *Participatory Culture in a Networked Era*, boyd asserts a similar concern when she references the "geeky" or "creative-class" parent who games with their kids, is tech-savvy, and "provide[s] meaningful mentorship that values an empowered identity in relation to media," which, she suggests, is "defining a new digital learning elite."[48] Many students don't recognize the power of social media; therefore, they need a caring adult who has embraced digital leadership to ask the right questions and provide scaffolded support. If this caring adult is an educator in a public school, then this levels the playing field for students who lack that influence at home.

Another sad fact is that for most of the student digital leaders you'll read about in this book, their passions were actually ignited *outside* of school. When we offer students the opportunity to be digital leaders *in* school, we help them develop the skills they need to become active citizens in their world, one that is increasingly digital and connected.

But know this: You don't need to be particularly geeky or tech-savvy to provide your students with these opportunities. You already engage your students in a variety of experiences through literature, art, poetry, and interesting topics, many of which may awaken passions and talents. The next step is to consider the extent to which technology and social media can augment these experiences. Consider the various examples presented in this book, and ideas about how to extend learning and sharing beyond your classroom's walls, so your students can connect, explore, create, and investigate, and foster digital leadership.

Student Vignette 🔊

Social media has been the single most important tool in help-ing me establish Developing Innovations, my nonprofit organi-zation. As a twelve-year-old scientist, I was so excited to win a gold medal at our regional science fair. To me, it was the great-est accomplishment of my lifetime. I had worked really hard to build a subsonic open-circuit wind tunnel and was heading to the Canada-Wide Science Fair in Prince Edward Island! A year later, I won gold again at my regional science fair, this time for my Advanced Aerodynamic Aircraft Wing System, which I'd tested in my wind tunnel. I went on to compete at the Canada-Wide Science Fair in Alberta, where I won silver. It was such an exciting time, but if you'd done a Google search for my name, you know what would have come up? Two goals that I'd scored in a hockey game way back in 2008. It was then that I realized that kids, like me, needed a platform to share their accomplishments, and that is how Developing Innovations started.

Since February 2014, I've had the honor of showcasing more than seventy brilliant STEM students from around the world. Finally, their digital footprint, as well as mine, started to reflect our accomplishments. I am always thrilled to learn the expo-sure that some of them are receiving has helped open doors for them in acquiring funding, lab time, awards, scholarships, uni-versity entrance, and even STEM-related job offers. I encourage everyone to search their name and see if their digital footprint truly reflects who they are. If it doesn't, get on social media and change it for the better!

—Aidan Aird, twelfth grade

In Summary ⬇

- Literacy today is more than just reading and writing. Being literate today means being able to critically consume and create a variety of texts.

- Understanding media literacy and how it works empowers students to learn about the world around them.

- A positive digital presence happens effortlessly when you embrace digital leadership.

Discussion Questions ✖

1. To what extent are we limiting our definitions of literacy based on our own experiences? What are barriers to this, and how might we overcome them?

2. Where and how might we be more intentional about teaching media literacy, digital literacies, and social media literacy in our practice, not as add-ons but as complements and/or replacements for other practices?

3. What support(s) do we need to model and explore social media literacies together in the context of English, history, or geography class? Are those at a school level? A district level? A department level?

4. To what extent do we need to embrace a different approach to entrepreneurship and career readiness?

Chapter 4 Notes

1. Burnett, C. and G. Merchant, "The Challenge of 21st-Century Literacies," *Journal of Adolescent & Adult Literacy*, 59(3), 2015: 272.

2. "The NCTE Definition of 21st Century Literacies," *National Council of Teachers of English*, February 2013, ncte.org/positions/ statements/21stcentdefinition.

3. Belshaw, Doug, *The Essential Elements of Digital Literacies*, p. 50, 2015, frysklab.nl/wp-content/uploads/2016/10/ The-Essential-Elements-of-Digital-Literacies-v1.0.pdf.

4. Schwartz, K., "Sir Ken Robinson: How to Create a Culture for Valuable Learning," *Mind Shift*, August 15, 2016, http://ww2.kqed. org/mindshift/2016/08/15/sir-ken-robinson-how-to-create-a- culture-for-valuable-learning/?utm_content=buffer00436&utm_ medium=social&utm_source=twitter.com&utm_campaign=buffer.

5. "Margaret Atwood says Twitter, Internet Boost Literacy," *CBC News*, December 5, 2011, cbc.ca/news/entertainment/ margaret-atwood-says-twitter-internet-boost-literacy-1.1057001.

6. Alrubain, Rusul, "How to Use Social Media to Strengthen Student Writing," *Edutopia*, February 13, 2016, edutopia.org/discussion/ how-use-social-media-strengthen-student-writing.

7. Belshaw, Doug, T*he Essential Elements of Digital Literacies*, p. 50, 2015, frysklab.nl/wp-content/uploads/2016/10/ The-Essential-Elements-of-Digital-Literacies-v1.0.pdf.

8. Williams, R. & Ricciardelli, L. "Social Media and Body Image Concerns: Further Considerations and Broader Perspectives," *Sex Roles*, 71(11-12), 2014: 390.

9. Ibid., 389.

10. Couros, George, "'Deficit Comparisons' to 'Abundance Introspection,'" July 3, 2016, georgecouros.ca/blog/archives/6460.

11. Lindsey, Daryl, "Social Media Is Not Real Life, but That's Not the Problem," *The Everygirl,* November 5, 2015, theeverygirl.com/ social-media-is-not-real-life-but-thats-not-the-problem.

12. "Media Triangle," Modified by Ken Pettigrew from the original by Eddie Dick, media education officer for the Scottish Film Industry.

13. Andsager, J. L., "Research Directions in Social Media and Body Image," *Sex Roles*, 71(11), 2014.

14. Hughes, J. & Morrison, L. "Using Facebook to explore adolescent identities." *International Journal of Social Media and Interactive Learning Environments*, Special Issue, 1(4), 2013: 370-386.

15. "Applying the Common Core," *Critical Media Project*, criticalmediaproject.org/resources/common-core.

16. Andsager, J. L., "Research Directions in Social Media and Body Image," *Sex Roles*, 71(11), 2014.

17. Merrill, C., Painchaud, B., et al, "The Power of the Selfie Center," ISTE Denver, June 27, 2016, conference.iste.org/2016/?id=100314011.

18. Riley, Amy, "The Power of the Selfie Center," smore.com/qemqd-the-power-of-the-selfie-center.

19. Silverman, Craig, "This Analysis Shows How Viral Fake Election News Stories Outperformed Real News on Facebook," *Buzzfeed*, November 16, 2016, buzzfeed.com/craigsilverman/viral-fake-election-news-outperformed-real-news-on-facebook?utm_term=.rxnPPBpXD4#.vp7bbNyPBZ.

20. Donald, Brooke, "Stanford Researchers Find Students Have Trouble Judging the Credibility of Information Online," *Stanford Graduate School of Education*, November 22, 2016, ed.stanford.edu/news/stanford-researchers-find-students-have-trouble-judging-credibility-information-online.

21. I learned this trick from *Master the Media* author, Julie Smith.

22. Molloy, David, "Meet the Seven-year-old Girl Tweeting from Aleppo," *BBC News*, October 2, 2016, bbc.com/news/world-middle-east-37535343.

23. Ibid.

24. Modifiable copy can be found at SocialLEADia.org.

25. Adapted from: edugains.ca/resourcesDI/TeachingLearningExamples/ ScienceTech/GR10ScienceAcademicSNC2DResearchingDiseases Appendix.pdf.

26. "Evaluation Information: Applying the CRAAP Test," *CSU Chico*, https://www.csuchico.edu/lins/handouts/eval_websites.pdf.

27. Pilger, Gerald, "Before You Believe It," *Country Guide*, January 17, 2017, country-guide.ca/2017/01/17/smell-test-helps-you-gauge-the-credibility-of-news-and-information/50193/.

28. Twitter curates the most popular topics users are tweeting about and calls them "trending."

29. Mehringer, Susan, "Attention and Other 21st-Century Social Media Literacies," *Educause Review*, October 7, 2010, er.educause.edu/articles/2010/10/ attention-and-other-21stcentury-social-media-literacies.

30. Rheingold, H., "Attention, and Other 21st-Century Social Media Literacies," Educause Review, 45 (5), (2010): 14-24, er.educause.edu/articles/2010/10/ attention-and-other-21stcentury-social-media-literacies.

31. Csikszentmihalyi, Mihály, *Applications of Flow in Human Development and Education: The Collected Works of Mihály Csikszentmihalyi* (1;2014; ed.), Dordrecht: Springer Netherlands: 2014, doi:10.1007/978-94-017-9094-9.

32. "Growing Success: Assessment, Evaluation, and Reporting in Ontario Schools," First Edition, Covering Grades 1-12, 2010: 11, edu.gov. on.ca/eng/policyfunding/growsuccess.pdf.

33. A sample of what this looks like can be found at SocialLEADia.org.

34. Aoun, Joseph, "Robot-Proof, How Colleges Can Keep People Relevant in the Workplace," *Chronicle of Higher Education*, January 27, 2016, chronicle.com/article/Robot-Proof-How-Colleges-Can/235057.

35. Dede, C., "Comparing Frameworks for 21st Century Skills," Bloomington, IN: Solution Tree Press, 2010: 51-76.

36. Fullan, Michael, and Geoff Scott. "New Pedagogies for Deep Learning," whitepaper: *Education PLUS*. Seattle: Collaborative Impact SPC. (2014), oucqa.ca/wp-content/uploads/2014/10/G.-Scott-Plenary-Talk-3-11.15-12.15pm-Churchill-Room-Handout-1-of-2.pdf, 1.

37. Ibid.

38. @KING_NAHH

39. "Nyeeam Hudson's Book Tour," Instagram, instagram.com/kingnahh/?hl=en.

40. Flanigan, Tara, "This 10-Year-Old Just Built a 3D-Printed Prosthetic Hand," *Mashable*, September 23, 2016, mashable.com/2016/09/23/3d-print-prosthetic-hand-kid/#4sN2B3tnkmqM.

41. Christensson, P., Digital Footprint Definition, *Tech Terms*, May 26, 2014, Retrieved 2016, August 21, techterms.com.

42. Ibid.

43. Gillooly, P., "Don't Quit Social Media. Put it to Work for Your Career Instead," *New York Times,* December 3, 2016, nytimes.com/2016/12/03/jobs/dont-quit-social-media-put-it-to-work-for-your-career-instead.html.

44. The full lesson is available at SocialLEADia.org in this chapter's "Resources" section.

45. Cohen, Stacey, "Why Every Personal Brand Deserves an Early Start," *Huffington Post*, Aug 3, 2016, http://www.huffingtonpost.com/stacey-cohen/why-every-personal-brand-_b_11285702.html.

46. "Outstanding Youth in Philanthropy: Aidan Aird," *AFP Toronto YouTube*, December 2, 2016, youtube.com/watch?v=TcJQ9ikfMQs&feature=youtu.be.

47. Ciabattari, Teresa, "Cultural Capital, Social Capital, and Educational Inequality," *Childhood Education,* 87(2) (2010): 119. Academic OneFile, Web March 13 2016.

48. Jenkins, H., Itō, M., and dana boyd, *Participatory Culture in a Networked Era: A Conversation on Youth, Learning, Commerce, and Politics,* Cambridge: Polity Press, 2015.

MEET THE STUDENTS
AIDAN AIRD

DevelopingInnovations.org

🐦 @Aidan_Aird

ⓕ /developinginnovations.org

ⓘ in/aidanaird

ⓞ Instagram: /aidan_aird

Aidan Aird is a seventeen-year-old student at St. Brother André Catholic High School in Markham, Ontario, Canada, and a four-time Canada-Wide Science Fair award winner and medalist. He is the founder of Developing Innovations, a nonprofit organization that inspires, celebrates, and promotes STEM learners, as well as a co-founder of STEM KIDS Rock, which aims to inspire the next generation of STEM learners. Aidan's accolades include: 2015 Eduzine Global ACE Young Achiever, 2016 Three Dot Dash Global Teen Leader, 2016 360 Kids Volunteer of the Year, SHAD Top 16 Stories for 2016, and the 2016 AFP Greater Toronto Youth Philanthropist of the Year.

Use Aidan's Story to Inspire Your Students

 Have students peruse the various inventors and inventions in DevelopingInnovations.org's "STEM Innovators" section, and then rank the top three student-created inventions. Determine the criteria for choosing these inventions together as a class.

 Aidan really wants to highlight other scientists' accomplishments. What have your students achieved? How and where could your class showcase these accomplishments?

 The "STEM Careers" section on Developing Innovations' website is "coming soon." Ask your students to research careers in science and technology and suggest them to Aidan.

SECTION II

WHAT DIGITAL LEADERSHIP LOOKS LIKE IN SCHOOLS

Connecting Students with Meaningful Projects and People

Why is it important for us to connect? Well, because we are in the twenty-first century, and nearly all of us are already connected at home. Being connected at school, through various groups and online communities, allows us to contribute to a greater and more authentic audience for a greater purpose.

—Alfred Lau and Catherine Zhang, sixth grade

When I was a literacy consultant and a member of my district's 21st Century (21C) learning team, we often invited students to present brief keynotes or "Ignite presentations" (twenty slides at fifteen seconds per slide) to offer us their insights and perspectives on how technology-enabled learning was supporting their learning. One year, we had two students demonstrate what they learned in their robotics club and how they felt it made them better students. Another student told us why she uses Google Apps for Education (now "G Suite") to stay organized and how using technology has made her more confident, despite her learning disability. Aidan Aird (whose student vignette you read in the previous chapter) discussed how he's promoting STEM within his community through social media and shares others' work.

Last year, two sixth-grade students, Alfred and Catherine, did their Ignite presentation in front of a room with more than 200 educators for an EdTechTeam Saturday event. The topic? Their connected classroom. They shared that in less than a hundred days of school, they had connected with students from five countries during a Global Edcamp event; reached out to Doctors Without Borders, a nonprofit organization that agreed to post five of their PSAs to the nonprofit's Twitter feed; and organized an impromptu bake sale benefiting Syrian refugees, during which they raised $700 (which was doubled when they donated it to Red Cross). Their teacher, Robert Cannone, had previously shared with me that even though the class had been advised the bake sale might not be a good idea because of allergy concerns, the students were so passionate about their cause that they went ahead and did it on the weekend.

Alfred and Catherine ended their Ignite speech[1] with this:

> To us, being connected is more than just connecting online. We connect at school, in teams, and with our teachers. When we connect, we feel that we are using our voice to make an impact in a positive way, and when we connect, we are also learning new ideas and perspectives. When you add these up, we are making a difference in our own world and maybe someone else's.

I looked around the room to watch the reactions of the educators who had given up their Saturday to learn. Many shook their heads in amazement, others couldn't stop smiling, while others seemed a little uncomfortable—almost as if they didn't know where to begin, but realized that begin, they must.

Every year I ask Robert, a passionate educator and friend (okay, a former student—I'm that old) from my own district in southern Ontario, about his current class and he tells me, "These kids are going to change the world." And every year, I ask him, "How it is that you got so lucky to get students in your class who are going to change the world?"

The fact is, it's not luck. Rather, Robert allows his junior-aged students the opportunity to inquire and to learn within a safe environment where questions are honored and they feel like it's okay to take risks and explore their passions, because he is there to support them. In his classroom, teams are responsible for a variety of tasks, which Catherine describes beautifully: "Teams are like a puzzle; every person is a piece of the puzzle, and everyone is needed to complete the puzzle." Rob doesn't see technology and social media as add-ons to his curriculum; he understands they can amplify the content he's already teaching. He knows kids can learn from experts across the globe, so he encourages them to do so. He has watched as his students have connected with peers the world over while working toward a common goal, and he's seen the effects this has had on their learning. He actively helps his students create their own personal learning network because he knows how much he's benefited from his. He has taught them how to behave appropriately online by allowing them to be online—to learn and share their learning, to address causes important to them, and to be a more positive influence in others' lives.

And his students? They have been so moved by the experiences they've had in his classroom. They have developed the poise and confidence to talk to adults, both virtually and in person.

The more I meet teachers like Robert who have embraced digital leadership and the student digital leaders they're nurturing, the more I see a direct correlation between students who practice digital leadership and being connected to people and organizations. Because when you meet a student whose teacher believes in using technology and social media to connect with others, you can't help but notice the confidence they exude and how engaged they are in school and in life.

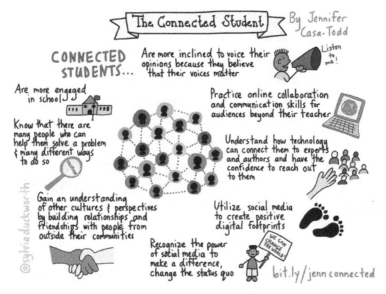

Figure 5.1, Created by Sylvia Duckworth and Jennifer Casa-Todd

Connecting our students to others via technology and social media is a sure way to practice digital leadership. In the following classroom examples, you can see how positive an impact this can have.

Ask an Expert

The year before Alfred and Catherine's Ignite presentation, I'd had the opportunity to work with Robert's sixth-grade students while they were studying space. He had been actively following Commander Chris Hadfield, the Canadian astronaut who became famous when he used social media to communicate from the International Space Station, and he'd been persistent enough to get the astronaut to agree to a live video stream with his class.

When Robert called upon myself and the 21C district planning team for tech support to live stream with Commander Hadfield, I asked him if he'd be willing to extend this opportunity to the entire district.

He agreed, so we set about planning a virtual visit with Commander Hadfield, ensuring Robert's sixth graders had ownership of the plan every step of the way. When we began talking about how we'd advertise the event, I immediately thought of Eric Fabroa, a creative teacher at the local high school who ran the film club. We connected virtually at first to plan and brainstorm and then physically connected to create a movie trailer. (Tip: If you're on the fence about connecting your students to the world right away, working with your local high school—or vice versa—is an awesome first step.) Eric had everything we needed: the video equipment, a green screen, and a group of students excited to share their expertise. The collaboration proved extremely valuable for both groups; the younger students learned from the older ones, who took the role of mentor. When these sixth graders are ready to graduate to the high school, they'll have already had a positive experience with the school's students and possibly even have an interest in joining the film club.

Next, we wondered how the other schools in our district could engage in the live-stream event, rather than just passively viewing it. We decided a Google Form (survey) would be the best solution, giving every student in every class in every school the opportunity to potentially ask Commander Hadfield a question. Robert's students created the form, and we distributed its link to all of the schools in our district. Then we opened the resulting Google Sheet that the form generated to track the students' responses and asked the students at all of the schools to vote for their favorite question. Rob's class asked Commander Hadfield the top ten questions. We also created a TodaysMeet virtual room so we could capture questions from the live viewing audience, giving every school and every student the opportunity to feel included, even if they hadn't contributed a question beforehand.

> Live-streaming a guest speaker really isn't much different or more technically challenging than arranging for a speaker to come to a class in person.

When the day of the live stream with Commander Hadfield came, more than fifty schools watched, and Robert's sixth-grade class "hosted" the event by asking the questions receiving the highest number of votes as well as those the viewing students were posing in real time via TodaysMeet. Afterward, teachers contacted me, describing how excited their students were when they heard Robert's class pose their question and Commander Hadfield answer it. It was an incredible, empowering experience for Robert's class, and by extension, the participating classes—so much so, in fact, that our district featured it on its website and Twitter account.

When you break down this activity, live-streaming a guest speaker really isn't much different or more technically challenging than arranging for a speaker to come to a class in person. But since it offered the hosting class's students additional opportunities to connect, the result was so much more powerful. And because Robert's students were involved in every step of the process, they truly took pride in and ownership of the event's success. Think about it: They got to speak to a famous astronaut on behalf of their peers, and they used technology and social media to extend the opportunity to hundreds of other students.

This wasn't the first time Rob used technology and social media for authentic learning experiences. When Robert taught a high school English course and his students were studying F. Scott Fitzgerald's *The Great Gatsby*, he reached out to a history professor who'd advised the film adaptation's director, Baz Luhrmann, on the historical accuracy of his 1920s portrayal. When Robert's students were studying *Man of La Mancha*, he reached out to the actress who had played "Aldonza" in the film. When his sixth-grade students were studying water sustainability, he connected with the Canadian Broadcasting Corporation (CBC) so that his students could participate in a live Q & A with famed environmentalist David Suzuki and Olympic kayaker Adam van Koeverden. And in May 2016, when Canadian Prime Minister Justin Trudeau announced that a woman would be the face of Canada's next bank note, Robert's students came to school eager to share whom they thought would be a good candidate. They were anxious to learn more about the selection process and what criteria would be used to choose this candidate. So Robert connected with the Bank of Canada through a simple e-mail, asking if anyone on the selection committee would be willing to talk to a group of curious students. What ensued was a project that involved several classes and schools learning more about famous Canadian women who might be the next "bank-note-able woman."

Are you noticing a pattern?

Robert believes his students' best teachers are the experts themselves, and by bringing these people into his classroom using a variety of technology tools, including social media, he is modeling and creating a culture of digital leadership. And, a result, he's creating students who are so very excited to learn.

Collaborating and Connecting Globally

Whenever I share an idea for a global project with my friend, Stephanie Corvese, a third-grade teacher in my district, she talks to her students about it and, inevitably, they try it. Even though her students are too young to use social media, she works with them to draft tweets and oversees their "posts."

Stephanie initially began her foray into social media by participating in the Global Read Aloud[2] project, created by educator Pernille Ripp. The annual event's premise is simple: Every year, teachers are invited to read selections from a list of books over a six-week period and then connect with other classes reading the same book. How the collaboration takes place (including the tool used) is up to the teachers, making it a wonderful opportunity for those new to using social media to begin connecting their classrooms with the outside world.

From there, Stephanie began taking advantage of other opportunities to connect. She started participating in many of the projects I was sharing on Twitter and subsequently even used the social media network to encourage her colleagues to participate as well.

When I asked her about her journey, she had this to say:

> *Connecting my learners to the world using a variety of social media platforms has been a transformative, exciting, and sometimes scary experience. My students create meaningful projects, such as videos about how to care for the Earth, and we publish them for the world to see. They engage in global projects where they learn from other kids and then feel inspired in creating something new and possibly better. When my learners know they will have an authentic global audience, the quality of their work improves.*
>
> *I've noticed a shift in how my third-grade students view the world. When they compare their lives with other kids around the world, they develop more empathy toward others. My learners are expressing more excitement and enthusiasm toward school. They are more curious and willing to take risks. They are moving beyond engagement to empowerment and are beginning to develop personal learning opportunities for themselves by pursuing their own interests. They feel they have been given a voice in how and what they learn.*
>
> *The best part of this journey, though, has been that I am no longer afraid to get my feet wet. I take risks, I make a few mistakes, and I learn from others, which is the mindset that I hope I am modeling for my students.*

I had a similar conversation with Sandra Coniglio, a high school teacher, who first began to engage in professional learning by joining Twitter, then took a leap of faith by having her students host a Twitter "slowchat" using the hashtag #AABSlowChat for the Global Read Aloud.

The thing that most inspires me about Sandra is that she admits to being in a place where she contemplated leaving teaching. She wasn't finding it fulfilling and thought she might be happier in a different career. Connecting dramatically changed everything for her, though. "Connecting with other teachers on Twitter has helped me to create more engaging and authentic assignments for students and get new ideas that have sparked my own passions as well," she says.

Engaging in the Global Read Aloud with her students and seeing their excitement reignited Sandra's love of teaching. But, more importantly, her once-reluctant readers were now reading in hallways before and after school to ensure they had something meaningful to say in class and online. And by posing questions through the slowchat over time for her students to answer using the #AABSlowChat hashtag, they were learning how to use more concise language, respond to others, continue an academic conversation, and act ethically and appropriately online. She also noticed that instead of simply giving a "like" to a comment, her students were becoming more confident and replying to their peers and even opening the novel to quote it. By giving her students the opportunity to take control of the Twitter chat, Sandra has shown them how Twitter can connect them with others who share a common interest.

In the Avon-Maitland District school board in southern Ontario, Leigh Cassell, Kerri-Lynn Schepers, and Nicole Kaufman moderate a kids' chat. The topic and questions are distributed to teachers so students have time to prepare their answers. Once a month, students respond to one another via Twitter. Up to 500 students have been involved and the topics, all around character building, range from unity to digital citizenship. This is another example of the power of how teachers can guide students as they connect and learn online.[3]

Making Someone's Life a Little Brighter

My friend and mentor, Lori Lisi, shared that she had attended a fundraiser for a young girl from her church community who had been diagnosed with a relatively rare malignant brain tumor, known as high-risk group 3 medulloblastoma. We had also recently lost a dear friend and colleague to cancer, and I remembered the helplessness that I'm sure lots of people feel when confronted with such a tragic and unfortunate reality. Lori expressed to me that she'd just wished there was something she could do. Because I fully embrace a digital leadership stance, and knowing what an impact my friend Shauna's #Unicorns4Molly project had on her students, I suggested we create a hashtag for Monica and try to get people from all over the world to rally for her and send her warm wishes and prayers. We asked Monica's dad, Tom, and he agreed.

When I initially put forth the idea, I leveraged my social media connections on Twitter. There was such a generous outpouring of support, including the sharing of inspiring and hopeful messages from Hawaii, England, Singapore, and across Canada. A few classes created video messages and cards. The hashtag #MonicaSitnikRocks became a source of community and where Monica's own school contributed many videos to her as well.

I then reached out via Twitter direct message to Robert Cannone, Stephanie Corvese, and Stephanie Viveiros—all who I knew might take some time with their students to connect more meaningfully. Initially, Stephanie Corvese's third-grade and Robert's sixth-grade classes created video messages for Monica, and Stephanie Viveiros' kindergarteners created posters.

Then, Robert's sixth graders, who'd had success with a previous bake sale, organized one so they could raise money for the bike that Monica had wished for. They advertised in the school and community, as well as on Twitter, and proudly raised enough money to buy her not just a bike, but a helmet, too. When I spoke to Jin, one of his students whose vignette is featured in this chapter, she told me that this was "the most special feeling."

When Stephanie Viveiros received my message, she knew her students would want to help Monica. She explained to me that in kindergarten, one of the big ideas is the conceptual understanding that "everything in our daily lives is connected and we are a part of a community of learners that supports people in different ways, and therefore, our actions can make a difference." Stephanie wasn't sure if her four-year-olds would be able to understand Monica's disease, so the following morning during her class's Tech Circle time, she shared some of the images from the hashtag and told them her story. As you can imagine, the students had many questions about Monica, including "What is it like to have to live in a hospital?" "Does she get to sleep with her favorite blanket?" "Is she warm enough at night?" and "What are some things she likes?"

Sixth-grade bake sale fundraiser

Despite the fact that they had never met Monica and only knew of her situation via the Twitter hashtag, the students felt such a connection to Monica that they felt compelled to do something to make her feel better. So they brainstormed ideas and collaborated, until they all seemed to gravitate toward one idea: making a quilt. Stephanie wasn't sure how this was going to take shape or form, but she knew that this was the idea her students felt most passionately about and that they all showed concern for her well-being while in the hospital. As one student explained, "I want Monica to be wrapped in our love and to know that we are cheering for her and for her to be warm at night."

And so, in Stephanie Viveiros' kindergarten class, an idea for a quilt started to develop. She shared the touching story about how her students brought in more than seventy-five T-shirts, each with a logo or picture they felt would either empower Monica or make her day brighter. As each student brought in their contribution, Stephanie asked them why they chose it. Many of the students responded with gestures of love and kindness. The students wrote a letter to Monica explaining why they selected that specific shirt to be used in the quilt. Some students wrote, "The picture of the tiger will make her feel big and strong like a tiger," and, "This says, 'happily ever after,' and I want Monica to live happily ever after, too."

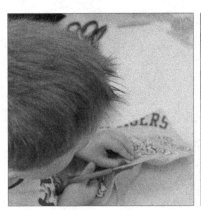

*Stephanie's kindergarten students preparing
their T-shirts for the quilt*

Stephanie was able to enlist the help of parent volunteers who assisted the students in preparing their quilting squares, with one parent sewing the entire quilt together. Each day, the students came to school excited to work on the quilt and help design the layout, choose the fabrics, and select the images. After much work and collaboration, the quilt was complete. The students were overjoyed as their idea had become a reality.

Their quilt was the most beautiful thing I've ever seen. The kids had made something, a tangible thing that could cheer up Monica. What was so remarkable was the sense of community that came alive in the classroom as a result of a connection that had been made on Twitter, for a little girl they had never met.

Presenting Monica with her bike, helmet, and quilt, June 29, 2016
(Twitter post)

In June, we received word that Monica was cancer-free and we rejoiced and shared the good news to the hashtag. We felt like, in some small way, we had contributed to helping her beat this thing, so you can only imagine our shock and dismay when we learned that Monica passed away in September. All of us had felt a deep connection to her, although we had never met her except through the wonder of technology and connecting people globally.

I know everyone involved in this campaign helped Monica when she was here to make her life a little brighter. Even a month later, the hashtag was being used to distribute Kindness Cards, which Monica's school community made in her memory.

The students (and parents and teachers) involved learned that their face-to-face actions helped to make a difference in the life of someone, but that technology and social media provide a way to build community, share their thoughts, and learn about people and causes.

Going Beyond Textbook Learning

So often, we rely on textbooks to help us teach our students important concepts. And while in some cases textbooks are necessary, when we challenge ourselves to think creatively about how we can connect our students to another class using technology and social media, we can create far more meaningful results.

In addition to sharing ideas with thoughtful educators, one of the primary ways I use Twitter is to connect with colleagues working on global projects I find interesting. I've met teachers from all over the world through the platform, many who have also embraced the value of connecting their students via technology and social media.

One such teacher was Norway's Barbara Anna Zielonka, who had come up with a project called "The World Is Made Up of a Million Tiny Stories Digital Storytelling." Although we didn't participate in the project in its entirety, one of my colleagues agreed to connect her students to Barbara's students to learn more about them. Barbara's class first shared a tweet: a "Tidbit" of information about their country. (Figure 5.2 is the Norwegian Tidbit Barbara's students created and shared via Twitter.)

To resolve the time-zone issue, Barbara asked her students to connect with Leigh's class at home as part of their homework. She'd assured us that her students love doing this and that it's a common task in the European community. So, at the designated time, Leigh's class came into the library to use Skype, and despite a few technical hiccups, by the end of the class, all of Leigh's students had "met" a student from Norway for the first time in their lives. This Skype session was amazing to watch, and several moments still stand out to me. Among them was when one young woman didn't want to press the "Connect" button. She admitted to me that she was nervous because she didn't know what to say, even asking me if she could "opt out." I am mindful of challenging and supporting students and knew that if she did connect, it would be a good experience, so I told her she had to participate. So at the end of the session, I made sure to come back to her and find out her thoughts on the experience. She told me she wasn't sure why she'd been scared because her partner student was so nice. And when I asked another one of Leigh's students what the most interesting thing she'd learned was, she said she couldn't pick just one. I wish I'd recorded the experience, because at one point, several of Leigh's students had their devices turned around and were taking their Norwegian peers on a tour of the library's learning commons.

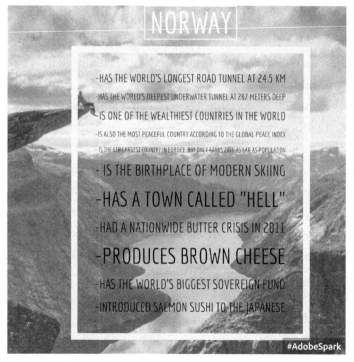

Figure 5.2

And then a boisterous group of boys came into the library. One student in Leigh's class began introducing the boys to her new friend. After a while, I asked the boys to leave because they were being too loud and the other students were having trouble hearing their partner students. As they were leaving, though, I realized they weren't trying to be disruptive—they were genuinely interested in what we were doing. The boys even asked what class this was and whether they could participate, and they remarked how unfair it was that this class got to do something so cool when they couldn't. What I found most remarkable was that students could not believe we were using Skype to connect to other students in the world; their only knowledge of that tool (and a surprising few of them had ever used it) was to connect with family. This experience opened up a whole new world of possibility for them and really made me think about the extent to which we make assumptions about how "connected" students really are.

Similarly, I began working with Ricki Machala, a religious education teacher at my school, to explore the idea of culture (how our faith is shaped by human experience, which extends beyond our own family and community and into other cultures) with her tenth-grade class. I tentatively asked her if she would be open to connecting with a class from another culture to explore this concept better. She had never done this before, but took a risk with me.

So we reached out to Fabiana Casella, an educator from Buenos Aires, Argentina, whom I know through Twitter. Fabiana was in the middle of exams at the time, but she's always looking for opportunities for her students to practice their English by connecting with English-speaking students. Everyone was so excited about the idea of connecting, but two problems quickly arose: First, Fabiana's school doesn't have access to technology (her students use their cell phones); second, because the classes didn't run simultaneously, they wouldn't be online at the same time. Initially, both of these issues felt like insurmountable obstacles, but we put our heads together and brainstormed how we could use the tools we

> Students could not believe that we were using Skype to connect to other students in the world; their only knowledge of that tool was to connect with family.

had at hand and connect anyway. The solution was this: Fabiana's students would create questions and share them to Google Docs, and then, using the Voxer app (which allows you to speak and share links, images, and videos), Ricki's students would communicate their questions, share pictures of themselves, and respond with answers. Fabiana would then take Ricki's class's work and upload it to Padlet (a virtual wall) so that all of the videos and images would be in the same place. A connection that Ricki originally thought would just be fun turned into an incredible and positive learning experience for everyone involved. Most notably, it led to our students wanting to connect with their Argentinian friends via their own personal networks (Instagram and Snapchat). Ricki summarized it best when she said, "We think our students are so connected, but I realized that their connections were so small and extended only really as far as their friends and family community, sometimes spreading as far as an out-of-school team or activity. For this project, my students were given the opportunity to open their community and idea of culture." She also noted a remarkable improvement in student achievement: Her Unit 2 summative assessment results improved by 20 percent because the content was real and meaningful to them.

Students started to "friend" each other on their personal social media accounts, and when I shared this with other teachers, so many of them were uncomfortable with the idea. I wonder why. Students can now stay forever connected with people, and the fact that our students now have friends in Argentina with whom to socialize or learn can only be a good thing.

Providing Students Opportunities to Care

One of the most powerful examples I've ever come across of how connecting globally can empower students to make a difference in others' lives is from my good friend, Leigh Cassell, a technology coach for Avon-Maitland and founder of the Digital Human Library.

Leigh shared with me a powerful story that she had originally shared on her blog.[4] When Leigh was teaching a second-grade unit, "communities around the world," she and her students traveled the globe, collaborating with classes in twelve countries through video conferences, blog posts, letters, and video exchanges along the way. One of the students' stops was in Lakka, Sierra Leone, where they "visited" Alusine's class. For several months, the classes exchanged letters[5] and learned about their respective communities' life, culture, and traditions, which was no small feat, considering Alusine's students had to walk two hours one way to reach an Internet café just so they could visit Leigh's class's blog and read her students' letters. When the year ended, Leigh's students celebrated their learning about the world—with the world.

The following year, when Leigh contacted Alusine, now her friend, to inquire about connecting and learning together again, she received a response that both shocked and saddened her. In her letter, Alusine shared horrific stories of loss resulting from the Ebola virus. In fact, most of the children with whom they had connected had lost their lives, and those who were fortunate enough to survive had lost their parents. And in a desperate attempt to escape the virus, many people from Lakka fled Sierra Leone on a boat, which later capsized. There were no survivors. Alusine's community was devastated.

Leigh thought a lot about whether or not to tell her previous students what had happened. But after much thought, she concluded that since they had spent months developing relationships with these kids, she needed to tell them. So one day, over lunch, they gathered and Leigh shared the devastating news. There were many tears shed that day, but as they hugged and consoled each other, one student spoke up and asked, "What are we going to do to help all of the people who are still alive in Lakka?"

Those words ignited the room, and soon, the students were abuzz with talk of how they could help this community. What inspired Leigh most about the conversation, though, was how what her students had learned about life in Lakka was helping them make a decision about how to assist. Together, the students decided that creating posters showing families how to wash their hands properly, sneeze into their arms, and stop the spread of germs would be the best way they could help. So they did just that, and soon word spread throughout the school and other classes wanted to get involved as well.

In just a few days' time, the students had put together several packages of posters, as well as donated pencils, markers, paper, and other supplies for the families in Lakka. When Alusine received their packages, she responded with a letter that brought tears to everyone's eyes: "Never before has the community of Lakka ever experienced such kindness from others, and your act of kindness will make a profound difference in the recovery of our community."

As Leigh reflected on her experience connecting her students with the world, she said she understood the application of that learning: "Empowering students to make a difference in the world is what teaching and learning is all about."

Time and time again, I come back to Leigh's story when I'm talking to someone about blocking students' access to social media or when a colleague tells me using technology in the classroom is optional and separate from their curriculum. Because once an educator embraces digital leadership as a pedagogical stance, everything changes. No longer can you look at an idea without wondering how you could use technology and social media to flatten your classroom's walls and make learning come alive for your students.

Finding Meaningful Connections

Although I can say that just being open to digital leadership will open up endless opportunities for you as they have for me, I understand that many of you might like a little more explicit direction. The following are a few of the resources I have tapped into to find meaningful connections for my students.

The Digital Human Library

The powerful connection her students shared with Alusine's class in Sierra Leone is, in part, why Leigh Cassell founded the Digital Human Library, a not-for-profit organization that connects teachers to hundreds of experts and organizations around the world completely free of charge. Not only has Leigh curated hundreds of experts with whom any educator can connect, but unlike any other resource I've seen, she also offers a catalog of multimedia virtual tours and links to resources so teachers can provide diverse voices within their classrooms. In fact, she's dedicated an entire page to helping teachers find global learning partners for their students ("Global Connections for Teachers and Students"), which includes one of my favorite resources: Connected Learning Partnerships. Created by Leigh and Sean Robinson, a science and digital literacy teacher, Connected Learning Partnerships aims "to help teachers and students connect with one another easily, so they can focus their time on working together—not finding each other."[6] When you register, you will become part of a community of educators wanting to connect students in meaningful ways.

Twitter and Other Social Media Communities

I've mentioned Twitter several times already, and I'll mention it several more times, because through it, I've discovered a community of educators who are passionate about teaching, learning, and amplifying students' voices. In fact, many of the projects I'm including in this book resulted from ideas that either I've shared on Twitter or someone has shared with me.

One of the educators I've met through Twitter is Jennifer Williams, EdD, a professor and literacy coach. After chatting with her on Twitter for a few years, we finally met in person at the Future of Education Technology Conference in January 2016. When she and Fran Siracusa, a Spanish teacher of more than twenty years, presented the idea of "building bridges" at the conference as a metaphor for our opportunity to connect students, I realized they were as passionate about connecting students as I was. Together, they founded Calliope Global Education Initiatives,[7] which aspires to connect international classrooms and serve as a catalyst "that will inspire transformational learning and teaching through global projects, travel, and professional development." In fact, it was Jennifer and Fran who introduced me to an incredibly supportive and resourceful group of educators on Twitter known as the #GlobalEd[8] community. The members' tweets range from discussing really cool global projects, initiatives, policies, blogs, and resources to wanting to connect students with others around the world. The hashtag has several regular contributors, whom I know would be just as happy to connect you to meaningful projects as I am.

Another group that has been personally supportive of me, and through which I have made a number of connections for my teachers and students, is EduMatch, founded by Sarah Thomas, a regional technology coordinator in Maryland. Edumatch's mission (no, it's not a dating site) is to connect educators from around the world who share similar interests.

> Through Twitter, I've discovered a community of educators who are passionate about teaching, learning, and amplifying students' voices.

Using the various social media channels, EduMatch builds more than a network of educators—it creates a family that learns and grows together. EduMatch has introduced me to educators from all over the world who see technology-enabled learning as an opportunity for students to have transformational experiences.

And if you're looking to open up your classroom's walls for your students, Sean Robinson's "connections-based learning" hashtag, #cblchat, is another great one to check out on Twitter (and Google+).

I was naturally drawn to Sean and what he calls "connections-based learning" because it complements my core beliefs about the relationship between digital leadership and connecting students to real projects and people. Sean says connections-based learning "celebrates the way connections are formed and leveraged through education. It reminds us to seek ways of learning that facilitate the building of relationships. It declares that significant learning requires a significant relationship. Connections-based learning makes it a priority to leverage interpersonal connection at each step of the learning process. Whether it is the teacher-student connection, the connection with members of the class, school, and community, or the connection with experts in the field of study, thought is given to maximizing these relationships."[9] Sean has also created a Voxer group, of which I am a part, which is comprised of passionate educators who share their learning and projects regularly.

Skype in the Classroom

When I first began helping teachers integrate technology into their classrooms, I joined Skype in the Classroom, where I learned about the many ways the platform connects teachers and students. Among those is "Mystery Skype," a (now) well-known geography activity (although any live video-streaming tool can be used for this) whereby classes from different parts of the world ask each other questions so they can figure out where in the world the class they're talking to is located. You can also use "Skype Lessons" to submit a lesson idea for your grade level or subject and find a matching teacher and class. And, as an added bonus, Skype in the Classroom also frequently offers informative group Skype opportunities with oceanographers, astronauts, authors, engineers, etc., which can make your curriculum come alive.

The Global Audience Project

Another easy way to connect your classroom is through the Global Audience Project,[10] created by Brian Costello, a technology integration specialist and Google Innovator whom I met through EduMatch. Brian says the Global Audience Project is the culmination of his desire to make it easier to connect teachers and classrooms. In 2015–2016, Brian developed a project to help his classes learn about communities by discussing their homes with other classes from around the world. Using connections developed mostly through Twitter, he helped his kids connect to fourteen classes in the United States, Canada, South Africa, and Mozambique, through the "Class World Tour." The project was a huge hit with his students especially, but also their parents and his colleagues. While presenting it at the International Society for Technology in Education Conference in 2016, though, one of the key questions Brian received was, "How did you find all the classes?" The Global Audience Project was his answer. Today, educators like us can share work and find a project or coach to support us as we connect our students.

Your Own Connections

No one ever said we can only forge connections online; rather, digital leadership simply means we look at social media and technology as opportunities for learning that go beyond the classroom. We have always brought guest speakers into our schools and should continue to do this. When I opened myself up to the possibility of positivity online, connections seemed to present themselves to me in person as well; the people I met on Twitter and through my social media connections are possible "experts" I could bring into my classroom.

Student Vignette 🔊

Social media can be used to spread a message, raise awareness, and bring the world together. In fact, just last year, the way I and everyone around me used technology drastically transformed. We shared our class's accomplishments online through our class blog and Twitter account, we organized an event about one of Canada's greatest milestones, and we even raised money for Syrian refugees and a child with cancer, all through technology and communication. The phenomenon of the Internet and social media had just become apparent to us, and I think the way we used it to make our own difference in the world is something worth sharing.

Along with our class Twitter account, which posted frequent updates on our classroom events to curious parents, we set up a blog, which had its own "public relations department" (that I was a part of)! Our blog included events that our school took part in, surveys to take with our classmates, sad farewells to some teachers, and warm welcomes to others. It was a creative and rewarding way to document our school year, as it trained our commitment and language skills, as well as gifted us with memories to keep with us as we advanced into seventh grade. Perhaps the most important element of maintaining these accounts, though, was that we could spread positive messages and inspiration to whoever read them. We could easily inform everyone about how we were using technology and, in turn, encourage others to find their own use of it as well!

My sixth-grade experience was impacted greatly by these events; they gave me opportunities to present my own opinions to others as well as to write about topics that I was passionate about. Adopting technology in this "new" way over the course of the year opened my eyes to how empowering Internet access can be. In fact, it inspired me to select the topic of "Internet access" for a poster I created on my NGO of choice. Personally, the most valuable lesson that I have learned, and that I think everyone should know, is that there is a good side to everything.

Last year, our class learned a useful lesson: Technology can bring us together and connect us. Through all the initiatives we did, we realized how technology doesn't make us unsociable (as is often said), but it has the ability to spread messages to people across the world, gather the people whom you know to celebrate great achievements in history, and to even make changes in the world as we know it. As technology advances, its uses will become more and more various. However, it really is up to us where this variety will take us and how it will truly change the world.

—Jin Schofield, seventh grade

In Summary ⬇

- Connecting your students to meaningful projects and people provide authentic learning moments and can help your curriculum come alive.

- Connecting to other educators (including those I've mentioned) via social media can inspire you, but more importantly, it can help students to see how they might use social media differently.

- There are numerous resources to help you on your journey.

Discussion Questions ⤬

1. Consider an existing lesson or unit of study. Where could there be an opportunity for your students to connect with an expert or another classroom?

2. Are there local issues or people needing support or cheering up? How could technology and social media complement face-to-face interactions?

3. Who could offer technical or curricular support as you connect with experts, organizations, or classrooms? Might your students help you with the "how" while you focus on the "why"?

Chapter 5 Notes

1. A copy of this is available at SocialLEADia.org in this chapter's "Resources" section.

2. "Global Read Aloud," theglobalreadaloud.com.

3. twitter.com/AMDSBkidschat

4. Cassell, Leigh, "What If?" EduBlogs, March 2, 2016, edublog.amdsb. ca/tlc/2016/03/02/what-if.

5. Cassell, Leigh, "Letter #3 from Sierra Leone," May 26, 2014, edublog. amdsb.ca/cassell/2014/05/26/letter-3-from-sierra-leone.

6. "Connected Learning Partnerships," *Digital Human Library*, digitalhumanlibrary.com/connected-learning-partnerships-clpedu/.

7. calliopeglobal.com

8. In the Twitter search bar, type #GlobalEd and follow the educators who contribute to it.

9. Robinson, S., "Connections-Based Learning," *Living Education eMagazine*, 2015: 33.

10. globalaudienceproject.com

Practice Digital Leadership with the "Other" Social Media Tools

For me, blogging is a passion. I do aspire to continue making an impact on the world and encourage young people to look into creating a blog, whether it is a book blog, a food recipe blog, a fashion-makeup blog, or any blog of any genre that expresses their passions.

—*Michelle Wrona, eleventh grade*

'm mostly an optimist, but even I know I can't just wave a magic wand and, suddenly, make everyone in every district realize that social media is an essential tool for learning and that they need to embrace digital leadership. Nothing is ever simple in education, and sometimes, things do take time.

Remember, social media is defined as tools or platforms through which people can engage "in a large-scale conversation, exploration, and opinion-sharing,"[1] and "*create* and *share* their own content."[2] So, in this chapter, we'll explore the tools that districts more than likely will not have blocked—because they don't understand that they are really social media—and how these can foster digital leadership.

Blogging

I remember when blogs first became popular. There was a great deal of controversy within our English department surrounding whether or not we should allow our students to read blogs because they weren't "credible" sources. However, the argument against blogs' credibility is becoming increasingly more difficult to make, as scientists, journalists, historians, artists, geographers, athletes—basically, anyone and everyone—are using this informal first-person narrative style to write about their perspective on a variety of topics. And they do so on a public platform—social media—that allows users to comment.

I consider blogging an excellent springboard for academic writing and an important genre of modern writing that should receive as much attention as the literary essay. What's more, it is far and away the simplest way for us to help our students develop their digital leadership skills. Unlike some of the social media platforms that place limitations on character counts or types of posts, blogs can include text, links, images, and practically anything else the writer would like to use to convey their message.

In this way, blogs allow for extended conversation and sharing ideas from multiple perspectives, which is impossible with other social media platforms. It's not just the teacher linking to articles, videos, images, or maps, but the students who can and should. And, as a result, the role of the teacher shifts to one who provokes thinking through questions in a personalized, more meaningful way.

Compare this to some of the more traditional ways we (and I'm including myself) have promoted thinking in the past:

- We post a provocation in the form of a question, an image, or a video link.

- We then engage our class in a discussion around the topic or theme.

- We assign additional resources so students can get a more fulsome understanding of the topic.

- Learning culminates in the form of a paragraph, a test, or an essay, which the student then submits for assessment or evaluation before moving on to the next project.

When you add a blog into the mix, though, students are engaging with the material and providing their own perspective and opinion. The moment they learn that they'll be sharing their blog with someone outside their school, the quality of their writing and thinking suddenly increases because the audience becomes authentic. Best of all, this audience's feedback can build upon the ideas already being addressed, which can then lead to a discussion. When all students have a chance to truly engage in a topic, they are more apt to understand it, to get excited about it, and want to talk about it.

Students can use blogs to demonstrate digital leadership through the following:

- Empowering others who have no voice

- Addressing societal inequality

- Promoting important causes

- Learning and share their learning

- Being a more positive influence in the lives of others

When I first blogged with my students, I didn't have a clue what I was doing. I'd read about other people's positive blogging experiences on Twitter, so I looked up YouTube videos to try and figure it all out. I honestly think my students bought into the whole idea because they realized we were all just trying this out together. I cannot tell you how many times I deleted something, posted something twice, and had my students show me something they'd figured out. When it came to content knowledge, I was a master, but blogging made me feel vulnerable and very human. I actually think most of that class's students would fall over from shock if they knew I now blog regularly and that I spent some of my time at the district level providing teachers with blogging support, both curricular and technical.

Julie Balen, a passionate, committed English teacher in northern Ontario, uses blogging as a way to give her First Nations school's students a voice and an opportunity develop their own digital presence. Julie has been working tirelessly to ensure her students, who have for too long been excluded from the mainstream conversation and felt powerless, know they can use their voices to express their ideas and opinions for audiences beyond their classroom and reservation.

Julie shared with me, through Twitter, a blog from one of her eleventh graders, Annie Wemigwans. Annie chose to respond to the project via her blog. I'd initially thought I would just quickly peruse Annie's post and provide a comment, but instead, I sat there poring over her blog and marveling at this student's articulate, pointed opinions. I was riveted. Reading Annie's blog taught me more about a First Nations perspective than I'd ever known.

In this example, she speaks to some of the stereotypes about First Nations communities:

> Our people are portrayed as buckskin warriors. This is true to some extent, as our traditional regalia resembles what I see on television on old cowboy movies. We do have loincloths, and leather dresses, and feathers in our hair and we do dance in a circle to the beat of a drum. The thing is, though, it isn't as comical as Hollywood makes it out to be. When we dance, we are celebrating life, death, and the gift of our ancestors. We honor the sky, the earth, and our spirituality. That and it is lots of fun, there's food like any festival. Think of us as not mysterious and powerful, but as a part of a society that is colorful and different from yours.

Julie has always encouraged her students to share their writing with others, assuring them she'd be there for support if they receive any "tough comments." She says Edublogs, especially, is a great platform for this because it allows her to see all of her students' comments. Julie empowers her students to have a voice, and she knows technology and social media are among the many ways she can do that.

Kathy Cassidy, a first-grade teacher and the author of *Connected from the Start* who lives in Moose Jaw, Saskatchewan, has been blogging with her first graders since 2005. In my professional learning workshops for teachers, I always have teachers peruse her (and other) classroom blogs to explore what blogging with young children can look like. If you go to it,[3] on the right-hand side, you'll see a list of her students' names, each linking to their personal blog, which provides a visible demonstration of the child's learning and thinking. In just first grade, these students are already demonstrating digital leadership by learning and sharing their learning with others, including their parents.

Creating a Successful Class Blog

Before students begin writing their first blog post, have them read a variety of blogs, particularly ones written by students. (For some great examples, check out the blogs of the student digital leaders in this book.) Students don't often get to read other students' perspectives, so providing them with this opportunity allows them to read authentic, student-generated work, which only naturally raises the bar for their own writing. Even young students benefit from looking at, reading, and commenting on other young students' work. And since each blog is unique to its creator, this may help students determine what they want like their own blog to look like.

If you're a leader providing workshops for teachers, I've seen success doing the same thing with teachers: I have participants look at a variety of class blogs, starting with Linda Yollis' third-grade blogs and Kathy's grade one blogs, and then determine which elements they deem "effective."

Success Criteria

When I introduced blogging to my class, I was amazed by the quality of the content they produced and how effective the comments they wrote one another were. However, I think this was, in large part, because, together, we determined what an effective post looks like and what an effective comment looks like. We would never skip these steps for a writing task, so we shouldn't skip them for blog writing, either.

Gradual Entry

If you're really tentative at first, remember this: Every blogging platform offers a moderator setting and the option of setting your blog to private. Honestly, when I initially set up my blog, I was nervous that students would post inappropriate content, so I thought moderating would be a good idea. However, I soon unchecked that little box because it became way too cumbersome to physically approve each and every comment someone posted before anyone else could see it, and, frankly, since we'd developed very clear expectations, it wasn't really necessary to moderate their comments.

I had also originally made the blog private, which, at the time, helped me feel in control of it; the platform was so new to me, and I didn't feel I knew enough about it to make it public. Gradually, though, I grew more comfortable with the public reading our posts. That said, I've learned that if you don't want the potential for an authentic audience, choose another tool—blogs should be public. Nonetheless, if to start blogging, you feel you need to begin with comment moderation and private settings, then go ahead—just make sure that by the end of the year, your students get to experience digital leadership and the joy of connecting with others through their blogging!

Blogging Incognito

Modern Learning and Digital Literacy Coordinator, Royan Lee, experimented with having his students blog "incognito" when he taught sixth grade. By this, I mean authors are anonymous to the world but not to the teacher or one another. When we chatted about this idea, he suggested that by blogging anonymously, students are encouraged to not only start the act of blogging, but to also take risks and stretch themselves further than if their identities were known. It shows them that social media doesn't necessarily need to portray the entire picture of who you are. His students were able to show their Star Wars side or their dance side without ever feeling the pressure to do anything else. And, as a teacher, Royan says blogging incognito allows him to test the notion of "whether you really have to be yourself to learn how to be yourself" while respecting the community in which he lives because "some families aren't comfortable (yet) with the idea of self-publication and intentional digital footprinting."[4]

Sharing with the World

Just because you have a blog and its settings are set to public, the whole world will not automatically flock to read your students' thoughts and ideas—cultivating a readership is definitely a process. One of the best strategies for this is to take advantage of your own connections to other educators and share your students' blogs with one another. If you want an extended relationship (and there are so many benefits to this), something I've found useful is to have your students first get to know one another, either through a video conference or by exchanging information in the form of a survey.

Another way to spread the word about your class's blogs—especially if their content speaks to a current event or issue—is to encourage students to share its URL with a person, organization, or company that might be interested in reading about the topic they're discussing.

A Collaborative Blog

One of the struggles we had in our 21C initiative was that so many teachers in so many of our schools were doing awesome and innovative things in their classrooms, but we didn't know about them unless we were working directly with the teachers or they happened to facilitate a session for us. Our solution was to create a collaborative blog,[5] open to any teacher in our district, which was prominently displayed on our website. Leigh McCarthy, a third-grade teacher, shared with me her experience with a live webcam of an eagle momma she had discovered. She had the live cam up constantly, and often people from other classes would pop in to see what the eagle family was up to. Watching this momma eagle care for her eaglets had completely transformed her class. She shared how excited her kids were and how much they loved to talk about eagles, read about them, and write about them. By contributing to our collaborative blog, other teachers were able to learn about this experience. Other teachers shared their reflections and how-to tips with Hour of Code, Global Day of Design, Google Expeditions, and Genius Hour. We found this to be a great way to share and celebrate innovative practices in our schools.

You could also use collaborative blogs in the classroom. You will recall that Jin, who shared a student vignette in Chapter Four, was a part of the public relations team where she, under the support and guidance of Mr. Cannone, was able to share the learning in their classroom; she loved this role!

Most schools have websites and, while we traditionally use them for information items or to celebrate school-wide achievements, they can also become a collaborative blog where teachers and students can take turns posting an entry. The beauty of this approach, which I have initiated at my own school, is the many levels of "awesome." The teachers and students who contribute feel valued, teachers get insight into what others at their school are doing, students gain experience writing for a real audience, and parents who visit the school's website have a clearer insight as to the happenings in classrooms or school events.

A Blog as a Digital Portfolio

A blog can also be an amazing way for students to curate their best work. I return to my own blog time and again to find an article I'd read

> A blog can also be an amazing way for students to curate their best work.

about a topic I wrote about. When I apply to present at a conference or for a job, I reference my blog, as it reflects my body of work and experiences. It is unlikely that we can say our students are leaving our schools with the same advantage.

Many districts are moving toward K–12 digital portfolios tied to a learning management system (LMS). If done well, students (as well as their parents and teachers) can see their cumulative growth over time. Many of these LMSs however, are secure systems, meaning they aren't publicly accessible. One of the questions George Couros has challenged me to think about when it comes to these closed LMSs is who owns the learning when students graduate? If the answer is that everything disappears when they graduate, then we have not really helped them distinguish between "school tools" and real-world tools.

Curation Tools and Digital Leadership

I'm currently a student in a master's program, so finding the right curation tool has been integral to my success. I realized, rather quickly though, that I'd been using these tools without ever considering them forms of social media. When I was creating a lesson for a writing project, my Minds On activity was to have students do a Google search for themselves so they could determine if the results aligned with what they wanted people to see and know about them. As I modeled the activity and searched for myself, I noticed some of the curation tools came up along with my name.

In *Library Reports*, authors Joyce Kasman Valenza, PhD; Brenda Boyer, PhD; and Della Curtis define "curation" as "the ability to find, to filter, to evaluate, to annotate, to choose which sources are valuable."[6] When incorporated into the classroom, curation tools can provide an easy way for students to develop a positive online presence while also allowing them to learn and share their learning. Beyond that, curating resources is a critical skill for students to learn because it involves evaluating and selecting the most important information.

In his article, "Content Curation: The Future of Relevance," Stephen Dale, who specializes in information management, says, "Curation in a digital world isn't a luxury, it's a necessity."[7] He also reflects on the fact that "social media sharing has enabled anyone to share anything with the world."[8] Modeling what content curation looks like for younger students by having a collaborative online curation space is extremely important. As they get older, we should gradually begin asking them to take on a more active role in selecting and creating content, with the goal of moving toward independence.

If we do the curating, then we are doing the thinking. Teaching students to curate information is as necessary today as having them read information. Such an approach would complement inquiry-rich classrooms, where research is based on student interests, but it could also happen in any independent unit as well. We need to shift this responsibility to our students.

Older students should be able to decide which platform to use to curate their work and then develop an understanding of why or how that platform best suits their learning style. They should also have a social networking opportunity that allows them to share their learning and actively learn from other students' curated resources. Then, once they reach the twelfth grade, students could reflect on their curated resources from ninth grade and the extent to which they feel they have grown as learners and information gatherers and seekers.

Placing an emphasis on curation not only helps students track the plethora of information available on the web and provide them with essential literacy skills, but it also gives them an organizational tool they can readily use if they choose to go to post-secondary school. Curating information also provides students with an opportunity to learn and share their learning and, as a result, hone their digital leadership skills.

When it comes to curating information, many schools are still having students cite or annotate resources for a specific unit or project, usually in the form of research notes, a bibliography, or annotated bibliography, and then submit the document to the teacher for review and sometimes even grading.

Adopting a digital leadership stance requires you to rethink what you've traditionally done. We are constantly seeking more efficient, more productive ways to find and organize information, but this hasn't quite translated to helping our students do the same. That's why, along with our students, we should select a tool that will not only help them develop their research skills and find relevant research but also become a repository for all of the resources they've found. Content curation requires students to think critically, use a number of different forms of literacy, make a fairly safe foray into using social media, and learn and share their learning, meaning they're practicing digital leadership. But the most incredible thing is that by empowering students to curate content digitally, they will graduate with a body of resources from throughout the course of their entire school career.

A Few Curation Tools

Wakelet (for ages thirteen and older) and tools like it, provide a great way for students to summarize and synthesize learning by allowing them to create something new out of online content, including social media platforms such as Twitter, Instagram, and Google+. What I love most about curating tools is that several people can draw from very similar information and their final products can end up completely different—the results are based entirely on a person's selection and interpretation of the resource, making the story or "wake" unique to their learning.

With that in mind, you could ask students to draw from a specific hashtag connected to a movement, an organization, an author, or a politician and then have them summarize their interpretation of the main messages. Older students could generate a thesis and use the artifacts and examples they find to prove it. Or, better yet, you could turn the traditional essay on its head by having students use a curation tool to write a persuasive "essay."

Professionals have also put together public *wakes* that would make a great springboard for a critical literacy discussion by asking questions like "Whose voice is missing?" and "Is there a bias?" Wakelet and similar curation tools allow for public sharing. That means students could share their wakes, or any of the public wakes, using another social media platform, and then comment on one another's work and further discuss the issues. This kind of activity would be far more insightful than any test we could ever give.

When students sign up for a Wakelet account using their names, their creations will come up in a Google search, which is a good way to intentionally improve their online digital presence.

Flipboard (ages thirteen and older) is another social media curation tool that allows for the co-construction and sharing of knowledge. I tried this tool out for one of my courses, and I really liked that I could add a comment or idea to the articles, videos, or photos that I "flip" and categorize and organize magazines based on a topic of my choice before ultimately sharing them. Similar to Wakelet, Flipboard allows students to collect and organize resources on any given topic and then share them with either their peers or the public. It was Lisa Noble, a French and music teacher from Peterborough, Ontario, who first shared the benefits of a class Flipboard account with me. She creates a class Flipboard account, and her young learners then help her curate resources. Once students learn the benefits of using a tool that allows for curation in a magazine style format like Flipboard, they could use the tool independently well beyond their school lives.

My sixteen-year-old daughter is on **Pinterest** all the time, looking for decorating and recipe ideas. And although I don't use this platform very much myself, I've talked to a number of educators who curate really valuable educational resources (especially posters) on their Pinterest boards.

So, if Pinterest is valuable for us, and many students are already familiar with the platform, then it would stand to reason that it would be a good choice to use in class. Because of its incredible visual quality, Pinterest would appeal especially to visual learners. If you teach students younger than the age of thirteen, you could also create a class Pinterest board for a topic you're studying. If your class is made up of students thirteen and older, they could create their own boards and consolidate their understanding of a concept by selecting and organizing resources.

Content curation competencies touch on so many skills and provide us with a wonderful opportunity to teach how to give proper credit.

More "Social Media" Tools We Can Use

The next set of tools provides a perfect springboard for learning about how to communicate effectively online. They are also tools that can be used in post-secondary education or in the workplace, because they are public. I've highlighted a few, but there are likely several dozen that do slightly similar things. The more creative we are with these types of tools and the more we use them to connect with others beyond the walls of our classroom, the more flexibly students will be able to transfer their learning to other contexts.

Virtual Walls

Before my district role, I was always at the front of the class, but I've learned when you sit in the back, you notice a few things. Like when you give a lecture to your class, and you have an amazing feeling, and you think, "Woo-hoo! Everyone gets this and is as excited about this as I am." And then you sit in the back of the class and realize only a handful of students are truly excited about it—everyone else is checking their phones or gazing off into space.

Enter virtual walls, online spaces where students can contribute their ideas, usually in response to a prompt given by either a teacher or another student. When we allow students to use a virtual wall, such as TodaysMeet, Padlet, or Dotstorming, every student has a voice, and every voice is visible and accountable.

Using these platforms in our classrooms without making the URLs public is an excellent way to establish norms around expectations and online behavior. But since a public URL is available, virtual walls could also potentially connect you and your students to a global audience. Like any technology or social media tool we use, however, we need to be intentional in determining which conversations are important to have face to face, which ones should stay in the classroom, and which ones are okay to share.

Virtual walls allow students to practice virtually sharing and collaborating and can be used synchronously or asynchronously, in the event of a time difference. Older students can create their own virtual walls to interact with the audience when presenting to the class or gathering others' ideas. I've also found them to be an excellent stepping stone for students before engaging in other forms of social media because they allow for practice on online collaboration and communication.

Robert Cannone uses **TodaysMeet**, a virtual wall, to complement his sixth-grade language arts/English students' presentations. He asks his students to select a topic they're passionate about and then present it to the class in a format similar to *The Social* (a Canadian talk show along the same lines as the United States' *The View*). Students then research relevant, thought-provoking news stories.

For example, one time, he tasked his students with discussing the story of Harambe, the silverback gorilla killed at the Cincinnati Zoo. Students engaged in authentic, thoughtful discourse around this topic as though they were members of an actual panel. While the students were presenting, the audience (Robert's class) actively participated, asking the panel questions via TodaysMeet. (In this case, Robert hadn't shared the TodaysMeet link with another classroom.) What's more, as part of this oral communications task, the talk show panel was asked to respond to audience comments in the moment, showing Robert just how much his students really understood about their topic.

If you were to follow Robert's lead and put together a panel discussion that incorporates TodaysMeet later in the year, you could broaden your students' audience and introduce new perspectives into the activity by partnering with another class within your district or anywhere in the world, for that matter.

Padlet is another virtual wall that has been around for a very long time and has become one of my favorite tools for sharing almost everything, inside and outside the classroom. Padlet makes it simple to create a "wall," where respondents can upload an idea (text), a link, an image, or a video, making it the ideal tool for sharing learning.

One of the most powerful examples I've seen of using Padlet to share learning was during Edcamp Global last year, when Calliope Global Education Initiatives' Fran Siracusa, an education strategist and global connector, introduced an activity she'd created called "Games We Play … Globally" (Figure 6.1). Each participating class was to upload a video of its students playing a game unique to their country or that they enjoyed. The project itself built on oral communication and procedural writing because students were explaining the how-tos of their game. Rob's students were excited to showcase the game "Octopus," and they had fun playing the other games students in Argentina, Spain, Italy, France, and other parts of North America, including Hawaii, had demonstrated.

Figure 6.1

The opportunities for incorporating Padlet into your classroom are as endless as your imagination, and although it's a tool we can use in school, the more flexibly we use it, the more students will see it as a place where they can connect with anyone, for any reason, in their own lives.

Video-Conferencing and Live-Streaming Tools

Skype, YouTube Live, Facebook Live, and Periscope, as well as the other video-conferencing and live-streaming apps and services available, may not initially seem to fall under the umbrella of social media, but they certainly do. After all, these are tools that allow for the creation of information as well as an opportunity to exchange ideas.

You may recall the connection with Norway's Barbara Anna Zielonka in a global digital storytelling project; I told her that because of time zones, it might be tricky for our students to Skype or use Google Hangouts on Air, in real time. She responded saying not to worry because her students were happy to connect with ours from home.

Barbara said:

> *Skype sessions are amazing. My students are not used to homework, but when I say that their task is to talk to other students who live abroad in the evening or during the weekend, they are extremely happy. I will ask everyone to download Skype on their computers and share their nicknames with you. It will be fun.*

I love everything about her response, but when I shared it with my daughters and their friends who were visiting our house at the time, they were tentative about the idea of connecting with other students from home. One girl actually said, "Wouldn't that be creepy?" I couldn't help but think of the fact that in North America, learning with others in another country isn't something our parents—or even our students—might readily accept as the norm. I wonder if I had asked students to connect with the students from Norway from their homes if I would have had to fill out waivers or get multiple levels of permission, when this is such a commonplace occurrence for them. We can learn much from our friends from Norway on the value of connecting students to one another.

Integrating video-conferencing and live-streaming apps into our classrooms can be an incredible way to bring in authentic learning opportunities, with the ultimate goal of teaching students they can reach out to anyone in the world who could help them solve a problem, at any time in their lives.

Periscope is a live-stream app (available for Apple iOS and Android smartphones) that provides opportunities for digital leadership if you think creatively and positively about the possibilities. When Periscope first came out, a principal approached me asking how we could block it because he was afraid students would use the app for nefarious reasons. While this is definitely possible (as I've said before, any and every social media tool can be used that way), once I shared some ideas for how he and his faculty could use Periscope for learning purposes, he actually changed his mind and tried it for morning announcements through the school Twitter feed. A live-stream tool like Periscope allows students to assume the role of journalist, providing them opportunity to connect and share part of a music concert, panel discussion, or school-wide event in real time.

I love "teacherpreneur" Valerie Lewis's #PasstheScopeEDU idea. Every month, there is a theme and participating classes "pass the scope" to share their learning and reflections. For example, on International Peace

> Live-streaming tools, like Periscope, allow students to assume the role of journalist and to connect and share in real time.

Day 2016, classes showed how they are working toward a more peaceful world,[9] and the "Attitude Gratitude," segment showcased things for which they were grateful.

"#PasstheScopeEDU," Valerie says, "is a community that allows teachers (novice to veteran) to share the great things happening in their schools, districts, and communities in order to promote innovation, personalized and professional learning, connectivity, and the power of a network that could transcend any building, city, state, and country." The community grows monthly, with a specific themed broadcast and special hashtag on the third Thursday of each month. The jewel here is that students also get involved in the process of sharing their learning with an authentic audience in meaningful and purposeful ways.

I have seen people Periscope others without their knowledge, which provides a valuable opportunity to have discussions about intellectual property, freedom of information rights, the importance of asking permission, and copyright laws. Many social networking platforms have livestream video capability (Facebook, Instagram, YouTube), which many students use for fun and frivolity. When we, as teachers, use these tools, we can empower them to use them for digital leadership.

Student Vignette 🔊

I've always been a reader. Reading, for me, is a part of my life, just like sports or musical instruments for some. I was always ahead of the game when it came to choosing new books to read. Sure, I read some novels in the nine-through-twelve-aged section when I fell into that age range, but I also found myself seeking new fictional worlds in the young-adult section pretty early on.

The first book that really caught my attention and prompted me to join the book community was, unsurprisingly, The Hunger Games *by Suzanne Collins. I was nine years old, on the plane coming back from summer vacation, and my love for dystopian fiction began at the very moment when Katniss' first story ended. Writing, on the other hand, is something I must admit I've excelled at since I was young, so it collaborated with reading into a gorgeous bundle. I was able to really discover the blogging community from a family friend of mine, who, fortunately, is also an author: Marta Szemik. She has blogged about her adventures in writing young adult fiction, and since we'd always bonded over books, she told me about blogging. I fell in love.*

Beginning in March 2013, I opened That Girl with Her Nose in a Book, *which eventually evolved to* A Thousand Lives Lived *(which was influenced by the phenomenal George R.R. Martin, who once said, "A reader lives a thousand lives before he dies. The man who never reads lives only one."). After beginning my blogging journey, I took part in different challenges, which caused me to feel the eagerness to post daily, whether it was discussion posts or reviews. Marta taught me the basics and some insider tips about book blogging as a whole, and I've carried out the rest on my own. I thank her every day for her encouragement.*

To create a base for my blog, I've used a variety of social media channels, including Twitter, Goodreads, Google+, Tumblr, Facebook, and Bloglovin', while at the same time, commenting on new blogs, reading new content, and creating ideas. These channels have led me to networking opportunities like attending conferences such as BookExpo America, the largest book event in North America, where bloggers, publishing professionals, librarians, and booksellers can meet, network, and learn about upcoming reads. I have been able to meet many New York Times *best-selling authors and network with some of the world's biggest publishers, all because of my vast audience, which allows me to intrigue people with my blog's content and create a name for myself. Although creating this impact has taken a lot of work and time, I feel it is completely worth it, because not only does blogging allow me to create a name for myself, giving me something to slightly brag about because of its uniqueness and communication opportunities, but it is something that makes me extremely happy. Some bloggers I know treat their review-writing as a job, but, for me, blogging is a passion. I aspire to continue making an impact on the world and encourage young people to look into creating a blog, whether it is a book blog, a food recipe blog, a fashion-makeup blog, or any blog of any genre that expresses their passions.*

—Michelle Wrona, eleventh grade

In Summary ⬇

- Blogging is a great way to promote digital leadership, as it provides students an authentic audience for writing and can be used to learn and share learning and talk about important causes

- Curation tools provide an excellent vehicle for developing a positive online presence and a portfolio of learning.

- Any tool that can be shared with students can be shared with the world, creating opportunities for digital leadership.

Discussion Questions ✖

1. What are some opportunities for incorporating some of these social media tools to meet your curriculum's goals?
2. How could you provide students with opportunities to share what they know with you and with others?
3. Is there another educator with whom you could partner so you could try some of these platforms and tools?

Chapter 6 Notes

1. Harvey, K. (Ed.), *Encyclopedia of Social Media and Politics,* 3 Vols. Thousand Oaks, CA: SAGE Publications Ltd, 2014.

2. boyd, danah, *It's Complicated: The Social Lives of Networked Teens*, New Haven: Yale University Press: 2014, 6 (emphasis added).

3. mscassidysclass.edublogs.org

4. Lee, Royan, "Blogging Incognito," *Royan Lee* (blog), September 29, 2011, royanlee.com/?p=909.

5. I first got this idea from a blogging workshop with George Couros many years ago.

6. Valenza, J. K., Boyer, B. L., & Curtis, D., "Curation Platforms," *Library Technology Reports*, 50(7), 2014: 60.

7. Dale, S. "Content Curation: The Future of Relevance," *Business Information Review*, 31(4), 2014: 199-205.

8. Ibid.

9. "Let There Be Peace on Earth WORLDWIDE!" storify.com/iamvlewis/let-there-be-peace-worldwide.

MICHELLE WRONA

thatgirlybookworm.blogspot.ca

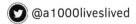 @a1000liveslived

Michelle Wrona is a sixteen-year-old dreamer, perfectionist, blogger, reader, peanut-butter obsessed, wanderlust-crazed, wannabe writer teenager living in Toronto, Canada, who is (almost literally) drinking maple syrup with a swirly straw, right by the fireplace in her igloo. She founded *A Thousand Lives Lived* in 2012 when she was twelve, fangirling over her love of books and the different fandoms which form the book community with her enlarging audience. Her favorite genres in YA are thrillers, horror stories, and contemporary romances. Michelle hopes to write a YA novel someday, and says that she will never switch to read just "adult" novels. Aside from her obsession with books, she spends her time being a neat freak, and contemplating where she would like to travel next.

Use Michelle's Story to Inspire Your Students

 Check out Michelle's blog and see what she is reading today.

 Ask students to respond to Michelle on Twitter about your class's favorite books, or to use your class Twitter account to share their learning about books being read in class.

SECTION III

How We Make Digital Leadership Happen in Schools

Digital Citizenship in Context

Adults are always telling us what not to do online. They never show us what we should do or how we should act.

—Najha Marshall, twelfth grade

The anchor of digital leadership is ethical and responsible use, and yet we aren't really doing a good job with digital citizenship in our schools. I really like the analogy that Dan Haesler, #SchoolOfThought author uses when he compares our current social media instruction to driving lessons. In it, he asks us to imagine what it would look like if we taught teenagers how to drive the same way that we taught them about how to use social media:

1. Driving lessons would be taught by adults (teachers or parents) with little or no experience of driving.
2. Driving lessons would only focus on what not to do.
3. Driving lessons would never take place in an actual car.[1]

His point is that students gain a far better understanding of digital citizenship as a result of an authentic, in-the-moment, and guided approach than when they learn through a booklet or unit taught completely out of context at the beginning of the year. As a mother, I've always subscribed to this approach, signing up for the same platforms as my kids so I can ask the right questions and be there just in case they need me.

For example, when my younger daughter, Kelsey, saw I had an interest in VSCO (a photo-sharing app I'd never heard of), she showed me how to use the tool and how she and her friends were using it. Our ensuing conversation was enlightening and much longer than the monosyllabic responses I'd been receiving as of late (if you are parenting a teen, you know exactly what I'm talking about). I asked her whether or not she used her real name or a username and whether or not she still had rights to her photos. The first question she had a ready answer for, but she hadn't considered my second, so we looked at the app's terms of service together. I also showed her the Creative Commons logos and we explored the idea of creating a watermark signature that she could put on her photos. I taught her more about digital citizenship in those few minutes than she would have gotten from a month of me preaching about what ethical and responsible use looks like. Now, she's curating photos that she is proud of on a social media site that she could use when she gets older if her passion for photography continues.

So, how does that teaching approach translate to the classroom? In my more than twenty years of teaching, I've come to understand that no matter how great the resource, if it doesn't match the group of students in front of me and the learning context going on in my class, I may as well skip it. That's not to say we should throw away all of the really awesome resources available—it's just that we should approach them as additional tools to help us teach how to navigate online spaces in creative, critical, healthy, and ethical ways in *context*, rather than as isolated lessons. I've seen digital citizenship lessons take the form of students talking about their digital footprints by coloring a footprint, or completing a worksheet about words associated with digital citizenship. Do we really expect this will transfer to when they are using devices?

This idea of in-context learning is supported by research surrounding the theory of Situated Cognition. It argues that knowing is inseparable from doing, and that all knowledge must be situated in a learning context. Consider these insights into student learning from a 1989 article in *Educational Researcher* titled "Situated Cognition and the Culture of Learning" by John Seely Brown, PhD, Allan Collins, and Paul Daguid:

- "Learning methods that are embedded in authentic situations are not merely useful; they are essential and knowledge must be applied in context in order to be used and made explicit."

- "Research around using vocabulary words from a dictionary to teach reading show learning to be ineffective because 'learning from dictionaries, like any method that tries to teach abstract concepts independently of authentic situations, overlooks the way understanding is developed through continued, situated use."

- "People who use tools actively rather than just acquire them, appear to build an increasingly rich implicit understanding of the world in which they use the tools and of the tools themselves."

- "Given the chance to observe and practice in situ the behavior of members of a culture, people pick up relevant jargon, imitate behavior, and gradually start to act in accordance with its norms and that despite the fact that cultural practices are often extremely complex, students, when given the opportunity to observe and practice them, students adopt them with great success."[2]

This theory holds true for literacy and numeracy and is absolutely applicable to technology tools, social media, and online behavior today.

Situated Cognition argues that knowing is inseparable from doing.

Focusing on Good Behavior— Online and Offline

Kevin Honeycutt, a technology integration specialist, aptly says, "Kids are growing up on a digital playground and no one is on recess duty." And while he speaks to the absence of an adult, I'd like to extend the analogy to the role an adult can and should play, regardless of whether kids are online or offline.[3]

When my children were young, I supervised them on the playground. I didn't necessarily expect them to be well-behaved or that the children around them would be well-behaved, but I'd taught them to be kind, respectful, empathetic, and patient. I accompanied them to the park on their playdates to ensure that, if there were any issues, I could help guide them. I played with them, and I was quick to celebrate when they shared, took turns, and played nicely, but I also stood far enough away so they could deal with conflict on their own. (If you're a parent, you know exactly what I mean.)

When my kids entered kindergarten, I had faith that their teachers would assume the playground supervisor role and that, if there were any issues, they would communicate them with me. I expected the teachers to respond encouragingly when all was well and to intervene and help problem solve when needed. As my kids got older, I stood back more and only intervened when necessary. Gradually, I let them venture out on their own.

Kids are playing in digital playgrounds and virtual meeting places at increasingly younger ages. Sometimes parents are there to help and sometimes they aren't. But if teachers aren't there either, who's guiding kids when something goes wrong or encouraging them when they are behaving positively? While students are quickly understanding that there is accountability for their actions offline, online, they seem to feel they can do and say what they like without the prying eyes of adults around.

Let's start with "Acceptable Use" versus "Responsible Use." There is a difference (Figure 7.1).

Acceptable Use Policy	Responsible Use Policy
• Is presented in the format of what the student "shouldn't do"	• Is presented in the format of what the student "should do"
• Defines the rules that learners and educators must follow and may limit technology use	• Increased student responsibility for use of technology to support learning
• Often restrictive, intended to control or prohibit particular behaviours	• Developed with students to create common understanding of the responsibility of accessing online technologies as part of the learning process
• Often operate on the assumption that students will lose the privilege of technology if they do not follow certain rules	• Can contain clear expectations regarding the use of technology in the classroom

Figure 7.1[4]

Since my daughters were little, whenever they'd go out the door without me, I'd always tell them, "Make good choices." So when one of my daughters made a very poor choice, I remember having a conversation where she challenged me by saying, "You always say make good choices, but half the time we don't know what that means!" She was, of course, absolutely right. It's the same in the classroom: When we're clear with our students about the criteria for success, they are much more likely do well because they know exactly what's expected of them.

In light of that, we need to be explicit about what it means to be a good digital citizen by modeling what good behavior looks like. Modeling digital leadership allows us to provide positive reinforcement, rather than constantly harping on the negative.

In my Library Orientation lessons, I start my discussions with the "Responsible Use of Technology Pledge" diagram (Figure 7.2), which shows an obligation to protecting and respecting ourselves and others and requires students to brainstorm what that means to them.[5] In my school, this format mirrors what the "Acceptable Use District Policy" details. I've found that when you ask students to discuss in pairs what each of these categories means and then co-construct the answers, they are more likely to hold themselves accountable to this policy because they helped create it and actually understand what it means. Because of the diagram's open-endedness, each K–12 classroom in a school (or district) can use the same template and language, adding nuances to the verbiage as students get older. For example, "Respect Others" may include a conversation about sharing or viewing pornography in ninth grade, while in third grade, it could mean simply asking permission to take someone's picture. Using this organizer at a staff meeting can help to clarify and be transparent about the collective understanding of what it means to use technology responsibly.

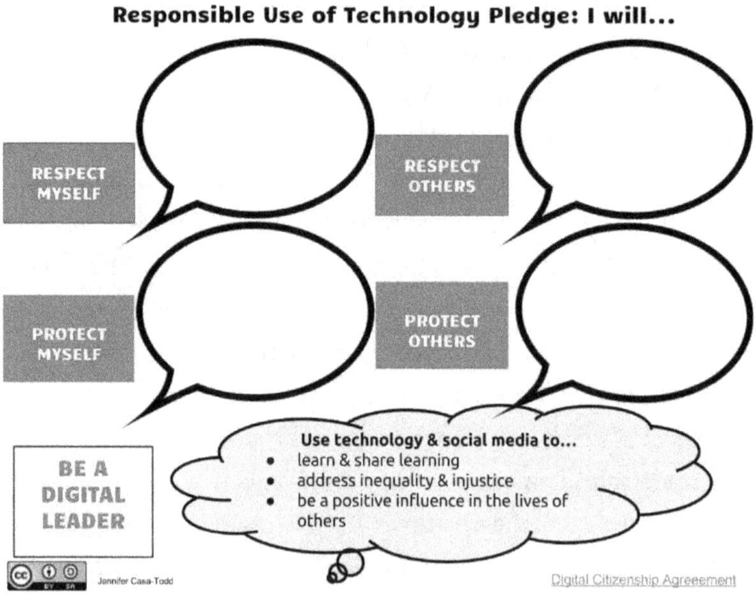

Figure 7.2

In addition to reviewing responsible use of technology, I intentionally outline what being a digital leader entails. Most students lean in when we explore this—likely because they have never heard an adult speak positively about social media. Part of what I do next is to ask students if they have seen or know of anyone who is using social media to exemplify digital leadership and ask them to brainstorm what each of the elements might look like.

This general "Responsible Use Policy" is a great launch pad, until a student makes a mistake. Then you can choose to either view these mistakes as disruptions, or you can look at them as incredible teaching opportunities, allowing you to offer your students greater depth and understanding about how to behave appropriately online.

Julie Millan, a fourth-grade teacher and former digital literacy consultant in Toronto, shared a wonderful story with me about an incident in her class. She'd been using Google Classroom (a private learning platform for students) but had forgotten to check off the "comment box." So one of her students decided to upload a "funny" video, and the ensuing comments ranged from amusing to inappropriate. But because Julie embraces a digital leadership stance, she didn't shut down the opportunity for comments; rather, she asked her students if they would like their very own for fun Google Classroom account where they could upload funny videos or share stories unrelated to school. She used this situation as a springboard for a persuasive writing exercise, requiring students to write a compelling letter as to why (or why not) a "fun" Google Classroom account was a good idea. She also used it as a moment to have a more in-depth discussion about respecting others by focusing on what's appropriate to share and what appropriate comments look like.

Using this approach does not shut down the opportunity to use technology and/or social media; instead, it allows for an incredibly rich, in-context dialogue with students and very clearly outlines of what they can do. Figure 7.3 shows what Julie used in her classroom. It's a an approach you can use for any social media tool. I know that Diana Hale, a teacher in Toronto, uses this same approach before students begin to actively use their class Twitter account.

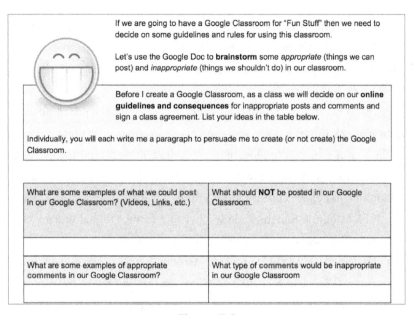

Figure 7.3

At the very heart of the responsible use discussion is, of course, relationships. When students respect you, feel loved and safe, and feel like their voice matters to you, they will unlikely misuse technology where explicit expectations have been co-constructed and continue to be referenced.

THINK

I'm sure you've seen a variation of this popular THINK poster. (Figure 7.4).[6] The problem lies in the fact that we plaster this on walls in classrooms and in hallways believing that, as if by osmosis, kids will begin to practice these behaviors.

One of the strategies I use is to have students modify the poster so that they feel ownership of it. Another strategy that works well is to place a variety of posters (Common Sense Media has so many excellent ones) around your classroom, creating a sort of "gallery walk," whereby students go from poster to poster using the "+/-/Interesting"[7] strategy. They would give a "+" and articulate everything they like about the poster, a "-" to everything they don't like, and an "Interesting" for, well, that's self-explanatory. You could then ask students to vote on one of the posters for their class to modify together. This way, every time you use technology and social media together, you could refer to the poster everyone created, allowing it to become more than just another decoration on the wall. And though this may take extra time at the beginning of the year, it will prove to save time and heartache because the expectations are clear and students are accountable for what they have co-constructed.

Figure 7.4

The Nine Elements of Digital Citizenship

At this point, you may be wondering how you could possibly balance yet one more thing on your already-full plate, especially considering apps and technology tools are ever-changing or you may not be familiar with many of the online spaces out there.

Mike Ribble, EdD, director of technology for the Manhattan-Ogden Unified School District 383 in Kansas, created a list of what he considers to be the "Nine Elements of Digital Citizenship."[8] These can apply to almost every online tool and app. Knowing what these are, so you can pull these out as appropriate, will help you to direct your questions and your teaching when practicing digital leadership. Where there are unique district policies or protocols in place, be sure to use those when using social media.

Here are Mike's nine elements, each followed by a question I have suggested pertaining to digital leadership:[9]

1. Digital Access: full electronic participation in society

- How can I help others to see the inequity and importance of digital access?

2. Digital Communication: electronic exchange of information

- How can my posts make a positive difference in someone's life?

3. Digital Law: electronic responsibility for actions and deeds

- How can my actions online not only follow the law, but also be a good model for others?

4. Digital Security: electronic precaution to guarantee safety

- How can I balance online safety with engaging in opportunities to learn from others?

5. Digital Commerce: electronic buying and selling of goods

- How can I help others understand that companies target us to make money?
- What opportunities are there for us to use social media to raise funds for a cause that is important to us?

6. Digital Health and Wellness: physical and psychological well-being in a digital world

- How can I contribute to my personal well-being as well as that of others?

7. Digital Literacy: teaching and learning about technology and its uses

- Which tool will best help me convey my message?

8. Digital Etiquette: electronic standards of conduct or procedure

- How will I demonstrate respect for myself and others with differing opinions?

9. Digital Rights and Responsibilities: those freedoms that extend to everyone in a digital world

- How does my behavior online acknowledge others' contributions?

Through discussions with my students, I've noticed some of the best conversations and lessons bridge several of these nine elements.

'Digital citizenship, digital leadership, and technology integration must happen at the same time.'

It seems as if every district and every organization is trying to come up with their own unique framework and definition of digital citizenship. In some ways, this makes sense, as every school district and every individual school has its own culture; but it can also be quite confusing and, truthfully, in some ways it overcomplicates matters and delays support. Far too often, what happens is districts spend months trying to develop a policy, continuum, or resource to ensure digital citizenship reflects their own "brand" or "culture," when, as each day passes, teachers are developing their own strategies and students are doing what they've always done.

We live in an age where information is abundant, and in many cases shared freely, meaning thousands of great resources are already available. It's important that a school's teachers discuss what a continuum for ongoing conversations about ethical and responsible behavior looks like and where they should go for help. *The Digital Citizenship Education in Saskatchewan Schools*[10] report, written in part by the University of Regina's Alec Couros, PhD, and Katia Hildebrandt, does this beautifully. This resource's K–12 continuum, with its open-ended, guided questions, helps us determine what students need to know, understand, and be able to do. And, of course, the many other books and resources on digital citizenship available provide the right lesson for the right moment.

The fact of the matter is districts can create an exemplary resource and send it to schools without ever really helping actual students in actual classrooms become better "citizens" in the online world.

Age Restrictions: Opportunity or Barrier?

Even at a young age, students know about and are experimenting with social media apps that aren't exactly in line with the age restriction set out by most companies. Of course, this is a parent and family responsibility. Yet when I look at my nieces, nephews, and family friends, I am deeply concerned about the extent to which hundreds of thousands of other kids are navigating these spaces mostly on their own, usually at a very young age.

So if an app says, "You must be at least thirteen years old to use the service," do we avoid using it in school because of the age restriction, despite the fact that many kids are using apps younger and younger? The most logical response seems to be "yes" because we would never want to be liable; however, we need to teach kids about the positive power of technology and social media in and around the same time they are playing in online spaces.

As I looked around and talked to people about how they were approaching this topic, I learned A.J. Juliani, an education and technology innovation specialist in Pennsylvania, allows his six-year-old daughter to use Snapchat as a means to accustom her "to using, navigating, and behaving in a social platform."[11] I had a similar conversation with Rafranz Davis, executive director of professional and digital learning in Texas, who is an important mentor for her nephew, Braeden, when he uses social media.

She says she gives Braeden the freedom to make his own choices, but that she also offers him guidance and support as he needs it.

Are you beginning to see a pattern? If these educational leaders think mentoring the young folks in their lives while they're on social media is important, then there must be a good reason. They know their kids need guidance. Parents and relatives who are already playing with social media spaces are helping the children and teens they love understand its nuances—this is a new reality for parenting today, and it should also be a new reality for teaching today.

A Class Account

The best way to mentor our students is to create a class Twitter, Instagram, Snapchat, Facebook, or _____ (insert the tool being used most by parents and kids when you are reading this) account. Let them use the class account to connect with experts, organizations, and other classes in a guided, contextual way so that you are practicing and discussing those crucial Nine Elements of Digital Citizenship. You might emphasize the following points at various points in the year:

- We recognize and empathize with the fact that not everyone has equal access to technology. (Digital Access)

- We only check our social media feed at certain times during the day to ensure a healthy balance. (Digital Health and Wellness)

- We don't turn our notifications on because we don't want to be distracted by them. (Digital Etiquette, Digital Health and Wellness)

- The classes and accounts that follow us are opportunities to connect with and learn from people in other classes from other communities. (Digital Communication)

- Our worth is not determined by how many followers we have, because it's more important to engage in conversations and relationships with the followers we do have. (Digital Health)

- We block anyone whose identity we are unsure of or who is inappropriate in any way. (Digital Security)

- We understand that some posts are "sponsored" or "promoted." (Digital Commerce)

- We pay attention to how "edited" a photo might be by asking, "I wonder how many times they had to try to get such a perfect photo?" (Digital Health and Wellness, Digital Literacy)

- We emphasize that a "like" isn't the same as making a comment and forging a relationship, and that when you "like" something, it means you agree with it. (Digital Literacy)

- Rather than making statements when we don't agree with something or aren't quite sure of someone's intent, we ask clarifying questions. (Digital Communication)

- We delete a post if we think it might be misunderstood or interpreted negatively. (Digital Communication)

- We regularly check our privacy settings to see if anything has changed and we talk about what should be private (stay in the classroom) and public (okay to share with the world). (Digital Security)

- We create a strong password and check for possible fake accounts following ours. (Digital Security)

- When we use a hashtag, we understand that anyone can see our post, even if they aren't following our class's account. (Digital Literacy)

- We never reveal personal information about ourselves or meet anyone privately. (Digital Safety)

This seems like a long list, but really so much of it is based on what we inherently want students to know anyway; but like with any learning, we need to be explicit about it.

Gradual Release of Responsibility

Ultimately, we want to empower our students to begin to use these tools on their own. One method I've been using for years when teaching literacy is the Gradual Release of Responsibility Model,[12] which involves the teacher modeling a behavior or task, then gradually releasing the responsibility for the learning to the students.

It goes something like this:

"I do it." (The teacher or expert offers direct or focused instruction.)

"We do it." (The class does it together.)

"You do it together." (Students work with a peer.)

"You do, I watch." (A student works independently.)

As a tried-and-true literacy process, it can also certainly help us frame conversations around social media use digital citizenship, and digital leadership. It is important to note, however, that whereas in the traditional sense, the "expert" is primarily the teacher, for our purposes, when discussing technology or social media, the direct or focused instruction can actually come from a student (or an expert outside of the classroom who visits through video-streaming).

This solid learning theory also reminds us that the most important thing we can do when engaging in connected learning using technology or social media with our students is to let them own it. When we gradually release the responsibility of learning, it is the student who benefits from using technology and social media, and it is the student who has the opportunity to practice digital leadership. When we post on behalf of students, though, we take that learning opportunity away from them and we assume it for our own personal gain, something we must be extremely careful to avoid. It is important that we travel alongside our students on this journey and be mentors for them. Ideally, the gradual release process begins in kindergarten and culminates in seventh and eighth grades, when students turn thirteen.

> It is important that we travel alongside our students on this journey and be mentors for them.

Beyond Your Control

In some cases you will have students whose parents do not feel comfortable signing a Freedom of Information form, or a principal who is extremely hesitant to allow social media. You need to tread very carefully here, because you want to respect the wishes of parents and you want to keep your job. A good compromise is to ask students to create a face or mask (this can be an art activity) and take a class picture, which becomes your profile picture. Be sure to always include those students by either giving them the camera or focusing on hands and feet. This is a great whole-class option for you if you are not quite comfortable either.

A Kindergarten Case Study

As you can imagine in a class of twenty-eight four-year-olds, everything takes time, repetition, and patience. What's more, kids need to play and explore in an environment that supports cognitive, emotional, social, and physical development so they can learn how to self-regulate, contribute, problem solve, take turns, and share in face-to-face situations. Kindergarten teacher Stephanie Viveiros understands that but also recognizes the incredible potential of technology and social media and thereby makes a point of introducing her students to ICT so she can make home-to-school, as well as global, connections. She takes a guided approach to teaching digital citizenship and sets the stage for her students to become digital leaders.

Stephanie began gradually introducing one of her class's two iPads to her students as a tool to capture student learning and thinking (or "pedagogical documentation," as we call it in Ontario). At the beginning of the year, during small-group guided instruction, Stephanie showed her students how to take a picture of their favorite work using the iPad, to document one piece of their work each day. She continued showing them how to take photos, ask their peers' permission to be in their photos, only take snapshots of those students who'd signed off on the district-required Freedom of Information waiver, then how to sign in to their Google account and upload their photos to the class's shared Google Drive folder titled "Documentation" before signing out of Google.

Over the course of the school year, as her students continued practicing their digital literacy skills, they were given options for how they wanted to present and document their work. They could share it in physical form in a folder that went home to their parents, on the classroom Inquiry Wall, in the Google Drive folder to be sent to their parents via e-mail, or to the Google Drive folder to present during their Tech Circle time using the projector and whiteboard. If a student wanted to share more than one photo, they would create a collage made up of several images using on online collage tool such as PicCollage.

Since her students already knew how to take a photo of their work and determine where they wanted to share it, Stephanie added another choice: They could share it with their parents and others on Instagram. With specific guided instruction, she worked with a small group of children on a rotational basis to create the Instagram posts, and every day a different group would select what sharing should stay private and what should stay public. She showed them how to delete a post if they made a mistake. She modeled how to share in a positive, constructive way and had the groups talk about what shouldn't be shared. She also took the time to see which new followers her class had and made sure the conversation was about the new classes and people the class could learn from and with. (I love that she reframed the idea of followers from popularity to classes and people and connections.) Stephanie also engaged in a "think-aloud" with her class about Internet safety and discussed what to do if people wanted to follow the class account with whom she didn't feel comfortable, show-ing them what that looked like a couple of times in the year. This allowed her students to gain insight into her thought process.

As an amazing (and unexpected) bonus, parents started contacting Stephanie to ask for help with Instagram, so she created tutorials and con-nected with them to facilitate their learning and promote parent engage-ment. The students were excited to share their knowledge with their par-ents, both at home and at school. While at home, students and parents would create photo collages featuring events, outings, trips, and celebra-tions and e-mail them to Stephanie to share during morning Tech Circle. She told me the parents were creating Instagram and Twitter accounts just so they could see all of the great learning the kids were doing. Best of all, I was able to see what Stephanie was doing and could share that learn-ing with others in our district (always asking for permission, of course). Whether it was building a gigantic bird's nest, designing and creating bird feeders, planting an herb garden, hosting a Father's Day soccer game, or watching caterpillars turn into butterflies, her kindergarten class was always doing and sharing something fun and exciting.

Think about the many elements of digital citizenship (health and well-being, security, literacy) that Stephanie and her students practiced and how she empowered her students to become digital leaders by giving them opportunities to make choices in their learning, and then sharing that learning through technology and social media. That communication created a powerful opportunity to connect with parents, the class's com-munity, and the world—so much so that it became a part of Stephanie and her students' everyday routine.

Digital Citizenship Boot Camp

Another great way to promote digital leadership and to ensure digi-tal citizenship is taught within a meaningful context is to use the model North Dakota third-grade teacher Kayla Delzer created, called "Digital Citizenship Boot Camp." (She even built excitement around the idea by dressing in camo!) To learn these essential skills, students engage in a series of lessons around how to be safe, ethical, and savvy online and are rewarded with a certificate for their efforts. But that's not the end of boot camp; rather, Kayla's students then practice the positive online behaviors they've learned by managing their class's Twitter, Instagram, and Snapchat accounts. Her use of the Gradual Release of Responsibility model begins with students becoming the "Tweeter of the Day," "Instagrammer of the Day," and "Snapchatter of the Day." Students then practice creating posts that are not only appropriate, but that also showcase their classroom and learning in a positive light. Each day, her students come to school excited and feeling empowered. (Ryley, one of her third-graders, shares his perspective in this chapter's "Student Vignette.")

Like Stephanie, Kayla also extends learning opportunities to her students' parents by offering them their own boot camp. The students all take pride in helping their parents set up accounts and teaching them everything them they need know, from how to retweet to how to use their district's hashtags. Good communication with parents always led to a better year for me as a teacher. What an empowering learning and community-building opportunity for everyone!

Classroom Committees

Rob Cannone's approach with his sixth-grade students is to have students work in committees on a rotating basis. The public relations team works on the class blog, the social media team updates the class Twitter account, and the tech team is responsible for the upkeep of Chromebooks, iPads, and/or any other devices in the classroom. Other teams include:

> Empower your students to become digital leaders by giving them opportunities to share their learning through technology and social media.

eco-team, responsible for ensuring the proper recycling of materials and the classroom design team, responsible for designing bulletin boards and creating anchor charts for concepts taught in class. This approach works beautifully because it makes everyone feel accountable for all aspects of the classroom, and social media is no more revered than any other responsibility.

Stephanie, Kayla, and Rob show us how it is possible to begin to engage students in real opportunities for digital leadership in guided ways while adhering to the terms and conditions of most social media apps.

Student Vignette 🔊

I use Twitter, Instagram, and Snapchat in my classroom using our iPads. I take photos of kids that are working productively and crushing it, and I type a tweet to tell about the pictures. I like to show our followers what we are doing and why it's important. I also like to send tweets to authors, creators of apps, teachers, families, and experts when I have questions or need more information. It is amazing knowing that there are 3,000 followers looking at my work. It's a once-in-a-lifetime opportunity to be on social media.

Using social media and going through Digital Citizenship Boot Camp helped me understand what to share online and what to keep private. If you're a parent, don't post stuff that you don't want to say in front of your kids. If you're a kid, don't post stuff you don't want your teacher to see. I know there is a whole world out there, and maybe someday, someone will see the tweets I wrote and hire me for the job I want. I want to be proud of my social media accounts.

—Ryley Hanson, third grade

In Summary ⬇

- Students benefit from adult mentors in online spaces just as they do face to face.

- Literacy strategies, such as Situated Cognition and the Gradual Release of Responsibility, are useful for integrating social media in the classroom.

- At any age, a contextual approach to digital citizenship is more effective than teaching lessons in the form of units or packets, as valuable lessons are embedded in classroom practice.

- Students need to be a part of the conversation when it comes to responsible use of technology.

- Digital leadership is an ideal way to demonstrate to students what is possible, while still focusing on the elements of digital citizenship.

Discussion Questions ✗

1. Does your school or district have a continuum of learning in place that encourages teachers to address the digital citizenship elements in context, rather than in discrete units, for students of every age? If not, how can you initiate these discussions?

2. How could your district, school, or department shift the focus from what kids shouldn't do to digital leadership (what kids can and should do)?

3. If you aren't comfortable with some of the ideas I've presented here, what are the concerns? With whom could you have a conversation to work through the things that make you uncomfortable?

4. How can you include parents in the conversation?

Chapter 7 Notes

1. Haesler, Dan, "Driving Down Social Media Way," October 2, 2012, danhaesler.com/2012/10/02/driving-down-social-media-way.

2. Brown, J. S., A. Collins, and S. Duguid, "Situated Cognition and the Culture of Learning," *Educational Researcher,* 18(1), 1989: 32-42.

3. My thinking around this really clarified as a result of a conversation with Diana Hale.

4. Couros, Alec and Katla Hildebrandt, "Digital Citizenship Education in Saskatchewan Schools," 2015, Retrieved from publications.gov.sk.ca/documents/11/83322-DC%20Guide%20-%20ENGLISH%202.pdf.

5. A modifiable version is available at SocialLEADia.org in this chapter's "Resources" section.

6. A modifiable version is available at SocialLEADia.org in this chapter's "Resources" section.

7. This is a literacy strategy I have used for years, so I don't know where it originated.

8. Ribble, Mike, "Digital Citizenship in Schools," Lecture, ITSE, Washington D.C., 2011.

9. You can find a resource with guiding questions for each element at SocialLEADia.org.

10. Couros, Alec and Katla Hildebrandt, "Digital Citizenship Education in Saskatchewan Schools," 2015, Retrieved from publications.gov.sk.ca/documents/11/83322-DC%20Guide%20-%20ENGLISH%202.pdf.

11. Juliani, A.J., "Why We Let Our Six-Year-Old Use Snapchat," *A.J. Juliani* (blog), n.d., http://ajjuliani.com/why-we-let-our-six-year-old-use-snapchat/.

12. Fisher, Douglas and Nancy Frey, "Better Learning Through Structured Teaching," ASCD, December 2013, ascd.org/publications/books/113006/chapters/Learning,-or-Not-Learning,-in-School.aspx.

MEET THE STUDENTS
HANNAH ALPER
CallMeHannah.ca

 @ThatHannahAlper

 /ThatHannahAlper

 /thathannahalper

Hannah launched her blog, CallMeHannah.ca, at the age of nine with the desire to inspire others to join her in the belief that the little things we can all do add up to make a big difference. Today, Hannah is an engaged global citizen pursuing a deeper understanding of and connection to the world. She seeks inspiration and motivation from those who have come before her and regularly features their stories on her blog and social media. On Twitter alone, she has more than 40,000 followers.

Hannah has found power in using her voice to motivate and empower people of all ages to identify their passion and take action. She is a writer for *The Huffington Post*, a ME to WE motivational speaker and WE ambassador, and an ambassador for Bystander Revolution, an anti-bullying organization.

Use Hannah's Story to Inspire Your Students

? Malala Yousafzai is Hannah's role model, but who is Malala, and what has she done that we should know about? (This a possible inquiry provocation.)

What is Bystander Revolution? What action(s) can your class or school take to support this cause?

Hannah supports environmental causes such as World Wildlife Fund and Earth Hour. What do these organizations do? Are there other organizations doing similar things that you could support?

8

Shift from Negative to Positive

It's really important that I share messages that
are hopeful, kind, and true. I also try to give
people something to think about and wrap up
my thinking in a message that's interesting and
thought-provoking.

—*Olivia Van Ledtje, third grade*

The most significant shift we can make in our schools
is to drown out the negative with positive. We have to acknowledge that negative things might happen on social media. But when we shift the conversation to digital leadership, we improve the chances that social media will be used to make positive things happen.

Olivia Van Ledtje has taught me what the next generation of kids using social media can look like. She is, hands down, the most inspiring nine-year-old I've ever met. In person, she is confident and spunky (and can do a mean walkover). She's working hard to promote a deeper understanding of what it means to be kind using social media, and her @TheLivBits Twitter account is definitely a role model for adults and students alike. Online, Olivia tweets messages encouraging kids to love authors, books, and big ideas about life, and she's as genuine online as she was when I met her in person. She shares her excitement about studying ballet, her love for sharks, and she expertly uses hashtags; I love to see what she comes up with. She refers to me as her #CanadianTeacher. In her keynote at the San Francisco DigCit Summit she implored us to think about how we can use social media to promote our passions. I was immediately drawn to her positivity.

It wasn't until I spoke to her mom, Cynthia Merrell, later in the evening, that I was shocked to learn Olivia's journey online began as a result of a bullying incident at school.[1] In her LivBits series about bullying, Olivia says that when she tried to seek help from her teachers, a few didn't believe she was being bullied and offered little support. Traditionally, the narrative around social media is that it causes pain and anguish via cyberbullying; however, Olivia's story makes you pause and rethink that notion because, for her, social media has been a place of acceptance and a source of joy—and she isn't the first student I've spoken to who has said this.

Interestingly, in Northwestern University's 2016 report, *The Common Sense Census: Plugged-In Parents of Tweens and Teens*,[2] 43 percent of parents were "moderately" or "extremely" worried about their teens' or tweens' Internet use, meaning 53 percent didn't have that degree of concern. Of the parents who expressed moderate or extreme worry about their child's use of the Internet, most did not cite cyberbullying as among their top four concerns, despite the media's attention to this issue. In fact, 44 percent of parents, in that particular study, said they believe social media benefits their children's relationships, versus 15 percent who believe it hurts them, and 41 percent who don't believe it makes a difference.[3]

The fact is that some adults, mostly those who have never used social media in ways that promote digital leadership as we've defined it, think the minute we allow students to go online, we open them up to a world of hatred and malicious bullying. Most cyberbullying, however, is an extension of the in-person bullying occurring in a classroom or playground, and much of the banter between kids online is no different than our own teenage banter on telephones and in hallways—but because it is in writing is feels more permanent and hurtful.

In a 2012 report from the Consortium for School Networking, *Making Progress: Rethinking State and School District Policies Concerning Mobile Technologies and Social Media*, 20 percent of the teens and 33 percent of younger teenage girls Pew researchers interviewed said their peers are mostly "unkind" to one another on social networking sites, and 19 percent of teens reported having been bullied within the last twelve months. While these statistics are somewhat disturbing, it's important to note that the number one form of bullying does not involve technology, as 12 percent of the teen respondents said they had been bullied in person, 9 percent had endured bullying via text messaging, 8 percent online (through e-mail, social networking, and so on), and 7 percent over the phone.[4]

Unfortunately, it's hard to know what to believe exactly, because in 2014, McAfee's "Teens and the Screen Study: Exploring Online Privacy, Social Networking and Cyberbullying" found that 87 percent of the youth whom researchers talked to said they'd witnessed cyberbullying versus the year prior (2013), when 27 percent said they'd seen cruel behavior online.[5] I realize it's not the same survey, and perhaps there is an increase in these behaviors, but it really does show just how inconsistent some of the information out there is and how media can feed people's fears in the form of sensationalism.

Having said all of this, I always take surveys and research findings with a grain of salt. I love chocolate, coffee, and wine, and on any given day I can find research to support my consumption of each of these items because they are "good for me." But if I wanted to quit drinking coffee, I could find an equal number of research studies to point to how unhealthy drinking coffee can be. In my own informal sampling of 103 students via

Twitter in June 2016, nearly 27 percent reported they'd had a "negative experience" using social media personally. When I asked them to clarify what "negative behavior" meant to them, the students said "just people being rude," "rude words," "coarse language," and "swearing at me." Now, by no means am I condoning this kind of behavior, but I think it's necessary to just pause for a moment and consider how many tweens and teens you've seen act this way in their face-to-face interactions (a walk through the hallways of my own school affirms that this number is quite high), or, if I may be so bold, how often you saw or demonstrated that kind of behavior when you were their age. With that in mind, do we take away opportunities for students to play together at recess or work in groups because they might be rude to one another? Of course not! We give them strategies to work cooperatively and collaboratively. The same strategies are necessary when it comes to social media use.

What's more, I've noticed during my library orientations that we may be overusing the term "cyberbullying" to the point where it has lost any real meaning. Just like when we differentiate between "bullying" and "mean behavior" (in person), we have to be careful about how we're defining cyberbullying and how often we use the term when talking about simply being mean versus sustained, malicious targeting online.

This is not to say that such behavior is okay, nor that cyberbullying isn't happening. I definitely acknowledge that when a child gets a reprieve from ongoing negative behavior by leaving school, those harsh words can follow them home via their device—it's one of the reasons why my own children have never been allowed to take their devices into their

> When students are rude to one another at recess or in class, we give them strategies to work cooperatively and collaboratively. The same strategies are necessary when it comes to social media use.

bedrooms. I also believe that just as kids can be mean in person, the fact that a screen separates them from the human being might prompt behaviors they may never have engaged in if they were looking at each other. As a result, we must continue to have conversations about how we can counteract the negative with the positive at every opportunity. We must also emphasize the fact that social media is made up of people who, like Olivia, are choosing to post positive content. Whenever possible, we need to remind our students that the person being targeted is someone's brother or sister or mother or son or daughter. This is a necessary reminder in person as well as when they are behind the screen.

One of the teachers in my PLN told me the tragic story of a child who was cyberbullied to the point that they took their own life. As a result of this incident, the school banned all cell phones. Don't get me wrong—this is absolutely horrible, and the school has a great deal of healing ahead of it, but I sincerely doubt that banning cell phones from classrooms and blocking social media would in any way have helped that child. In fact, if the student did have social media access, might their peers or the teacher have noticed something was amiss?

You may be thinking that I am being flippant about a very serious incident. Believe me when I tell you I do not take the issue of bullying lightly. I know firsthand how incredibly mean people can be to those who are different. In elementary school, I was cross-eyed. I wore the wrong clothes. I allowed everyone's opinion of me to doubt my own gifts and abilities. I was bullied so terribly that when I was thirteen years old, I consciously set out to take my own life—and we didn't have cell phones back then. Thankfully, there were only five pills remaining in the bottle of Tylenol I took, so that when I naively cried myself to sleep thinking I would never wake up, I was so incredibly grateful to actually open my eyes that my entire outlook on life changed. What would have helped me more than anything would have been for a teacher to notice. To teach empathy and kindness to my peers. For my own parents to notice. For a caring adult to have tapped into one of my passions or strengths. For me to know someone believed in me. For me to know just because I looked different, it didn't mean I wasn't valuable or worthy.

What was my miracle ends in tragedy for way too many kids. When I became a teacher, I made sure to teach and model empathy and multiple perspectives and to be particularly attentive to those students who might be targeted because they're different. I know all too well that our problems with bullying do not stem from social media. Although they may be amplified by social media, bullying is about cruelty, power, and an apathy for other human beings. We need to be observant of our students' needs and well-being, regardless of whether or not we're allowing social media in our classroom.

We need to also consider another perspective. I spent every single recess by myself. I distinctly remember when I stopped trying to be included. I was "invited" to play hide and go seek (likely because my teacher told my peers to be "nice" to me and to include me). I was "it." After spending over thirty minutes looking for people, I realized that they had hidden away to play another game, never intending to include me. I sometimes brought a book and sat by myself, but then I was mocked for being a nerd. When I see a student sitting alone and looking at their phone, I don't see what you see. I see a person who is able to pass the time and perhaps avoid being harassed or perhaps someone who is at least able to connect with an online friend group. I wish I'd had a phone back then so I could have saved face or at least played a game to take my mind off my loneliness and despair.

Using Social Media for Good

Another inspirational young person who is forcing us to reconsider our notions of social media is thirteen-year-old Hannah Alper. I met Hannah when I attended an evening with the Amanda Todd Legacy Society's founder Carol Todd, hosted by the Bully Free Community Alliance of York Region. Since the tragic suicide of her daughter, Amanda, Carol has dedicated her life to educating people on the dangers of cyberbullying and sexual predators. She is truly an inspiration and believes in the power of ensuring there is awareness of the potential dangers and that dialogue and conversation about online issues remain at the forefront. Much of the conversation that evening centered around the dark side of social media, and justifiably so. However, I tentatively put forward the notion that social media could be also used for good, and that if we were far more intentional with its use, then it could greatly benefit students who don't know any differently. Then, suddenly, a hand emerged from the audience. It was Hannah, a petite young lady, who very confidently expressed that social media can be used to promote positive action and to stand up against bullying. At the end of the evening, I introduced myself to Hannah and commended her for her courage to speak up in a room full of adults.

All one needs to do is take a look at Hannah's blog and her Twitter feed to realize not only how much she believes kids can promote positive action, but that she leads by example. She rallies for causes around the environment and is a spokesperson for organizations empowering others, including Bystander Revolution and WE. She is an incredible role model and an exemplary example of what being a digital leader means.

This is what Hannah has to say about social media:

> Don't underestimate social media and the Internet. If you just took a minute and looked at the things that students are doing online to change the world, you would be so blown away. It's actually really cool. Social media allows us to share our voice and issues that we care about and let our voice be heard by people in different cities, provinces, and countries. Yes, we can do bad things online, such as cyberbullying, but we can also prevent the bad things, reverse them, and do things on the Internet that will help us change the world for the better. Social media is also a place where we can connect with other like-minded young people and organizations. Because when we connect, we can get and give support and encouragement, and share ideas and information with others who share our passion and drive to create change.

So often, the media draws our attention to the negative aspects of social media—the cyberbullying, distractions, social ineptitude, and so on. And, while, yes, this may be based in truth, it sometimes prevents us from seeing an alternative narrative. Hannah and Olivia are perfect examples of what that alternative narrative can look like.

Another student who has taken her firsthand experience with cyberbullying and used technology and social media to combat negative with positive is Natalie Hampton, a sixteen-year-old from Sherman Oaks, California, who created an app called "Sit With Us." The social networking app came about after Natalie's own bullying experiences included some terrible actions, including her having to eat alone. Once a user signs in to the app, students can become an "Ambassador," then a student who doesn't have anyone to sit with can access the app and find a table that they are welcome to join.[6] *Seventeen* magazine featured Natalie's story in an article titled "I Made Kindness Go Viral,"[7] which I love as a classroom prompt: How can we help kindness go viral? Natalie is demonstrating digital leadership by using technology to make a positive impact on others and solve a real-world problem.

In their 2013 research article, "Integrating Social Media in Education," Hadewijch Vanwynsberghe and Pieter Verdegem, PhD, of Ghent University, contend that if something is presented as negative, then a student will respond accordingly.[8] This not only refers to presenting social media itself as negative, but also cyberbullying and the role of the bystander. On social media, just as in person, it may be tempting to respond to a negative person (the bully), when what we should do is model and teach our students to respond to the target (the bullied) instead. It is so easy to support someone who is the victim of negativity, either privately (via most apps' direct-messaging system) or publicly. And if others follow suit, this show of support will help to combat the negative, and more importantly, prevent the bullied person from feeling hopeless.

Students as First Respondents

Matt Soeth is a co-founder of #ICANHELP, a nonprofit organization empowering students to become "first respondents" who stand up to their peers when they see unacceptable behavior taking place. I met Matt at the DigCit summit in San Francisco, where he shared examples of the work #ICANHELP is doing in schools and spoke about student empowerment through reporting. He also told us about a problem his organization is seeing where students are creating fake webpages to target individuals. Some, he said, are created as a "joke," while others are intended to be more malicious. He said that, in one instance he'd seen a fake page come out for a teacher that had more than a thousand followers and was creating a lot of drama. The page was up for more than two weeks before a student finally turned in the person who'd made it. As a result of their work emphasizing the power they have to combat negativity and solve their own problem, Matt notes that a year later, another fake page went up targeting the same teacher, but this time, it had zero followers and was down in about forty-five minutes. In his presentation, he showed slides of students commenting in support of the teacher, asking the person to delete the page, and one student even saying they would tell the school secretary.

Matt believes, as I do, that conversation around how to empower students is the only way we can change the current trajectory of apathy and negativity. "That's the goal," he said, "for kids to handle it as the problem arises and eliminate the amount of drama taking place on a school campus."

#ICANHELP offers students support through its hashtag and website, which offers direction, gives advice, and keeps students on course. Students can also tag or direct message #ICANHELP directly to report a malicious page. Matt said, every once in a while, they will receive a message, but the page will have already been taken down because students start reporting it and get it removed themselves.

Matt said:

Types of pages include fights, harassment, cyberbullying, voting/rating students, shaming. It runs the gamut. What we have learned is that kids know when something is wrong or inappropriate, but they are cautious to do anything for the same reasons we don't do anything in real life when confronted with harassment: shame, "I want it to go away," bizarre curiosity with "Why are they saying this?", or they don't want to get in trouble and lose access to the services that connect them with their friends. However, when we work with students, it's like a light comes on. It's a mini-community of support where they know it's okay to report negative content and it's okay not to have that negative content in their lives.

The website for #ICANHELP also has a list of twenty activities[9] that provides a great starting point for students to identify how they can spread kindness and positivity on their campus. You could even use some of these ideas within your classroom, or if you have a digital leadership team, at your school.

Screenshot, Block, and Report

If nothing else, students need to know how to take control of the negativity they see online directed toward themselves and their peers. If we're going to create a generation of "first respondents," then it's imperative that we start teaching our students at a very young age how to take a screenshot of something that might make them feel uncomfortable.

And whereas I couldn't stop the negative comments against me when I was young because they always happened under the teacher's radar, it is very different today when bullying happens online, as every app has "block," "mute," and "report" buttons. If you "mute" someone, you don't see what they are posting. If you "block" someone, that person cannot contact you or see your profile. These are powerful tools for students to use so they stop seeing the negative. It's the "report" button that I feel is needed most. We need to emphasize that when we see inappropriate things being shared to demean and target someone, that we must report it. It takes very little effort and no risk (the user never knows the identity of the person reporting), but it is the most crucial way to see online spaces become not just safer, but better. I'm not naive enough to think every student is learning how to be a positive influence, so equipping our students with tools they can use and the confidence to use them is yet another way to empower them.

Create a Different World on Social Media

Engaging in digital leadership is a proactive way to ensure our students know that, in as much as the online world can potentially offer risks, it can also be a pretty positive place that is influencing people's lives for the better. To see this, look no further than our young digital leaders' Twitter feeds, and you'll see messages of encouragement and positive action. For example, Hannah advocates for Bystander Revolution and Curran helped found DigCitKids, which encourages children to #BeTheDigitalChange. Both students and the organizations they promote offer quick, proactive, and positive activities and strategies that can make huge differences in people's lives.

The more positive behaviors like these that we can find and model, both online and offline, the better off everyone will be. This could be as simple as asking our students, "How can we make someone's day special today?" This can then take the form of an in-person or online action, which could even become a daily or weekly routine that not only creates a positive culture within your classroom, but also shows your students how they can have a positive effect on someone else's life.

Scientists Nicholas Christakis, MD, PhD, and James H. Fowler, PhD, make a number of interesting observations about how we can affect other people's behaviors within our social networks (albeit face to face) in their book, *Connected: The Surprising Power of Our Social Networks and How They Shape Our Lives.* They say, typically, "A student with a studious roommate will be more studious, a diner sitting next to heavier eaters will eat more food."[10]

Have you ever held a door open for someone and then seen them open a door for someone else? Or have you ever smiled at a perfect stranger and seen them not only smile back but, in turn, smile at others? When I say I've had mostly positive experiences in every online space I've occupied in the past six years, this may be because I exemplify digital leadership in my own interactions. I hear from alternative perspectives by following a variety of news sources, but the people I follow and with whom I interact are not negative. Now, this isn't to say I don't challenge ideas that I perceive to be wrong—I do—but I ask questions rather than making inflammatory statements.

What if every school followed the example of Jeremiah Anthony and Konner Suave by creating "anonymous" accounts with the sole purpose of complimenting and celebrating students. It would be extremely interesting to see how such actions positively influence school culture and result in different social media behaviors.

What Happens After the Negative?

The summer I was writing this book, I had a not-so-positive experience for the first time. I'm including this story not to frighten you, but because I want you to know that when you engage in these spaces with your students, there is a risk involved—but it's a risk worth taking because having your students encounter a situation like this one on their own would be far worse.

It happened at 2:30 a.m. on Blab, a now-defunct live-streaming platform. (I suspect that the late time had something to do with what happened, but I can't be sure.) I was a guest panelist for Edcamp Global's Good Brings Good: Harnessing the Power of Connections for Social Change webcast. Other featured guests included Spanish teacher Fran Siracusa, Matone de Chiwit founder Karishma Bhagani (whom you'll learn more in chapter 10), Connected Learning Partnerships co-founder Sean Robinson,

French and Spanish teacher Tracy Brady, Flipped Learning Network member Manel Trenchs i Mola, and certified Microsoft Innovator Educator Expert Fabiana Casella, and other live participants. We all stayed up for the time slot to share our enthusiasm for the powerful connections we were making.

It began with negative comments put forward by "Dawn," which we later realized was a fake Twitter account someone had created just to be negative and anonymous. There were extremely anti-male sentiments and harassing statements directed at Sean. I proceeded to say in the chat box how disappointed I was that such an important topic was being sabotaged by negativity. Fran removed and blocked "her," and we continued.

Shortly thereafter, another "user" entered the Blab and spewed hateful anti-male sentiments toward both Sean and Manel, who had joined us from Barcelona. I believe it was the same person under the guise of a different username because the abuse was along the same lines. Fran tried to remove the user once again, but this time, she couldn't, possibly because she was nervous. I tried to post positive comments but I also made the mistake of addressing her directly, asking her to leave and stop being negative. Getting the attention she wanted and realizing how upset I was, the user sent me threatening messages, likely because I had stood up to her. Fran and the panel of guests addressed the issue but continued with the presentation remarkably well. Because Blab did not record the chat part of it, the average viewer wouldn't have had any idea what was happening.

Between 3:00 and 4:00 a.m., we each set out to report and block both users. I e-mailed Blab and contacted Twitter. Fran meticulously deleted all of the negative comments so they couldn't be seen in the replay. The group of amazing educators who had been in on the planning for the Good Brings Good Global Edcamp session got together on our group direct message on Twitter to talk about what happened and support one another with words and images. The conversation then extended to Voxer, where I received additional words of encouragement and support and we talked about what we could do differently next time.

As distressed as I was, this incident has convinced me, more than ever, that we need to help and guide students and navigate these spaces together. This negative experience has probably pushed my thinking more than would have been possible if I'd only continued to know the positive.

Principal Sean Gaillard shared an image similar to the one in Figure 8.1 with me on Instagram, and it immediately resonated. After all, it is what happens in the classroom after a wrong note is hit that makes all the difference. Being thoughtful and proactive will ensure that the next note is good and the experience is one of growth and learning.

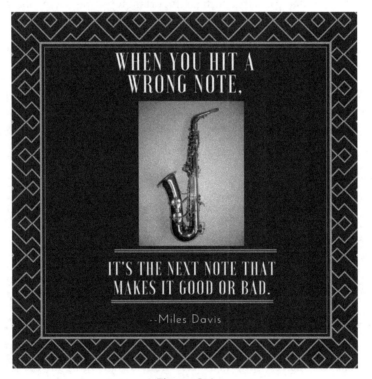

Figure 8.1

Planning for the Worst: An Action Plan

After the incident, I spoke to Marialice Curran about my feeling of helplessness and how I wished I had set up a proactive action plan. She made the analogy of a fire escape plan, which she said her dad always went through "at home and at a hotel."

Of course! We have our students practice fire drills and lockdowns because we know that when we anticipate something could go wrong, then talk about it as a class, we're empowering our students to take that action if it's ever necessary. We need to do the same when it comes to our social media use to prepare them to deal with something negative if it happens. A simple question like, "What could go wrong if we use this tool, and what will we do about it?" may suffice. Knowing your students well is important here, as you want to minimize their anxiety by using a calm, reassuring manner, and ensure that blame and shame are never emphasized.

Jahmeelah Gamble did just this when she encountered a negative situation while using Snapchat with her five-year-old student with autism:

> When we started using Snapchat, I would hold my phone and swipe through the filters so I could control which one she came across (as some of them are definitely not child-appropriate). Well, one day, I didn't pre-check the filters and, as we were swiping through them, there was a ghost one that screamed when you raised your eyebrows. Poor "E" screamed and hid behind my shoulder.
>
> "I do not like!" she yelled, and I quickly exited from the app.
>
> Instead of distracting her with another activity, I used this opportunity to talk about emotions, as it was a concept we'd been working on. "How do you feel? Happy, sad, or scared?"
>
> "Scared!"
>
> "What scared you?"
>
> "The monster."
>
> Surprisingly, when I asked her if she wanted to see it again, she said yes. From that day on, anytime we used a filter, we would talk about what it looked like, what we were pretending to be, and how it made us feel. This definitely helped develop her expressive language and role-playing skills!

When you use social media in the context of digital leadership, 99 percent of the time, nothing will go wrong because you're only putting the positive out there. Nonetheless, here are a few important strategies in the event that something does go wrong.

Stay calm. Think aloud.

If you have children, I'm sure you're familiar with this scenario: Your child falls and you screech, cry out, or gasp. Your child, in turn, sobs and wails uncontrollably. But if you purposefully suck in your breath, carry on, and offer support in a very even-keeled voice, as if nothing really frightening has just happened, the incident is unremarkable: My children tended to miraculously brush themselves off and continue to play.

The same applies in the classroom and to social media. As the teacher, your response is crucial. So if you respond to a negative incident by panicking, you'll only make things worse. The most important thing to do when something unexpected, unfamiliar, or negative happens is to take a breath and think things through logically. Anyone who watched the replay of the Blab would have seen Fran as the model of composure, even though she was panicking while trying to block and eject the offender.

Your coolness will instill calm, while your panic will make everyone anxious and fearful. Model for your students that taking a deep breath and thinking during times of stress is an important defense mechanism.

Use this "Think Aloud" as a guideline:

- "First, I will need to take a deep breath. I always take a deep breath to calm myself down when I'm nervous or something unexpected happens." (Take a deep breath and ask your students to do the same.)

- "I will take a screenshot of the username and the negative things they've said so I can have a record of it."

- "Next, I will look for a way to block this user because this is extremely inappropriate and uncomfortable. Blocking them will make sure we don't see them anymore."

- "I will need to report this to the company and talk to the principal about this. I can send the screenshots I took."

- "I think I need to change my password and make it stronger, just in case this person tries to get into my accounts."

- "I wonder what we could do differently next time so this doesn't happen again."

- "I'm feeling a little less anxious now that I've followed all of these steps. Let's talk about how you're feeling. Who else should we talk to?"

Making this thinking visible to our students gives them a frame of reference if they ever encounter a similar scenario while using social media (which we all know they do at younger and younger ages).

Do not engage.

As much as I always try to give everyone the benefit of the doubt, someone who is being negative on social media is not likely going to turn around and be grateful to me for helping them be more positive. Trying to reason with someone who is belligerent is futile—it definitely didn't work for me. In fact, in retrospect, standing up to the person is what prompted the threatening messages. I should have followed my own advice and concentrated on being positive towards Sean and Manel. It is important to continue as if nothing is happening and not engage in any way. If you do feel compelled to say something, questions are always better than statements. As difficult as it is, we must remind ourselves that hate is not stopped by further negativity and hate. Love and understanding are far more powerful.

> Hate is not stopped by further negativity and hate. Love and understanding are far more powerful.

Drown out the negative.

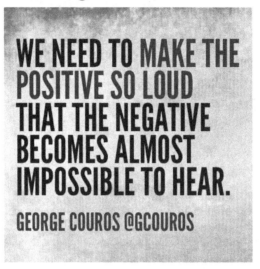

WE NEED TO MAKE THE POSITIVE SO LOUD THAT THE NEGATIVE BECOMES ALMOST IMPOSSIBLE TO HEAR.

GEORGE COUROS @GCOUROS

Figure 8.2

George's words in Figure 8.2 were all I could think of during the Blab. Unfortunately, although I started by being positive, I reverted back to being accusatory. I was also trying to take screenshots, so I was distracted. I keep thinking how different it would have been if the group had talked about this beforehand, how much more effective and powerful we could have all been at drowning out that one negative voice with positivity. To me, creating a game plan for how to handle the negative is the most important thing we can do to empower our students in a similar situation.

Use it as a way to instill empathy.

Calliope Program Director and professor Jennifer Williams, EdD, also reached out to me at the time of the incident, saying, "Breaks my heart to think that there are people out there that are hurting so badly that they intentionally try to cause harm to others. Just another reason to spread #goodbringsgood in our world the best we can."

Whether we're online or interacting with our students, we always need to remember that behind the negative comment could be someone who's hurting or lashing out. Knowing this doesn't make the situation go away, but it does help provide a perspective of empathy, something we absolutely need to teach our students. We need to emphasize that there are actual people behind the screens.

Make the company accountable.

Some companies really have no idea that educators are thinking of innovative ways to incorporate their apps into classrooms, so they aren't creating their products with kids and safety in mind. So if something negative happens, talk to your class about what action they'd like to take. For example, "Should we contact the company with our suggestions for how this tool could be safer?"

Again, the intent is to empower. Students need to know that if something needs to be fixed, they can be part of the solution. It could very well be that the company had never even considered the suggestions that the kids come up with. If we let them, our students can often surprise us, and their learning should lead to action—this is digital leadership.

Forge a positive connection with parents.

If an incident happens in class, it's important to communicate the situation with your students' parents and families and tell them how they can help. It is also important to think about what and how you communicate with them. Parents need to know something happened that made everyone uncomfortable, as well as the steps you took at school and which ones they can take at home. Providing a summary of the students' learning and their agreed-upon plan of action moving forward will reassure parents that you and your school's administration are being thoughtful and diligent about the choices you're making.

It's also extremely important that the tone of your message and word choice reflect the fact that students learn important lessons by engaging in the guided use of social media as a class, which they will then take with them as they navigate tools on their own. If your tone wavers with uncertainty, parents will pick up on that. But if your message truly conveys your belief that engaging in digital leadership is for the best, your students' parents will believe it as well.

Make wise choices.

Having said that, using technology and social media always requires critical thinking as educators. Once you establish your purpose, either you (or your students) should select a tool that would most easily and effectively help you arrive at your learning goal. Understanding how the tool works is a good idea, and the best way to do this is to find a buddy (teacher-librarian, instructional coach, consultant, administrator, peer, or student) with whom to explore. Or begin with your settings on "private" until you feel comfortable with the tool.

Consider this statement from the 2014 *Children's Rights in the Digital World* report:

> *Without the agency needed to participate and exercise rights, children can neither take advantage of the opportunities digital media afford nor develop resiliency when facing risks. They must be encouraged to think critically and develop their own language, views, strategies, associations and interests as users of connected digital media.*[11]

We can't let the possibility of negative experiences keep us from engaging in online spaces with our students. I shudder at the thought of a child or teen going through what I experienced all alone, just because their teacher didn't feel comfortable going there. I'm grateful to the community of friends that reached out to me regarding this incident, and I am ever mindful that it is a community of friends whom I know mostly only virtually—by way of social media.

Student Vignette 🔊))

I'm Olivia, the creator of LivBits, and I use social media to share my thinking with the world. LivBits is my social media identity, and it allows me to share big ideas with an audience outside of just my classroom. Each week, I make short videos that share my thinking from books, life, or the world. Social media is not just a bunch of posts and pictures for me—I use it to share messages about what's important to me and to seek feedback from other people.

Sometimes, my videos are hard to make because the topics are difficult to talk about or understand. This is why LivBits is so important: Making my videos forces me to think about what I've learned from something hard, and it encourages me to help others by teaching them from my experiences.

My mom, Cynthia Merrill, was doing research with teachers, and together they created the "Selfie Center." I would see her watching videos from kids all over the country, and I was so interested in making my own. She encouraged me to make my own selfie videos to make sense of things, and that's when I started LivBits. I didn't begin with any videos on bullying. Instead, I focused on making videos from messages I got out of books I loved. It wasn't until I got the confidence from my first videos that I had the courage to talk about topics that were tougher, like bullying.

Actually, one of the hardest videos I've ever made is about my bullying story. I had to do it in parts, like a series, because I don't like my LivBits to be too long and I had so much to say. I want people who watch the bullying series to see a hopeful message. The important thing to know is that LivBits started because of the bullying that I experienced.

Just recently, on Twitter, one of my followers commented saying my videos really showed my commitment to social justice. I didn't even know what that was. But the comment made me want to know more. When I learned about this big idea, I was proud that a follower was encouraging me and learning from my posts, and it made me want to do even more LivBits.

I learn something new about myself, my followers, and the world almost every time I post a video. My mom says LivBits is helping me live out my dream, and I think she's right. Without LivBits, I wouldn't be a piece of the thinker I am becoming. With LivBits, I can be the kind of learner I was meant to be. LivBits connects me to the world in such a meaningful way. I can use my kid voice to make ripples of change and show the world that #kidsCANteachus!

Keep reading! Keep thinking! And keep watching LivBits for more ideas about books, life, and the world!

—Olivia Van Ledtje, fourth grade

In Summary ⬇

- We need to provide students with strategies to combat negativity online and help them become "first respondents."

- When we focus on building empathy, we stand a better chance of supporting students who are victims of bullying.

- Using social media and having an action plan for how to handle possible negative scenarios will help students know what to do if they ever face some of these dilemmas on their own.

Discussion Questions ✖

1. What are some ideas you have for empowering students to become "first respondents"?
2. What are the proactive steps you could establish so that you and your students feel comfortable?
3. How could we highlight (or at least balance) positive conversations about social media to counteract the negative?

Chapter 8 Notes

1. You can watch Olivia's story at vimeo.com/178834653.

2. Lauricella, A. R., Cingel, D. P., Beaudoin-Ryan, L., Robb, M. B., Saphir, M., and Wartella, E. A. *The Common Sense Census: Plugged-In Parents of Tweens and Teens*. San Francisco, CA: Common Sense Media, 2016, commonsensemedia.org/sites/default/files/uploads/research/common-sense-parent-census_whitepaper_new-for-web.pdf.

3. Ibid, 8.

4. "Making Progress: Rethinking State and School District Policies Concerning Mobile Technologies and Social Media," *Consortium for School Networking*, nsba.org/sites/default/files/reports/MakingProgress.pdf.

5. "Cyberbullying Triples According to New McAfee 2014 Teens and Screen Study," *McAfee*, June 3, 2014, mcafee.com/us/about/news/2014/q2/20140603-01.aspx.

6. Itkowitz, Colby, "This Once-Bullied Teen Has a Simple Solution So No One Has to Eat in the Cafeteria Alone Ever Again," *The Washington Post*, September 14, 2016, washingtonpost.com/news/inspired-life/wp/2016/09/14/this-once-bullied-teen-has-a-simple-solution-so-no-one-has-to-eat-alone-in-the-cafeteria-ever-again/?utm_term=.6c8ba345e41d.

7. Abidor, Jen, "I Made Kindness Go Viral," Magzter, magzter.com/article/Fashion/Seventeen-US/I-Made-Kindness-Go-Viral.

8. Vanwynsberghe, Hadewijch, and Pieter Verdegem, "Integrating social media in education," *CLCWeb: Comparative Literature and Culture* 15.3 2013. Academic OneFile.

9. "20 Activities to Do at School," *#ICanHelp*, icanhelpdeletenegativity.org/wp-content/uploads/2016/02/ICANHELP-20-Activities-To-Do-At-School.pdf.

10. Christakis, Nicholas A., and James H. Fowler, *Connected: The Surprising Power of Our Social Networks and How They Shape Our Lives*, New York: Little, Brown, 2009. 21.

11. Third, Amanda, et al., "Children's Rights in the Digital Age: A Download from Children Around the World," Young and Well Cooperative Research Centre, Melbourne, 2014, unicef.org/publications/files/ Childrens_Rights_in_the_Digital_Age_A_Download_from_Children_ Around_the_World_FINAL.pdf.

MEET THE STUDENTS
OLIVIA VAN LEDTJE
TheLivBits.com

 @thelivbits

Olivia (aka LivBit) is a nine-year-old reader, thinker, and kids' voice believer. She is knowledgeable about all things shark-related and hopes to one day be an ichthyologist. She is an ambassador for the Gills Club, an organization promoting girls in science through inquiry-based experiences meant to grow enthusiasm and activism for sharks, and is a passionate advocate for books and using social media to promote digital citizenship, voice, and audience. Olivia's work on social media has been recognized around the world, and she has been honored to present with accomplished authors at national conferences, including the National Council of Teachers of English, Association for Supervision and Curriculum Development, International Society for Technology in Education, and International Literacy Association. Handpicked by best-selling author and educational technology leader Alan November, she was the youngest featured child keynote speaker at his international Building Learning Communities conference. Olivia is an accomplished ballerina who also plays the violin, loves eating pizza, and has an incredible heart for all things Disney.

Use Olivia's Story to Inspire Your Students

 What is Olivia reading? Explore her latest @thelivbits video to find a book that your class might enjoy.

 Olivia wants to be an ichthyologist and is an ambassador for the Gills Club. What is an ichthyologist? What does your class know about sharks?

Build Bridges:
Crucial Conversations

My school would say they do give me digital access because we have access to Chromebooks, but this is not digital access.... We only use technology to prepare for testing. I wish my school would take the time to see the difference in how I learn at home and apply it in my classroom and school, so my classmates can have the same opportunities I do.

—*Curran Dee, fourth grade*

What young Curran expresses is an unfortunate reality in too many districts. By the time he was in first grade, he'd started blogging at home as a way to complete the traditional assignments he was receiving in school. Unfortunately, he didn't have access to his blog at school, which is what inspired him to advocate for connected learning opportunities in classrooms around the world.

We, as educators, need to do the same: start courageous conversations with stakeholders, identify barriers, and provide viable solutions and tangible ideas for how to include social media in our schools so we can connect students to experts and to one another. For schools like the ones Curran is describing, there needs to be a shift to using technology and social media in the service of digital leadership; for schools that are already doing this work, there are always ways to continue to learn and grow. The following are a few conversations I believe to be crucial to help us move forward.

District-Level Conversations and Professional Learning for Teachers

Social media should be a part of professional learning opportunities.

In order to truly empower our students to be digital leaders, districts need to support teachers' efforts to integrate social media in context. They need to not only provide them with open access, but also professional learning so they can gain a better understanding of what this type of teaching should look like. These are the tough conversations we need to inspire, whatever our role and whatever the table at which we sit.

Under the leadership of its chief information officer, Mark Carbone, Ontario's Waterloo Region District School Board has taken this stance for years. Their model was chosen as a case study for the United States' Department of Education's Office of Educational Technology.[1] The district offers its teachers access to a variety of social media platforms, which they then leverage to encourage student learning, community building, and modeling effective and appropriate use. Mark says he's witnessed the positive effects this open system has had on Waterloo's teachers and students, and he truly believes that building capacity with teachers and students is important because "connected learners need connected leaders."

> "Connected learners need connected leaders."
>
> —*Mark Carbone*

The Futures Forum project, which Carbone spearheaded, equipped teachers with the tools they needed to leverage social media in their teaching and learning in order that they would explore these tools with students. Important to note is the fact that the classes in the Futures Forum project were not 1:1 classrooms. An example of one of their tasks was to use Twitter to break down silos by creating "TED Talk Fridays." Classes from different schools would watch a TED Talk and then tweet their responses to it. They also explored Facebook as a collaboration tool.

As a result of the Futures Form project, Waterloo District staff has come to understand that:

- Students learn at all hours of the day.

- When given the opportunity to collaborate online, students provide one another with feedback and help and use social media positively.

- Even when students are absent, they can still contribute.

Thus, they solidly believe in the idea of 4-ANY learning: learning that can happen anytime, anywhere, with anyone, about anything. The district's open thinking hasn't always been easy, but Carbone believes it's a necessary road that Waterloo needs to travel with its teachers so, together, they can support their students' futures.

It is essential for IT and curriculum departments to work together.

When you look at some of the most progressive, innovative school districts, you'll notice that the IT and curriculum departments work together. Typically, IT personnel primarily concern themselves with locking everything down to ensure the school's digital security, so they don't really have a sense of what the end user (the student) requires. However, since digital leadership depends upon students leveraging technology and social media, it's essential for the curriculum and IT departments to form a true partnership and have a mutual understanding of what is in the students' best interest.

George Couros offers some good advice about questions to ask the IT department in *The Innovator's Mindset*:

> *A collaborative partnership, which places student learning at the center, allows the perspective of the other, the balance of risk and reward as well as tough conversations about making blanket policies for a few exceptions may limit the overall best interests of student.*[2]

When I worked with our district-level 21C planning team, it consisted of brilliant people from both IT and curriculum. When we offered professional learning opportunities to teachers, we always invited IT personnel to attend as well. This had never been done before, and it was really interesting to watch and listen to the "aha" moments as IT understood what teachers were doing with the technology they were supporting. We even joked about how the IT folks were talking "education," while we curriculum folks started talking like "tech nerds."

Learning together is the best way to move forward.

As I continue to discern thoughtfully when to use technology and how to help teachers engage in technology-enabled learning, I've noticed something disconcerting: An "us" versus "them" attitude pervades our hallways, boardrooms, and staff rooms. That is, those who are open to technology are pitted against those who supposedly aren't. It's "connected educators" against those who have no idea what "connected educator" even means.

In my experience, teachers who don't embrace using technology and social media are usually just afraid to do so. They never anticipated teaching would involve anything other than sharing their knowledge of and passion for a subject with kids. This whole move to student-centered learning, coupled with technology tools with which many are completely unfamiliar, is scary. Rather than isolating these teachers, we need to support them.

It's important for us to acknowledge and talk about the fact that adding technology to a lesson won't make the lesson more engaging—a poorly designed lesson is still a poorly designed lesson, regardless of whether or not it incorporates technology or social media. When technology is used as a direct substitution, no one receives any added value. Teachers who may seem anti-technology may in fact be the best at planning lessons and may know their curriculum well enough to be able to apply it flexibly to meet their students' needs exceptionally well.

I know this to be true because, to be honest, I'm not young. I mean, I'm not old, but I didn't grow up with technology, nor did it come to me intuitively when I started using it. In fact, things like coding still don't come easily to me and I have to try really hard to understand them.

I have another confession: I've never taken a computer course. I have never even taken a "computers in education" course, although I did offer teachers professional learning opportunities about a variety of technology-enabled learning topics for years. So when people often ask me, "How do you know about so many tools?" In truth, I learned almost everything I know about tech tools from Twitter. When people come to me for help, I go to YouTube. When I see someone sharing something, I think about

> Adding technology to a lesson won't make the lesson more engaging—a poorly designed lesson is still a poorly designed lesson.

how I could apply it in the service of learning and use it to promote digital leadership. I've also learned from colleagues trying interesting things in their classrooms, and every time I have an opportunity to learn from kids (including my daughters), I take it.

So why am I telling you all of this? Because if I can learn technology, so can you. If you're reading this and you are part of the generation that knows these tools well, chances are, you never had the opportunity to use them for learning when you were in school either. We need to dispel the myth that teachers who don't intuitively know technology can't use it effectively, just as we must accept the fact that simply because a young teacher knows social media's codes and conventions, it doesn't mean they know their curriculum or how to effectively teach with technology for deep learning. We need to encourage mentorship and community building. So called "early adopters" should be encouraged to collaborate with "non-techy" teachers and share about teaching, technology-enabled learning, and good pedagogy. We're all striving to do the best we can for our students, and pitting one group against another doesn't help anyone. But this should not be limited to a school: Superintendents, administrators, and directors of education must all engage in a learning stance so we can make the best decisions and move forward.

School-Level Conversations with Teachers

Time is needed for deep learning.

You will recall Julie Balen, who encourages blogging? Well, I immediately thought of her English class when I was looking to facilitate a connection between a school in my district and her First Nations school for a Ministry of Education project I was working on. The two teachers agreed to teach the same series of lessons centering on the theme, "Tolerance in Canada," with an explicit focus on discrimination against First Nations people. Although the original lesson was the same, each teacher adapted and modified its content to meet their students' and courses' needs.

The classes video conferenced via Google Hangouts once, and they spent most of their discussion talking about the instances of discrimination the First Nations students had experienced. They didn't have the opportunity to talk about indigenous ways of knowing as lived experiences, other than as textbook definitions, nor was there an opportunity for them to share their culture in ways that would help build reconciliation. Several weeks later, I suggested the classes continue the conversation on Google Docs using the following prompts:

"What I know now and how it makes me feel."	"What will I do, now that I know what I know?"	Comments

In this Google Doc, the students wrote and moderated the comments themselves while the teachers and I observed the interactions. So while one student from our district talked about awareness in general terms, a student from the northern district challenged this by saying there is awareness out there and that true reconciliation requires more than this. To me, this was far more powerful than the Google Hangout itself.

When we asked my district's students to reflect on their learning experience, many of them commented on how powerful it had been for them. One student said, "It's one thing to read about something or watch a video, but knowing and talking to an actual person made this local issue real to me and makes me want to do something about it." And after the Google Hangout, another student told me, "Thank you for opening up a whole new world to us!" It had never occurred to her that video conferencing could easily connect her class with another one.

However, the students also expressed their disappointment that the classroom connection was too brief. Many students in my district said they truly wanted more—they wanted to continue the conversations, to extend the inquiry, and even to connect personally with the First Nations students via their own social media outlets.

What if we'd taken the time to continue the learning and abandoned some of the other things we felt we "needed" to cover? In truth, many teachers are so conditioned to deliver content that it's difficult for them to think flexibly about how to connect with other classes and why it is worth their time. What is often viewed as an add-on to their already full days can actually be an authentic way to explore important issues—and make their curriculum come alive for students.

While, yes, district leaders and administrators need to support teachers as they embark on these journeys, teachers also need to look at the time they actually have in the classroom, the ways connections build upon curriculum expectations, and how that time can be best used for learning experiences that go beyond content and textbooks. The students from the First Nations school could have taught our students so much about ways of knowing and the extent to which tolerance in Canada and reconciliation are being misrepresented in the media.

Don't get me wrong: Even the brief connection the students shared helped them understand one another a little better and recognize that no matter a person's race or color, they have more in common than not. They also came to understand that technology can provide learning experiences textbooks or videos can't. And I truly believe the students when they said that the next time they hear a derogatory comment made toward someone of First Nations origin, they won't sit by and let it happen because they realize how false the stereotypes are.

Connecting in thoughtful and meaningful ways requires some investment of time. When we let constraints (perceived or real) get in the way, though, we prevent our students from truly capitalizing on what technology and social media offer us. Administrators and district leaders need to honor this and support teachers' efforts to do this, and teachers need to give themselves permission to let other content go by the wayside if it means giving their students a deeper, more meaningful learning experience.

Smart phones are tools for learning.

Figure 9.1

As an educator, I acknowledge cell phones are learning tools and invite students to use them responsibly. In fact, I have Figure 9.1 posted in my library's learning commons. Think of how significant this is compared to the "no cell phone" signs students typically see. But if we don't see cell phones as learning tools, how can we possibly get our students to see them as such?

Every idea and example in this book can be accomplished with the powerful tool students possess in their pockets. Where equity is a concern, students can buddy up, or use a class device. We have to stop fighting cell phone use and instead show students how they can use smartphones for digital leadership. The more we incorporate their use in our classes (for accessibility purposes, to organize themselves using calendars, participate in class discussion, as ways to access formative assessments, to create collages, videos, podcasts, etc.), the more they will recognize their potential and the less we will have to "police" their use in our classroom. The guidelines around responsible use (Chapter Seven) will help you in the event that students are using their phones inappropriately.

Differentiation and student choice are best.

Sometimes in our zeal to incorporate interesting tools or social media into our classes, we revert to a one-size-fits-all approach. For example, "Everyone needs to upload an image to Twitter (*or* Instagram *or* Snapchat) that reflects the theme in the story we're exploring together." This means those students who don't have accounts on that specific platform would need to create one to complete the assignment, which I don't know if I necessarily agree with. My experiences in special education have taught me that sometimes, students understand what the curriculum says they are supposed to know, but the way we ask them to demonstrate their learning limits their ability to show us what they know. When we ask our students to make their own choices, we're empowering them to engage more and practice critical thinking, a skill the World Economic Forum says students very much need today.[3]

Teachers often ask me, "How can I assess a product if everyone is using a different tool?" As teachers, we need to know the *why* and the *what* (our curriculum's expectations), but *how* kids get there can be flexible. Assessment should not be based on anything other than how students have met the standard (at least not in Ontario or using the United States' standards-based grading). Have we ever traditionally evaluated students' ability to glue pictures onto a Bristol board or assessed their coloring abilities for a graph or poster? Font choices and focal points are excellent opportunities for feedback from us or their peers, but unless the standard or curriculum expectation we're evaluating involves creating a media product, they shouldn't count toward a mark. When I see "demonstrates an understanding of" as a curriculum expectation, the tool a student uses to demonstrate their understanding doesn't matter—the critical understanding of the concept or big idea itself does. As a result, we need to engage in conversations about how accepting a variety of iterations on a variety of platforms could be an excellent way to tap into our students' strengths and interests.

Admittedly, how to do this may seem confusing. I suggest you begin with a modified RAFT template (Role, Audience, Format, Topic).[4]

Think about "Audience" for a moment. Technology and social media have changed it so the audience no longer needs to be static, which is why I ask students to consider how they might share with their audience. The other modification I have made is to add a "T" for "Tool." The technology students use to share with their audience is integral to them demonstrating their understanding of a big idea. And, third, I've added a reflection section, as we can't ignore the research surrounding metacognition—it's necessary for students to reflect on their choices at the end so they can determine whether or not they made the best ones.

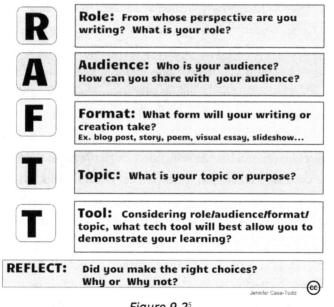

Figure 9.2[5]

You'll notice that the onus and responsibility for each of these stages falls on the student—and that's no accident. When we support students through modeling and guidance, we allow them to make decisions on their own and then to reflect on their decisions. This applies to their use of social media as it would to any other learning resource.

This modified RAFTT template may just help you to feel more comfortable offering your students more choices so they can ensure their best learning shines through.

We need to acknowledge and tap into the strengths of students within our classrooms.

One of my school's history teachers, Sheri Burke, asked me if I could help her create a website for a special project to honor war veterans. Of course, I said "yes," but before we could meet, she canceled. While she waited for time in my schedule to open up, a student in her class, Victoria Shi, volunteered to fill my spot and help her peers put the resource together. You see, Victoria had already created a beautiful website to showcase her passion for photography. I was not in any way disappointed that a student would be assuming the role I was going to play—in fact, I was ecstatic.

Every classroom has at least one Victoria, a student with a special talent or interests outside of school who, when given the opportunity, is willing to help their class and teacher with technology or social media. I've seen some teachers identify their classroom's experts ("techsperts") and then direct questions about specific tools or platforms to those students, and I've even seen others give these students badges. This not only frees us up, but empowers our learners by helping them to see their strengths and talents (which may not be shining through academically) as valuable.

As ancient Greek philosopher Heraclitus said, "The only thing that is constant is change." If our students can help be a part of the learning process when it comes to technology and social media tools, not only will they feel empowered, but we will feel less overwhelmed about embracing change.

We need to use our informed professional judgment to make decisions involving the use of social media in the classroom.

There are literally millions of apps and tools available, so rather than concentrating our professional learning on specific ones, we should focus on a framework of questions to determine which tool is best to achieve a specific purpose. Our 21C planning team came up with a "reverse stop-light" (Green, Yellow, and Red) tool framework for our district. I would say that this is a good approach for teachers to take when they are considering a tool for the classroom. Red means stop. Do not use a tool which sells personal information or which has explicit content for which there is no reporting or blocking mechanism.

Yellow means proceed with caution. Just like you would never show a video or film without previewing it first, start slowly and tentatively at first, and preview what you are going to share before going forward. And when you have done your due diligence and see the positive impact that is possible, and your students are thoroughly engaged, then green means go!

For our professional learning sessions, we created complementary case studies[6] to encourage our district's teachers and administrators to engage in crucial conversations surrounding important topics concerning safety and security and think critically about what they can do to support their colleagues, parents, and students. Mostly, though, we gave everyone *time* to have these tough conversations. Our intent was to inspire experimentation and innovation, while ensuring they would be thoughtful and proactive in how they use social media in their classrooms and schools.

So, what can and should we do? Just like we focus on what kids shouldn't do, we need guidance as to what we can do on social media.

While this book offers many ideas, here is a good list to share with colleagues:

- Share thought-provoking articles and resources that extend the learning taking place in the classroom.

- Connect students with organizations and people who could extend their learning in the classroom through social media and then teach students that they can do this, too.

- Share positive and motivational quotes, images, and sentiments.

- Encourage students to strive to be their best.

- Provide feedback and support (privately or publicly, depending on the situation).

- Celebrate students' successes and the success of others with whom you are connected.

- Engage in positive dialogue with your own students and others. Invite others to solve a math problem together, share what it looks like outside your window, invite others to share their favorite quote about peace, learning, gratitude, etc.).

Fortunately, we're already doing many of the things on this list in our classrooms. But by deliberately using social media when it makes sense to do so to achieve this, we're modeling good practices and extending relationships, while meeting many kids where they are.

When do I use my real name vs. a username?

When I was co-teaching in a tenth-grade careers class, we were exploring the idea of setting up a YouTube page like a learning portfolio. One of the questions I asked was, "Would you use your real name or a username?" A couple of students very adamantly said a "username" or "stage name," citing several YouTubers they knew who did this. Another student challenged that by saying, "If we are going to create a professional online presence for career purposes, then we need to use our real names." That student cited other YouTubers who use their real names. The resulting debate was exactly what I wanted to instigate. A name in and of itself is not considered private, but when information accompanies it, such as a student number, location, etc., this is considered to reveal private information. You can use your real name, but skip the part where you need to include private information, such as age or address. In order to keep young children safe, a class account using first names only (where parents have signed off on this) is appropriate, but as students get older, we need to engage them (and parents) in critical thinking about this issue in order to make the best decision for them. Aidan Aird and Hannah Alper use their real names, whereas Olivia Ledtje, Michelle Wrona, and others prefer "usernames." None of these students have had anything bad happen to them thus far as a result of their decision. This is likely because they are only sharing positive things connected to what they are learning, so there is minimal risk. Kayla Delzer, in her keynote at the Digital Citizenship (DigCit) Summit, made an interesting point: We teach our kids to memorize their name and address at a young age so that if they are ever lost, they can find their way home; yet online, their name and address is personally identifiable information that should never be shared. This is definitely an increasingly gray area and, thus, a crucial conversation that I believe needs to be had at a young age.[7] For older students, this would be such a powerful provocation for inquiry and debate because there is actually so much written for and against the use of real names vs. pseudonyms.

Crucial Conversations with Parents

Parents need to understand the role social media can play in their child's education.

Although they rely on districts and schools to make decisions for their children's own good, our students' parents are our partners in education, and they need to feel as such. With that in mind, at every opportunity, every board meeting, and every parent-teacher event, we need to help these parents understand that access to social media and technology is necessary. Why? Because education is different today than it was when we were all in school because the world is different. No parent can argue with that.

If parents complain, saying social media shouldn't have a place in schools, it's our job to help them understand that to empower their children to become active participants in their society, we need to leverage the tools that can help them do that. Learning and living together in this global community requires that our values, attitudes, and behaviors be the same face to face and online, and without opportunities to practice both, we cannot educate the whole child.

But I wonder if we perceive that parents would be against the use of technology and social media, or if we know this to be fact. I say this because in a 2016 study by Common Sense Media, 94 percent of parents agreed that technology positively supports their children with schoolwork and education. In particular, the study found:

> *Parents also felt that technology can support their children by supporting them in learning new skills (88 percent) and preparing them for 21st-century jobs (89 percent). Parents agreed that technology increases their children's exposure to other cultures (77 percent), allows for the expression of their children's personal opinions and beliefs (75 percent), supports their children's creativity (79 percent), and allows their children to find and interact with others who have similar interests (69 percent).*[8]

You'll find some parents are very adamant about not wanting their child's face anywhere on the Internet, and that is well within their rights. In some cases, it could even be a matter of the child's safety for reasons to which we aren't privy. Whatever the case, we need to be respectful of parents' wishes and assure them that their child can still practice digital leadership without having their face online. Many teachers work around this concern by taking pictures of heads and hands when sharing work,

We need to help these parents understand that access to social media and technology is necessary.

while others give students who haven't signed parental waivers the camera so they can still very much be a part of the activity without compromising their dignity. We can't force parents to see our point of view, but when we create positive, meaningful learning experiences for the children they leave in our care, parents will see the merit in these opportunities and, unless there is an extenuating circumstance regarding safety, begin to appreciate them.

New Castle, Delaware, Principal Douglas Timm has implemented an innovative approach: His school's parents only sign a waiver if they do not want their kids featured on social media. Think about that for a second. Instead of wading through 1,400 waivers (the current enrollment at my high school), he might have to deal with twenty, maybe thirty, if that.

More importantly, Douglas is telling his school's parents:

- Social media is a reality in our world today.

- Social media is a powerful tool for communication and learning.

- We are committed to presenting students in a positive light so they can begin building a positive digital presence.

- We are transparent and connected.

- We wish to celebrate your child.

I recently asked Douglas how this policy was going and if he had any negative experiences. His response? He hadn't had a single complaint about it in the three years since it was implemented.

Parents can and should take part in the learning.

Another benefit of digital leadership I've found is that not only does it help provide a counter-fear narrative but it also invites parents to learn more about using technology in the school setting. A 2014 research study titled *Children's Rights in a Digital Age*[9] notes how there is an increasingly widening gap between children's use of technology and their parents' use of technology. (But if you're a parent, I don't think you need a study to tell you this.)

Digital leadership changes after-school, parent-child conversations from "What did you do at school today?" to "So, I noticed you mixed paint colors in art today. Tell me more about that." When parents know what their child is learning, they can ask about a specific activity and become more involved in their child's school life; they no longer need to wait for parent-teacher interviews or for work to be sent home at the end of the unit. As a result, students have the opportunity to teach their parents a little bit more about the tools they use, something you already saw with Stephanie and Kayla's classes. This has been incredibly rewarding for the teachers, the parents, and the students highlighted in this book.

At All Levels: Students need to be true partners in the journey.

Students can lead change. I believe this with every fiber of my being because I see it time and time again. But as I look around our schools, never before have I seen such a disconnect between how our students are using technology and how uncomfortable so many adults are with it. I've never liked the terms "digital immigrant" and "digital native," but I readily acknowledge that our kids are fearless when it comes to learning how to use new technology tools, and they can often figure them out pretty quickly. The only real way forward is to move together, to engage our students as partners, and to trust them to do some of the work (as you saw in the RAFTT template and as referenced by teachers who have "techsperts" in the class).

At the District Level

In the final two years in my district-level position, I was honored to spearhead a student EdTechTeam initiative, together with the 21C District planning team. We had been working with teams of educators (administrators, teacher-librarians, special education, core resource teachers, and classroom teachers) from each of our district's elementary schools to integrate technology-enabled learning for three years. We believed having student teams at each school as partners would empower student leadership and help us move forward more efficiently.

We ran it two years consecutively with some modifications:

- Each school was invited to bring one team of two students from fifth through seventh grade.

- The event was held on a school day so students could learn alongside an administrator or teacher from their school. (Side note: Busing everyone in from all of our elementary schools was a bit of a headache, but it was worth the cost and effort.)

- Student leaders from the high schools took on prominent roles in the day, including facilitating some of the sessions.

- We brought in a high-energy, positive presentation and made digital citizenship the focus of each lesson. For example, for one of the Tech Quests, we asked participants to contribute to a collaborative Google Slides presentation discussing what they'd learned about being a positive presence online using only free-use images or photos they'd taken with permission.

- Throughout the day, we placed less of an emphasis on the tools themselves and a greater emphasis on critical thinking, creativity, empathy, research skills, and collaboration.

- Student teams were invited to share to the large group how they were helping their peers and teachers integrate technology in the classroom and how they were demonstrating leadership at their school.

- We demonstrated the virtual environment where they could stay in touch with us, complete challenges, and provide feedback on an ongoing basis, beyond the one-day event.

Sixty-seven of our eighty-eight schools participated, and we challenged each participant to become a positive influence in their online and face-to-face school communities. Not only was this a successful initiative, but it demonstrated and modeled the extent to which our district values its students' voices and leadership.

At the School Level: EdTech Day

As an offshoot of our district-wide event, one of the schools organized its own local EdTech event providing its students the opportunity to teach their peers about the tech tools they used for learning. A group of teachers (Fab Grossi, Laura Bagnara, Melissa Alonzi, and Jason Pacheco) and three students from the district-wide student EdTech team organized the event's logistics, and Denise Dupuis, an administrator at the school, not only supported the event, but ensured any and all obstacles were overcome. In fact, when it became clear the event would have more than fifty presenters and over a hundred kids attending, Denise extended it from one day to two.

Here's how it worked:

- All third through eighth graders were invited to submit a proposal for what they would teach.

- From these proposals, the organizers selected a variety of tools and projects and created a schedule.

- Each class in the school was invited to come into the library for approximately twenty minutes and go through the stations based on interest.

- In the Discovery Center, students could play with augmented reality (AR) or practice a tool they'd just learned how to use.

- In each case, the students didn't just show their peers, but got them to do something with them.

The excitement was palpable. Teachers accompanying their classes felt safe to peruse and learn as well, and the students were anxious to share their learning with them. That day, the school's educators certainly realized students are much more capable than we often give them credit. It was the perfect risk-free environment. The organizers say the school is excited to make this event an annual one and that they're planning to model this same format for a Parent EdTech Day.

At the School Level: Social Media Team

I was fortunate to have the opportunity to plan and facilitate a pilot project for one of our district's high schools with my colleague and friend, Terri Romeo, the school's teacher-librarian. Unlike a class or school social media takeover, whereby a group of students would be responsible to tweet or post to the social media accounts for one day (I've seen this option offered as a prize incentive), the principal allowed a student-run media team to assume responsibility for the social media accounts representing the school for the entire school year. Our task was to ensure the students had the skills needed to fulfill that responsibility.

We wanted to allow the students to create their own vision and goals for the project, using the school's and district's as guidance. To balance autonomy and responsibility, the team assumed full ownership for how they would achieve those goals. We knew that if the team was going to be responsible for the school's branding, it needed to have a good sense of how to leverage social media to meet its goals as a team in collaboration with the school's goals.

We began by asking the students to imagine how a parent, director, student, administrator, or community member might perceive a negative comment tweeted at the district's Twitter account, then brainstorm the best strategy for responding. We then showed them a positive tweet and asked the same question. This activity taught students that when you send a positive message, it will be well received, no matter your role.

Next, we gave the students a series of school tweets and asked them to determine which account relayed their message most succinctly, creatively, and effectively. This activity resulted in some excellent conversations. We also talked about how Instagram posts are the same/different and what considerations they needed to take into account with that tool. Then, we gave them a "what if," and had students compose a response to a negative comment on their tweet or post; we discussed if this was the right approach and how we could have made the response better.

We spent the rest of the time learning about design elements with the school's graphic design teacher, Dave Chen; discovering what the job of our district's communications manager, Sonia Gallo, entails; and observing the types of social media policies and practices a local post-secondary institution follows.

After much interactive learning, the team created a vision and mission and brainstormed how they could connect with their school's clubs and organizations. Terri and I sat back and listened to the students contribute ideas and suggestions, and we watched as a couple of students assumed leadership roles and moderated the conversation extremely well. We had done enough sharing, modeling, and talking—it was their turn to lead, and they didn't disappoint.

This is a model that could easily be implemented at the high school or middle school level to empower students. The fact is, when students are given responsibility like this, they rise up to the challenge, and often exceed our expectations.

Student Vignette 🔊

As a fourth-grade student, I have opinions on how I wish I could learn at school, but no one there has asked me to share the story I am going to tell you today.

I don't have digital access at school; I only have it at home. At home, I have opportunities to learn from the world using a variety of tools. At school, I'm bored. I fill in a lot of worksheets. My school life and home life are so very different. I wish I could learn the same way at school as I learn at home.

When I was in the first grade, I was assigned a rainforest animal project. The project had a list of rainforest animals to choose from, but I knew I didn't want to learn about the animals on that list—I wanted to learn about other animals in the rainforest. So I went home and blogged about my project. I received comments around the world with suggestions for animals I never knew existed. I probably got over twenty different rainforest animals to research, and I researched every one of them and I looked up every location. I then put the animals into categories and came up with my top ten, my top five, and finally my top choice: the binturong.

I would never have known about the binturong had it not been for having digital access at home. I had so much fun learning about rainforest animals—more than I would have if I'd just completed the packet the way the rest of my classmates did. In fact, this project made me realize just how different my learning at school is compared to at home. It's not fair. My entire first-grade class could have had the same experience if we'd all had digital access at school.

My school would say they do give me digital access because we have access to Chromebooks, but this is not digital access.

We don't blog. My teacher doesn't tweet what we're learning throughout the day. We don't get to participate in Mystery Skypes or the Global Read Aloud. We only use technology to prepare for testing. I wish my school would take the time to see the difference in how I learn at home and apply it in my classroom and school, so my classmates can have the same opportunities I do.

—Curran Dee, fourth grade

In Summary ⬇

- Conversations with every stakeholder need to be ongoing to give the appropriate push and support needed to make a change regarding how we use social media in our schools.

- It is not enough for the teacher to use social media; students need to be empowered to do so as well.

- There are ways to empower students at every level when it comes to using social media; it doesn't matter how slowly you start or how small a step you take, so long as it is a step forward.

Discussion Questions ✖

1. What crucial conversations would you add to this chapter?
2. Who might help support you or their peers in your classroom or school? What role can students play?
3. What courageous conversations could you have (or have you had) with parents about the changing world?

Chapter 9 Notes

1. "Albemarle County Public Schools," Department of Education, tech.ed.gov/case-studies.

2. Couros, George, *The Innovator's Mindset*, San Diego, CA: Dave Burgess Consulting, Inc., 2015.

3. Soffell, Jenny, "What Are the 21st-Century Skills Every Student Needs?" *World Economic Forum*, March 10, 2016, weforum.org/agenda/2016/03/21st-century-skills-future-jobs-students.

4. "RAFT Writing Template," *Read Write Think*, readwritethink.org/classroom-resources/printouts/raft-writing-template-30633.html.

5. Copy of template (Google Docs). An image for student use can be found at SocialLEADia.org.

6. Available at SocialLEADia.org.

7. Lauricella, A. R., Cingel, D. P., Beaudoin-Ryan, L., Robb, M. B., Saphir, M., and Wartella, E. A. *The Common Sense Census: Plugged-in Parents of Tweens and Teens*. San Francisco, CA: Common Sense Media, 2016: 10, commonsensemedia.org/sites/default/files/uploads/research/common-sense-parent-census_whitepaper_new-for-web.pdf.

8. Third, Amanda, et al., "Children's Rights in the Digital Age: A Download from Children around the World," Young and Well Cooperative Research Centre, Melbourne, 2014: 29, unicef.org/publications/files/Childrens_Rights_in_the_Digital_Age_A_Download_from_Children_Around_the_World_FINAL.pdf.

9. Fleischacker, Blake, "My Life Online," mylifeonlineworkshop.com.

MEET THE STUDENTS
CURRAN DEE
Around the World with Curran

@CurranCentral, @DigCitKids

Curran is the founder and "Chief Kid Officer" of DigCitKids, Digital Citizenship for kids by kids, as well as a TEDxYouth speaker, an international speaker for Digital Citizenship Summit UK, and a student ambassador for Buncee. He has written for veteran educator Angela Maiers' blog and moderates chats about digital citizenship and student voice on Twitter. He has also been invited to speak as a guest lecturer to graduate courses about embedding social media tools into curriculums, and his TEDxYouth Talk is part of teachers' professional development. His wish is for all students everywhere to have digital access, and he sees DigCitKids as a way to amplify students' voice in classrooms. He plays hockey, baseball, lacrosse, and golf, and in his free time, and he enjoys building in Minecraft and learning how to code.

Use Curran's Story to Inspire Your Students

 Check out the DigCitKids website. What kinds of challenges can you find there and which ones might be worthwhile for your students to help solve?

 Curran loves Minecraft and often contributes to the #MinecraftEDU chat on Twitter. What opportunities are there to use Minecraft in your classroom?

Instill Empathy, Justice, and Character

I use my blog and social media to share my story, reach out to sponsors, and network with other kids who are doing amazing things. Even though I can't drive places, social media helps me reach out everywhere so I can share how important hunger relief is to me and also find out who might need help so I can give them Brae's Brown Bags.

—*Braeden Mannering, seventh grade*

Braeden Mannering is a remarkable young man, and, like Joshua Williams, he feels so strongly about ending hunger that he spends all of his free time working to change the world. He leverages his blog, Facebook, and Twitter to share the awesome things he is doing and to compel others to take action against hunger.

Breaden was moved to take action after a summer 2013 trip to Washington, DC, when, at just nine years old, he attended First Lady Michelle Obama's Kids' "State Dinner" at the White House as part of her Healthy Lunchtime Challenge. During the event, she and then-President Obama challenged the students to think about what they could do to help the less fortunate in their own communities. Once he returned home, Braeden took up the torch against this social injustice that leaves so many unsure of where or when they'll get their next meal and founded Brae's Brown Bags (3B), a nonprofit organization on a mission to provide healthy snacks to people in need.[1]

In May 2015, Braeden, with the support of his mom, developed an eight-session conference agenda and cohosted the first of what would become a biannual "hunger conference" in Delaware. Nearly two hundred students, ages six to eighteen, from across the state learned about food insecurity, the importance of eating and living healthy, and how to connect with local officials and legislators. As a result of 3B's work, Braeden has been given a platform to speak about food insecurity, homelessness, and poverty at schools, conferences, and legislative sessions. And in September 2015, he launched "3B Ripples" to help schools and youth organizations start their own 3B student chapters in their communities.

Digital leadership is anchored in the idea that we can improve other people's lives, well-being, and circumstances, even if momentarily. And for many of these digital leaders, including Braeden, digital leadership means becoming passionate about a cause. Because when students explore their passion for helping, when they stop thinking about themselves and start thinking of others, they feel better about themselves. In addition, they have an opportunity to test their voices and power to see how they can create a better world.

I often wonder if empathy and altruism, a genuine regard for others before self, is a result of nature rather than nurture. Are Breaden, Joshua, Khloe, Hannah, Aidan, and some of the other digital leaders mentioned here the exception because they just happen to have good genes?

Abigail Marsh, PhD, an associate professor of psychology and researcher at Georgetown University, has dedicated her life to uncovering the motivations of people who engage in extremely altruistic behavior. In her 2016 TED Talk, "Why Some People Are More Altruistic Than Others," she says she's discovered evidence that altruistic people's brains are made up a little differently than the average brain. She also, however, cites Harvard experimental psychologist Steven Pinker, PhD, and others who have studied cases ranging from animal abuse to domestic violence and capital punishment, and says these researchers have noticed people are becoming less and less accepting of suffering, which has led to declines of all kinds of cruelty and violence. She believes the human capacity for humility is much more prevalent today.

She says:

> Even as the world is becoming a better and more humane place, which it is, there's a very common perception that it's becoming worse and more cruel, which it's not. And I don't know exactly why this is, but I think it may be that we now just know so much more about the suffering of strangers in distant places, and so we now care a lot more about the suffering of those distant strangers. But what's clear is the kinds of changes we're seeing show that the roots of altruism and compassion are just as much a part of human nature as cruelty and violence, maybe even more so. And while some people do seem to be inherently more sensitive to the suffering of distant others, I really believe that the ability to remove oneself from the center of the circle and expand the circle of compassion outward to include even strangers is within reach for almost everyone.[2]

As teachers, we work hard day in and day out to promote empathy in our classroom communities, and from the moment children enter our schools, we attempt to teach them right from wrong, how to share, how to be a good friend, how to embrace everyone from every culture, and how to collaborate. We emphasize the fact that, as Atticus Finch in *To Kill a Mockingbird* so eloquently put it, "You never really understand a person until you consider things from his point of view ... until you climb into his skin and walk around in it."

However, we often talk about these skills in a vacuum, as if social media couldn't be a powerful medium for character-building. Social media affords us an incredible opportunity to expand our students' circle of care and to help them to see how they, in turn, have the capacity to contribute to the common good.

Robert, Stephanie, Leigh, Julie, and all the teachers we've met so far know, love, and care for their students, as most teachers do. These teachers are culturally responsive, as most teachers are. They know students don't just develop powerful, empathetic voices online—students' voices must first be valued in class and then offered opportunities to demonstrate collaboration and caring, and technology and social media can help.

So does this mean building a culture of caring in our classrooms directly corresponds to altruistic behavior online? Not necessarily, but it certainly can help if we explicitly model and teach this kind of culture.

Creating opportunities for empathy and community-building in our classroom takes many forms. For example, Justin Schleider, a physical education teacher and technology integration specialist in New Jersey, shared his "3H" strategy with me. He says he asks kids if they would like a high five, handshake, or hug when he sees them demonstrate positive behavior toward him or a classmate. He's noticed that this has really affected the culture of goodwill in his class and sense of celebrating others.

And California high school teacher Victor Small uses an "Awesome Referral" chart to record his students' good behavior. He comments on things like helping and respecting others, courage, and resilience, as well as academic excellence, and says he, too, has noticed positive effects in his classroom. He also speaks very highly of restorative justice[3] practices, or bringing students together in peer-mediated small groups (often in a circle) to talk, ask questions, and air grievances. He says this has positively changed his classroom's—and school's—overall culture and has reduced the number of school suspensions as well. Listening to Victor speak about restorative justice reminds me of a First Nations talking circle I took part in, where every participant had a chance to talk while holding a sacred object (in our case, a feather). Victor says engaging in this practice shows students that their voices matter in the classroom and that any conflict can be resolved with open dialogue and attentive listening.

My daughters' elementary school had a "Gotcha" program, whereby teachers "catch" students demonstrating good behaviors and recognize them with a small certificate. Another example comes from #ICANHELP's Matt, who shared his idea for a "Compliment Wall," prominently displayed in a school common area to which students can contribute.

These are all awesome ideas. I love listening to Justin talk about the fact that his students have started high-fiving one another with greater frequency and that students are recognizing their own capacity to support their peers. The "Gotcha" certificates (provided that students are not just engaging in positive behaviors for the reward itself) and Awesome Referral chart could also be made available for students to use rather than just being teaching tools.

Now let's take it further, and make the Compliment Wall, "Gotchas," high fives, and Awesome Referrals optional for sharing on the class Twitter, Instagram, Facebook, or Snapchat account. Students could ask permission to share, and students could accept or decline. Everyone who follows the account could then celebrate along with the students or take the idea and use it in their classroom.

In fact, my younger daughter shared a powerful story with me on International Women's Day (March 2017). A student decorated her elementary school's bathroom mirror with empowering and positive quotes. There were Post-it notes for girls to add their own quotes. For the entire day, girls added notes, took selfies in the mirror, and spread positive messages on Snapchat, Instagram, and Twitter.

Positivity spreads, and building community and empowering students in the classroom can be either an essential first step or a complement to building a community online. Digital leadership does not preclude our face-to-face practices both inside and outside of the classroom—it extends them.

Changing Someone's World

Kerri-Lee Langer, an Ontario kindergarten teacher, shared with me that her young students had been having difficulty with treating their friends nicely, so she engaged her young class in a collaborative project to help them understand how their actions, both good and bad, can make a difference in a person's life.

She introduced the project by showing a video created by FreeHugsCampaign.org, featuring a man holding a "Free Hugs" sign in the middle of a street, and then asked her class if the man in the video made a difference in anyone's life. She wanted her students to see how they could potentially change the world through just one kind act. They were interested in the effect their kindness could have if they were to use social media to spread the word within their school community.

Her young students brainstormed short phrases they thought would most effectively send their message and then designed posters, ultimately creating a video.[4] They then shared their video on Kerri-Lee's Facebook page, along with the question, "How did the message make you feel?" The class watched as the responses came in. She says they really liked reading what the viewers said, as well as the fact that people from all over the world were watching their video.

Kerri-Lee says that even at their young age, her students understood the project's message of sharing understanding and compassion and this project made a difference in how the students treated their peers.

You could also go a much simpler route and do an art project similar to the one my own family did. My husband learned about Crafting for a Cure, a nonprofit organization that aims to help children in the hospital

"Wherever there is a human being, there is an opportunity for a kindness."

—*Lucius Annaeus Seneca*

have a more positive experience (CraftingForACure.ca). They were in need of cards written in French, so my daughters set out to create a bunch. I shared a picture of our cards on Instagram and Twitter and received positive responses from many classroom teachers who, in turn, did this with their own students.

Think about all the art projects we ask our students to make over the course of a year. Students take great pride in creating pictures, paintings, and collages, and they love it when people proudly display their work. But what if we asked ourselves and our students, "Who else in our community would also enjoy our artwork?" Could your local hospital benefit from cards like the ones my daughters made for Crafting for a Cure? What about a senior center?

When you share your gesture with others via social media, allowing your class's Tweeter, Instagrammer of the Day, or school social media team to talk about what you're doing, this idea spreads to several others in your own community—and maybe even across the globe. However, it is important to remind students that "good deeds should be done with intention, not for attention."

Building Empathy through Authentic Connections

We've already talked about meaningful connections in Chapter Four, but connecting classrooms is another powerful way to teach students about other cultures in an authentic, relevant way by helping them see other races and cultures as human beings. This can only be a good thing.

Remember the connection one of our local schools made with Julie Balen's First Nations class? Our students said they really had no idea that First Nations students were "sixteen-year-olds just like us," and a student from the First Nations school admitted to thinking everyone outside of her reserve was white, so she was surprised to see the class had so many "colors." And Shervette Miller-Payton, EdD, an administrator in Atlanta, Georgia, told me about how her class enjoyed connecting with one in Brazil because her students had so many assumptions about what kids outside the States would be like. She says they were shocked to learn the Brazilian students knew about the American culture. Connecting students from different backgrounds allows everyone to get to know and understand one another.

The following are a few more examples of how we could inspire our students to think within and beyond their own communities to embrace digital leadership.

Virtual Reality and Real Experiences

My school's community is home to student refugees from around the world, including Syria. In fact, we've had hundreds of families from the war-torn country settle in the Greater Toronto area. So understanding the plight of refugees is a local issue which is of concern.

A friend of mine, Stephanie Wilson, MA, a psychological associate in my district, introduced me to the VR film, *Clouds Over Sidra*, which follows the life of young Sidra as she takes you through her refugee camp housing 130,000 Syrian refugees. When you wear VR goggles, you actually feel like you're in the camp with her. So, for our district's Mental Health Symposium's maker fair, we provided students with cardboard, scissors, and various other items to create a product that would make Sidra's life better. Some made a prototype of a soccer field, while others created a backpack filled with items that could help Sidra at school. Both elementary and high school students engaged in the design process by brainstorming, prototyping, and making products. More important than the creations, though, this activity prompted our students to ask questions, generate ideas, and really empathize with Sidra and her situation.

So when Ricki Machala, a tenth-grade teacher at my high school, was looking for an opportunity to have her kids explore the concept in her religious studies class, I suggested *Clouds Over Sidra*. I have to tell you, hearing Ricky's students say, "This is sick," (an idiomatic expression for "awesome") made us both really excited. After the students watched the film using the Within app, we gave them a Q-chart so they could formulate questions they had about Sidra and her life. We found students were more interested in researching the topic as a result of the film's immersive experience because they could see, hear, and feel what a refugee camp looks like—something they would never likely experience in person in their lifetime—and seek answers to their own questions.

A wonderful next step could be for students to connect with someone in their community or from the Digital Human Library and ask questions, which is what Fabiana Casella's students did when they connected with The Writing Project's executive director Rusul Alrubail for a cross-curricular project about "world refugees."

Although we have yet to meet face to face, I have much respect for Rusul and all that she shared, and her story of fleeing Iraq during the Gulf War has touched both my and Fabiana's hearts. In fact, Fabiana told me that when she read Rusul's article on PBS titled, "I Am a Refugee. I Am Haunted by Images of Child Refugees,"[5] she wondered how she could incorporate Rusul's words and message into her classroom.

Now, you may recall that Fabiana teaches English as a foreign language and has limited technology access, but that doesn't stop her from thinking creatively about how she can connect her students with other people and classes. So she asked Rusul to record herself reading the article, which Rusul then shared via Facebook Messenger[6] and Fabiana downloaded it onto a CD.

Fabiana told me her students couldn't fathom how Fabiana knew Rusul. And she says she was impressed with how Rusul's "shocking story of her life" caught their attention and moved and saddened them. She was also struck by the questions her students had generated that day while listening to Rusul's recording, including "How did you feel when they said you were in war?" "Did you know what that meant?" and "What were the most difficult things to leave behind that you couldn't have back?" Rusul replied to the students with her answers. Beyond the fact that this connection gave Fabiana's students the opportunity to practice their English, they also had an incredible chance to hear from someone who had experienced the topic firsthand.

I always think about these stories when I hear people balk at the idea of connecting globally because "we should be worried about local issues." When we ask students to meet and learn from people beyond their normal experiences and communities, it can lead to them taking powerful actions and empathizing with people within their own communities.

For example, in this case, you could ask, "How many of the students in our own school or community have fled their homes for safety?" and "What can we do to make their lives better?" Fabiana's classes were moved to act in ways that students simply hearing about these issues in the news or reading about them in a textbook could never be moved; the fact that she was able to connect with Rusul, and share the experience so I could learn about it, is an incredible benefit of teaching today.

When we embrace digital leadership, we recognize that technology is another possible vehicle for powerful learning and understand how it can help us promote awareness and be a positive influence on others' lives. This transcends tools. You see, while virtual reality and social media, in addition to in-person relationships, can connect our students to people and other perspectives right now, there is no way of knowing what that will look like in the future.

My friend Fran was literally able to go into a "Portal" and talk with children from Iraq and have what she describes as "a completely surreal experience." Created by Shared Studios, each portal is "a gold shipping container equipped with immersive audio and video technology inside.

"I am only one; but still I am one. I cannot do everything; but still I can do something; and because I cannot do everything, I will not refuse to do the something that I can do."

—*Edward Everett Hale*

When you enter one, you come face to face with someone in a distant Portal and can converse live, full-body, and making eye contact, as if in the same room."[7] In short, technology is ever changing, and opportunities to connect our students to others in the world and empower them to connect to others will only increase if we open ourselves up to the possibilities.

Promoting an Important Cause

If at the heart of student digital leadership is that our students learn and share their learning, empower others who have no voice, address societal inequality, promote important causes, and become a positive influence in the lives of others, then we must encourage our students to share their voices when opportunities arise. Remember, leadership has no age limit. This generation of kids cares so much about other people, and many of them want to help.

Teachers who embrace a digital leadership mindset don't just limit their discussions to novels, stories, textbooks, or learning demonstrations within the classroom or school fairs. Instead, they leverage technology and social media to extend their reach and empower their students. And student digital leaders recognize that, through social media, their voices can be heard in an adult world. They promote their message through social media and organizations and are strong advocates for the voices of the voiceless.

Sensitive Issues

I've always tackled current events, even if they're sensitive issues, in my classroom head on, through the lens of gathering multiple perspectives. I'm sure you do this as well. I'm never surprised, though, when teachers are reluctant to do so because not only is the possibility for parental backlash real, but the students themselves may be sensitive and unable to handle the grim realities the media portrays. But this doesn't mean we should shy away from local issues that are at the forefront of our own communities or that our kids are asking questions about in the classroom (it's the right thing to do, after all); rather, we just need to do so through a lens of making a positive impact.

After the death of a close friend of my family's, my younger daughter became extremely anxious that something would happen to me and my husband. We spent a few months shielding her from the news, worried about the implications, which, in retrospect, we now realize may not have been the best thing to do. If her teacher had tackled a current event around death, I don't know how she would have responded, but I do know her teacher would have to have needed to include a message of hope as well as action.

I found the perfect example of balancing tragedy with hope and action in my Twitter feed in the form of a "Happy Jar." Sarah McLeod and her students were creating one for a First Nations school that had been touched by suicides, so she tweeted a link to a Google Form explaining the Happy Jar project:

> "If you give kids the inspiration and tools to change the world, it will change their own lives in the process."
>
> —*Craig Kielburger*

Students at [our] school were saddened to hear of the youth suicide crisis in indigenous communities in northern Saskatchewan [Canada]. They decided to take action and have been in contact with the First Nations school. Later this week, one of our students will be traveling to Loon Lake, Saskatchewan, to bring breakfast program items to the school. Along with the breakfast items, we would like to send warm thoughts and positive words in the form of a "Happy Jar." This is a jar filled with motivational sayings, positive words, and kind quotes meant to uplift people in a time of need.

We would like your help in creating this jar! Please fill this form in and send us your favorite quote, words of wisdom, or positive thoughts. We will include your words in the Happy Jar for the staff, students, and parents of the First Nations school. You can send us as many entries as you like—the more the merrier![8]

I sent the link to primary and secondary school teachers because, to me, this project is the perfect example of truly teaching empathy. A teacher interrupts their classroom's regular routine to have students think about others and, as a result, has a conversation about an issue that may be sensitive, but is extremely important to the students' overall understanding of an issue concerning social justice. And, because of the positive action, the discussion doesn't adversely affect the students (or my daughter, if she'd been in that class).

However, there is some controversy around addressing "hot-button" issues in the classroom because critics suggest students may feed off their teacher's bias. Kids are impressionable, they argue, and sometimes the message delivered and the message received may be very different.

In a 2012 *Maclean's* article titled, "Why Are Schools Brainwashing Our Children?" one father says, "Schools have no business covering hot-button topics. That's the parents' call."[9] Though I don't necessarily agree with him, the article does make the case that we need to be mindful of these tensions. This same father says his first grade's class had a PETA poster hanging up and asks what would happen if a child in the class were from an agricultural family? Would the family then have to explain why it kills cows? Knowing our students and our school culture and checking our own biases at the door can definitely help us make the best decisions.

One classroom strategy I always use (and that can be modified for any age group) is, "I don't agree with this."[10] Sometimes, I ask students to read an article or other text with the sole purpose of highlighting ideas or statements they don't agree with. This is really a lot harder than it sounds for one simple reason: We all have an inherent cognitive bias, or, that is, we all instinctively gravitate toward ideas with which we agree. Bringing attention to this tendency can bring greater neutrality and perspective to controversial issues, and it is a great way to get students thinking critically about their assumptions. This strategy will certainly serve students well when they respond to others or promote causes that are important to them online.

Activism and Slacktivism

The term "slacktivism," which comprises the words "slacker" and "activism," is increasingly being used to describe the disconnect between awareness and action through social media.[11] In fact, slacktivism is defined as "a willingness to perform a relatively costless, token display of support for a social cause, with an accompanying lack of willingness to devote significant effort to enact meaningful change."[12] What's more, critics say slacktivists are more about "'feel-good back patting' through watching or 'liking' commentary of social issues without any action," time, effort, mobilization, or demonstrable effect in solving a social issue.[13]

But isn't awareness a goal of education? If a young person learns about deforestation and then researches organizations doing something about it and either "likes" their page or demonstrates a positive response, isn't that exactly what we want? Could these actions eventually lead to the child taking a more active stance as they get older?

The Ice Bucket Challenge comes to mind as an example of how

awareness can go viral on the Internet. If you don't remember, the 2014 movement required that you record yourself throwing ice water over your head and challenging others to do so as well. You were then supposed to donate to the ALS Association to help them fight amyotrophic laterals sclerosis (Lou Gehrig's disease). At the time, the craze was criticized because many people were just interested in the fun of the challenge, which, by definition, is slacktivism. Yet there is no way millions of people would've known about Lou Gehrig's, nor would the ALS Association have raised $115 million in such a short time period, had the Ice Bucket Challenge not become so popular through social media. Just recently, the donated money led to a breakthrough in ALS research. So, in this case, even despite its negative connotation and criticism, slacktivism turned out to be very positive.

Ultimately, we do want to show students the difference between activism and slacktivism. In one tweet (Figure 10.1), for example, Curran emphasizes the difference between the two when he asks people to support students in Houston with their attempt to make their city bag-free.

Figure 10.1

In a 2010 article, UC Berkeley lecturer Howard Rheingold wrote, "Today's media enable people to inform, persuade, and influence the beliefs of others and, most important, help them to organize action on all scales. In doing so, people move from the literacy of participation to the literacy of collaboration."[14] He further speaks to how, in general, doing things together gives us more power than going at something alone.

Now, I'm not suggesting the role of the classroom should be political, but, unlike any other time in history, it is possible to mobilize people to take action. With that in mind, we need to consider the extent to which our students can create (or already are creating) a positive change, and how that positivity can spread via social media.

Another important point to note is that when we bring social media into the classroom, we can also help students learn a healthy skepticism of the tools themselves. In fact, technology and new media specialist Stephen Downes criticizes Snapchat for its filters that play upon stereotypes in an article titled, "Hey, Snapchat, Enough Is Enough." Stephen offers us a great opportunity to discuss portrayals of diversity in media and social media, which could be an excellent starting point for action. Students could contact a company and share their opinions, teaching them that they don't have to passively stand by when they recognize injustice. And, going back to Stephen's commentary on Snapchat, to keep the conversation positive, you could suggest alternative filters that would be more inclusive.

Students could learn about their favorite tools' privacy and security policies by reading the terms of service, which are often filled with difficult-to-understand legalese, and petition the companies to ensure a reader-friendly version of their app's or tool's policies is available. Or we could have students unpack some of social media's "unwritten rules" that sometimes create undue pressure. For example, take the fact that when a student "likes" something, they're agreeing with it but that "like" can affect someone's dignity. These are all important causes affecting students' well-being as well as that of others. And when students investigate some of the ways through which social media can, in fact, take away their rights, freedoms, or happiness, they are more likely to do something to rectify the problem than if we were to simply lecture about it at the front of the classroom.

Rallying Around a Cause

We can easily build awareness of issues that would not be considered sensitive topics but that are issues that would be of concern to communities. For example, while writing this book, I learned about the contaminated water crisis in Flint, Michigan, which made just a brief appearance on the Canadian news. Interested, I learned more about the issue, thanks to the help of my EduMatch friends living in Michigan. They spoke about the events as they unfolded, and eight-year-old Amariyanna (Mari) Copeny, aka "Little Miss Flint," on Twitter (@LittleMissFlint), gained national attention when she wrote a letter to then-President Barack Obama, urging him to address this major issue facing her city.[15] He responded by going to Flint and meeting Mari. A year and a half later, Little Miss Flint is still tweeting (her account is co-moderated by her mom) and bringing attention to the fact that Flint's tap water is causing rashes and still hasn't been fixed.

So often, while in pursuit of the next most interesting story, the media forgets about issues that are still very much a problem for those living them. However, Mari continues to promote this important cause that's directly affecting her and her community, and for that reason, she exemplifies digital leadership. Mari is using her voice to stand up for others. She has since become the youngest ambassador for the Women's March on Washington DC (January 2017) and has her sights on running for President of the United States in 2044!

Another issue is water scarcity. In this case, Fran Siracusa introduced me to Karishma Bhagani, a student studying at New York University, who, as part of a high school project while at home in Mombasa, Kenya, invented a water-filtration system that can purify water for a family of five for eighteen months. When we met, Karishma was in the process of getting her organization, Matone de Chiwit, recognized as a not-for-profit and was very excited to share her project with our students.

Karishma says in Kenya, 17 million people are without access to clean drinking water. So, to solve this problem, she designed a cost-effective water purifier using traditional elements, including sand, gravel, charcoal, cotton cloth, and moringa oleifera, a local plant known for its natural anti-oxidants and drought-resistant properties. Each unit costs a mere $25 to build. And through Matone de Chiwit, she hopes to provide these purification units to more villages in Kenya, and eventually the world.

Creating a water-filtration kit is actually one of the Ontario Curriculum's suggested activities for seventh graders, and the issue of water scarcity comes up in both science and geography, so it only made sense to bring Karishma in via a video conference so she could speak directly to the students about Matone de Chiwit, her invention, and Mombasa.

Fran shared the project with me and I, in turn, helped her to share it via our connections on Twitter, and we learned Sean Robinson, a teacher from British Columbia, was also connecting his ninth-grade science class with Karishma. The students' resulting projects ranged from social justice fairs and sharing videos about water scarcity to, in the case of Sean's high school class, even helping Karishma create a website for Matone de Chiwit as well as videos for the organization's fundraising campaign. Sean said he couldn't believe how motivated his students were to work on this initiative well beyond school hours, and even the school year. This is because they didn't just learn about something, take a test, and move on—they understood the issue and deeply cared about it. They used the vast reach of technology and social media to make a difference and promote a cause that had become important to them. This only goes to show that when students from different cultures and grades come together to explore an issue, the result is a better understanding of not just the issue itself, but of our common humanity.

Talking to Strangers

I've come to reevaluate the necessity of talking to strangers, which, as a mom, has felt so very counterintuitive. Think about the extent to which we trust "strangers" online today: We order an Uber ride and get into a car with a relative stranger. We use Airbnb and choose to live in a stranger's house instead of an established hotel. We trust strangers' advice when we go to sites such as Yelp and TripAdvisor for opinions about where we should eat, what we should do, and where we should stay. Of course, we need to help kids understand the real dangers of strangers, but talking to them is, in fact, necessary to understanding other people's perspectives. I would add that our classroom interactions with strangers are important because they provide a reference and model for what constitutes talking to strangers in appropriate and safe ways.

In her 2016 TED Talk, "Why You Should Talk to Strangers," author, consultant, and speaker Kio Stark says, "When you talk to strangers, you're making beautiful interruptions into the expected narrative of your daily life and theirs."[16]

The area where this has resonated the most is in my connections with my EduMatch Voxer group, which comprises teachers, technology integration specialists, media specialists, and teacher-librarians from all over the world. We use Voxer, a web tool and app, to communicate via text, links, videos, and photos, but most significantly, our voices. Whereas I spend most of my face-to-face time in very homogeneous groups (Catholic, white), this group literally has educators of every religion and every color. I have never in my life been so privileged to hear other people's perspectives on such a variety of topics. We talk about ethnicity, politics, education, and the environment, and we compare weather and cultural practices and holidays. My friend Justin Schleider said it best: "We can't but help look at the world differently as a result of being in this group."

For example, when we were having heated discussions about whether or not we should assign homework, Trix Barnachea from the Philippines told us about her culture's practices around homework, which helped me understand Filipino parents and students so much better.

The more I learn and grow in my learning as a result of the various people I've come to know virtually, the more I believe that teaching empathy in our classrooms must begin within our classroom walls but necessitates having our students connect with people outside their communities and personal realm of understanding. Fortunately, technology and social media afford us those opportunities.

Practicing Perspective Taking

Before students take any action or stance or engage in a response on social media, they must first look at the issue at hand from multiple perspectives in the classroom and in face-to-face discussions and scenarios. This not only helps them develop a "brain frame" around perspective taking, but it also ensures meaningful dialogue happens in the classroom and helps students avoid extremist responses. Karen Wolffe, PhD, a career counselor for people with disabilities, calls this "social thinking," or the ability to assume the role of others and understand actions affecting them. She also stresses that kids' ability to do this changes with age.[17]

I recommend doing a perspective taking activity as a cooperative jigsaw. Give each student one of four perspectives to role-play. After writing from the perspective they have been assigned, students share and discuss the various perspectives in a group of four, before sharing as a class.[18]

If you are looking to do this virtually, Flipgrid, an asynchronous video-recording tool, is great for allowing students to fully express an opinion about a topic. It allows for users to respond and reply to videos and thus there is a wonderful co-construction of knowledge that is possible with the tool. For any topic, a teacher can set up a Flipgrid and a thinking prompt, then students can submit a video reply and thus invite outside perspectives into the conversation. The reflection prompt, "I used to think, and now I think" is an important step, as it exemplifies the learning and growth.

Perspective Taking

I am _____and I think...

I am _____and this is my perspective:	I am _____and this my perspective:
Respond as the perpetrator's son, daughter, sister, brother, or mother:	Respond as the perpetrator's victim's daughter, sister, brother, or mother:
I am _____and this my perspective:	I am _____and this my perspective:
Respond as a community leader:	Respond as a bystander or community member:
Reflect: I used to think, and now I think…	

Figure 10.2

Julie Millan, a fourth-grade teacher, uses the concept of "thinking hats" in her classroom, and she says it has made perspective taking easier for her young students to understand. You could use this framework in any subject and in any K–12 grade. So many negative and mean responses and online shaming stem from a lack of understanding—or forgetting the fact that behind the screen is a real person who is important to and loved by someone. We need to remind students that our responses need to be tempered with empathy and respect, and we need to model this behavior.

Keeping It Positive

Even when students consider other people's perspectives, they may, depending on just how passionately they care about an issue, want to take action—which is exactly what you want them to do. Just explicitly remind them they once they've put something on social media, they may lose control over the sharing of it, and in some cases, can't take it back.

As a class, create a possible action plan using the think-aloud method we've already discussed. Always be on the lookout (and teach your students to be critical as well) for any comment with a negative undertone. A good think-aloud for this might be: "*Hmm*, I like the way this part sounds, but I'm wondering how it could be more positive."

Sometimes, teacher questions are useful as well:

- "If I were _____, how might I interpret that message?"
- "Will anyone's feelings be hurt by this?"
- "Will this help us to reach our goal of awareness, understanding, etc.?"
- "What suggestions do you have?"

Since I began using social media, my mantra has been something George Couros articulated: "Always err on the side of positive."[19] When I engage in discourse with others with whom I may not agree, I think of what my friend, Lori Lisi, a retired coordinator of secondary programs for the York Catholic District School Board, says: "Always presume positive intentions." If we ensure that what we post online is positive, we can rarely go wrong, and when discussing issues around social justice and activism, I think we should always err on the side of a few more things as well (Figure 10.3).

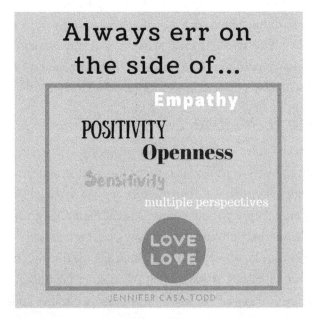

Figure 10.3

I also think that there is much power to build community and positivity by using a hashtag. When we collectively share to a hashtag such as #CelebrateMonday, created by Sean Gaillard, or #ShareTheAwesome," created and promoted by Nicholas Provenzano, for example, we're helping ensure that positivity overpowers the negativity online. We can contribute to #MotivationalTuesday, #MightyMonday, #TerrificTuesday, #WonderfulWednesday, "#ThrillingThursday, and "#FabulousFriday," which allow us to #TrendThePositive (all real hashtags). You could also create your own hashtag for a cause, which is exactly what *Creating Classroom Magic* author Shauna Pollock did when she created #Unicorns4Molly and I did for #MonicaSitnikRocks. This is a great opportunity for students to see a hashtag as an extension of positive face-to-face interaction. A school hashtag builds community and unity as well, especially if there are several social media accounts in a school.

Critical Literacy

With social media, we can also easily apply critical literacy, or as EduGAINS' 2016 *Adolescent Literacy Guide* (ALG) says, "critically analyzing and evaluating the meaning of text as it relates to issues of equity, power, and social justice to inform a critical stance, response, and/or action."[20] I think this is so important to our understanding of the world in an age where anyone can produce and share information.

These are some of the essential questions that come from the ALG which I ask students (and help teachers with) when they are applying critical literacy to text:

- "Who created or produced the text?"
- "What does the author want me to know, think, or feel?"
- "What assumptions does the author make about my beliefs?"
- "What voices, points of view, and perspectives are missing?"
- "How significant is their omission?"

- "What information does the author leave out?"
- "Who will likely benefit from this text?"
- "Is the text fair?"

And here are some critical literacy questions to prompt action in response to a text, which I believe is integral to digital leadership:

- "How can I find out about other perspectives on this topic?"
- "How have my attitudes changed? Why?"
- "What action might I need to take to address a concern?"
- "How can I use literacy to support those who are treated unfairly?"
- "How can I use literacy to make a difference in the world?"

Learning in context with your students and being equipped to ask questions—even if you don't know the answers—is very powerful. Sometimes discovering knowledge together is far more effective than providing answers.

Resources to Help You Start

Kid President

I have been a fan of Kid President's for many years because his character relays extremely well the fundamental belief that kids have voices worth listening to and also because he promotes actionable projects in which to get involved.

Brad Montague says of the project:

> *The idea for Kid President came a few years ago. My wife and I had just launched a summer camp for kids who want to change the world. We were blown away by the ideas and the hearts of the students there. These students wanted nothing more than to leave the world better than they found it. After seeing their creativity and compassion I couldn't help but think—wouldn't it be cool if we*

listened to kids more? When we got home we filmed the very first Kid President video.[21]

Kid President convinces us that kids and adults alike can be a positive influence on others and change the world when we work together. His videos are always inspiring, and they embody what digital leadership means. Check out his YouTube channel and Twitter page for class-appropriate ideas and inspiration for how you can discuss social justice issues and campaigns in your classroom. As Kid President says, "Love changes everything. So fill the world with it."

There is no greater testament to the power of Kid President than the story of Mia Clayton, aka Mia's Boxes of Love, Inc.[22] Nicholas Clayton, her father, and I know each other through Twitter and Voxer, and he shared with me the story of his five-year-old daughter, Mia, who wanted to help others and gathered a box full of her toys and told her parents she wanted to give it to homeless children. She came up with the name and logo design herself. Together they contacted a local shelter to find out what was needed. Mia wasted no time! Her first outreach was a backpack drive whereby they were able to donate over a dozen backpacks, along with supplies and $500, with the help of schools and social media. At the same time she was a YouTube fanatic and watched/loved Kid President, where she heard about his #Socktober campaign which invited people to collect and donate socks for the homeless. Mia decided to work on a #Socktober campaign at her school. She reached out on Facebook to her family and also received donations of socks from relatives. Her parents followed Mia's lead. It is a rare occasion when you hear about children leading their parents, but their inspiration for helping to create the project, which is now a nonprofit, was through the drive that Mia had to help others. Her parents wanted Mia to know it is important to "do awesome" with the gifts of fortunate circumstances and having their basic needs met. They were touched by the reactions of others via social media who wanted to help Mia and mentored her using platforms like Facebook, Twitter (where Kid President and Brad follow her and they share ideas), Instagram, etc. The

> "Love changes everything. So fill the world with it."
>
> —*Kid President*

result? A family charity that has worked to provide 18,000 plus pairs of socks over the past three years to local people in need. Kid President is sure to inspire a response from your class, and you can be that adult mentor who helps to guide them.

Kids Are Heroes

Kids Are Heroes believes kids are heroes and each one has the power to change the world. Whether it's drilling water wells in Africa, feeding and clothing orphans in India, or standing up for their causes, Kids Are Heroes "strives to empower children from all cultures to become social change agents."[23]

The organization's heroes are recycling and cleaning up their neighborhoods, helping their local animal shelters, and making life better for their neighbors. And, best of all, these kids are just like the students in your class! Reading the stories of young changemakers will inspire your own students to take action, or at least provide them with an understanding that age is not an obstacle for leading. Or maybe it will lead you to discover that your students are already doing wonderful things to lead change in the world.

The Harry Potter Alliance

The Harry Potter Alliance uses the Harry Potter book series to create challenges that will inspire fans to change in the world. Paul DeGeorge and Andrew Slack founded the nonprofit organization in 2005 to draw attention to human rights violations in Sudan, but since then, its campaigns have focused on social issues including literacy, immigration reform, economic justice, gay rights, sexism, labor rights, mental health, body image, and climate change.[24] The organization's "fans-turned-heroes" have been the subject of multiple academic studies on fan activism and civic engagement among youth, and its website is a great place to find a cause that may interest your students, especially if they're Harry Potter fans.

Teach SDG's

As part of an effort to take action to meet the seventeen Sustainable Development Goals of the UN by 2030,[25] educators have assembled resources and projects to help address these goals in the classroom. Many of the examples shared in this book, and the students highlighted, are already making strides to address these goals, which include No Poverty, Zero Hunger, Quality Education, and Clean Water and Sanitation, just as examples. Follow the hashtag #TeachSDGs or visit teachsdgs.org for sample projects and to spread the word about how we can all work towards making the world a better place through education.

Student Vignette 🔊

I got the idea of paying it forward from First Lady Michelle Obama. Then, when I saw a homeless man near my home, I couldn't stop thinking about him. I decided I wanted to make sure he was fed, and it had to be healthy food, because that's really important and everyone should be able to eat healthy. My mom has helped me really build and expand Brae's Brown Bags.

I use my blog and social media to share my story, reach out to sponsors, and network with other kids who are doing amazing things. Also, most of the donations we receive all come through online, either from my blog or Facebook. Even though I can't drive places, social media helps me reach out everywhere so I can share how important hunger relief is to me and also find out who might need help so I can give them Brae's Brown Bags.

The student chapters pack bags of healthy food, which they collect, unless they are in a high-poverty school, in which case we provide funding to help them get food. Then we help them connect with shelters and soup kitchens in their community and they deliver the bags, either as a chapter or by sending them through a school rep. The chapters report to us, but we tell them to make the bags their own by coloring them and putting notes in them—things like that.

It is tricky starting the chapters while I'm in school, but the ultimate goal is to have lots of chapters. Kids are doing amazing things every day, and 3B Ripples gives them a platform to become changemakers.

—Braeden Mannering, seventh grade

In Summary ⬇

- Although school is not meant to be a political place, we can teach empathy and social justice in the classroom, which can be extended to an authentic audience using social media.

- Connecting your students to experts and other classrooms for a common cause can help them gain diverse perspectives, but we also have to explicitly teach perspective taking.

- Looking at your existing curriculum resources and technology tools with a digital leadership lens can help your students see that others outside their immediate communities care about the same issues they do.

Discussion Questions ✂

1. How could you use the student digital leaders' stories in this chapter in your lessons?
2. Where could you extend an existing inquiry about a current issue to an authentic audience through social media?
3. How could you use any of the ideas from this chapter to help students see diverse perspectives surrounding an issue that, to them, may seem very black and white?

Chapter 10 Notes

1. braesbrownbags.org

2. Marsh, Abigail. "Why Some People Are More Altruistic That Others." *TED Talk*, September 16, 2016. ted.com/talks/ abigail_marsh_why_some_people_are_more_altruistic_than_ others?utm_source=newsletter_daily&utm_campaign=daily&utm_ medium=email&utm_content=button__2016-09-16.

3. Davis, Matt, "Restorative Justice: Resources for Schools," *Edutopia*, October 29, 2015, edutopia.org/blog/ restorative-justice-resources-matt-davis.

4. Langer, Kerri-Lee, "Digital Literacy & Social Justice," YouTube, https:// www.youtube.com/watch?v=BmGnLo6tLP0

5. Alrubail, Rusul, "I Was a Refugee. I Am Haunted by Today's Images of Child Refugees," *PBS Newshour*, October 2, 2015, pbs.org/newshour/ updates/family-refugees-see-images-refugees-haunts.

6. A real-time chat app connected to Facebook.

7. sharedstudios.com

8. "Happy Jar for Our Friends at Makwa Sahgaiehcan First Nation School," Modified from the original: https://docs.google.com/a/ycdsb.ca/ forms/d/e/1FAIpQLSddmFJ7KELGgd830Vnnzgrotbadqn9va5HxAT9Ce ergzktD_w/viewform.

9. Reynolds, Cynthia, "Why Are Schools Brainwashing Our Children?" *Maclean's*, October 31, 2012, http://www.macleans.ca/news/canada/ why-are-schools-brainwashing-our-children/.

10. I'm sure I got this from a book somewhere, but I have been using it for so many years that I cannot say with certainty where it originates.

11. Glenn, C. L., "Activism or 'Slacktivism?': Digital Media and Organizing for Social Change," *Communication Teacher,* 29(2), 2015: 81-85. doi:1 0.1080/17404622.2014.1003310.

12. Ibid.

13. Kristofferson, K., White, K., and Peloza, J., "The Nature of Slacktivism: How the Social Observability of an Initial Act of Token Support Affects Subsequent Prosocial Action," *Journal of Consumer Research*, 40(6), (2014): 1149-1166. doi:10.1086/674137.

14. Rheingold, H., "Attention, and Other 21st-Century Social Media Literacies," *Educause Review*, 45(5), 2010: 14-24.

15. "Little Miss Flint Meets the President, Is Adorable," *The Washington Post* Video Channels, May 5, 2016, washingtonpost. com/video/politics/little-miss-flint-meets-the-president-is-adorable/2016/05/05/aa1172e4-12f2-11e6-a9b5-bf703a5a7191_video.html.

16. Stark, K., "Why You Should Talk to Strangers," TED Talk, February 2016, ted.com/talks/kio_stark_why_you_should_talk_to_strangers?language=en.

17. Wolffe, Karen, "Teaching Social Thinking and Perspective Taking," *Powershow.com,* powershow.com/view/3b7389-ZWRmY/Teaching_Social_Thinking_Perspective_Taking_Dr_Karen_powerpoint_ppt_presentation.

18. I have included both print and electronic modifiable templates for this at SocialLEADia.org in this chapter's "Resources" section.

19. Couros, George, "Err on the Side of Positive," *iPadPalooza*, June, 2016. Retrieved July 31, 2016, youtube.com/watch?v=zoMn4063yc4.

20. "Adolescent Literacy Guide: A Professional Learning Resource for Literacy, Grades 7-12," *Adolescent Literacy Learning*, 2016, 9, edugains.ca/resourcesLIT/AdolescentLiteracy/Vision/AdolescentLiteracyGuide_Interactive.pdf.

21. "Who We Are," *Kid President,* kidpresident.com/whoweare.html.

22. "Mia's Boxes of Love," Facebook, facebook.com/miasboxesoflove.

23. kidsareheroes.org/pressbox.htm

24. thehpalliance.org

25. "The Sustainable Development Agenda," *UN.org*, Jan 2016, un.org/sustainabledevelopment/development-agenda.

MEET THE STUDENTS
BRAEDEN MANNERING

braesbrownbags.org

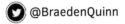 @BraedenQuinn

Braeden Mannering, a thirteen-year-old from Bear, Delaware, is the founder of Brae's Brown Bags (3B), a nonprofit organization providing healthy food to homeless and low-income people. Through this organization, he has activated more than 3,200 volunteers; provided nearly 10,000 "brown bags" of healthy food; and raised more than $58,000 for hunger relief.

His ongoing mission is not only to feed people, but to raise awareness of food insecurity and poverty and empower and inspire youth across the nation to become part of the solution.

Use Braeden's Story to Inspire Your Students

 How could your own students organize a brown bag drive to address hunger in your community?

 What organizations address food insecurity and poverty in your own community?

Ignite Students' Passions

I am thinking and concentrating on my future career as an animator, possible scriptwriter, and video game designer. I want to be successful. Social media has helped me to focus on a bigger picture. Not just my career goals, but how I can contribute my talents and gifts to others."

—*Gabe Howard, eleventh grade*

About eight years ago, a student named "Allan" took my cooperative education (co-op) class. This experiential learning opportunity allows students to earn traditional school credits (English, science, and math) by working at a job placement. Allan had been in my English class the previous year and really struggled. He was the kind of kid who didn't want people to know he couldn't read at grade level, so he'd often skip school or act up. I knew he was embarrassed to be in a workplace English class while the rest of his friends were in academic or applied English. (And I'd be lying if I said that when I saw his name on my roster, I didn't inwardly groan for a split second.)

As I expected, he found the in-class reading and writing tasks difficult those first few weeks. But then something remarkable happened. I visited Allan at the car garage where he was working (part of my role as his co-op teacher) and asked him to tell me about what he was doing. In that moment, he became a different person. With a vehicle on a hoist, he confidently began to explain what he thought was wrong with the engine, why he thought this, and how he was planning to fix it. The level of technical vocabulary he was using was, at times, to me, embarrassingly incomprehensible. I really thought about the implications of this experience on my teaching. Before visiting him at the garage, I'd only ever known Allan as the young man who hated Shakespeare's work and equally hated writing about it.

Have you ever had an experience like this? When you hit on a topic someone is passionate about and they become animated—almost a different person? Despite my advocating for mandatory co-op (which is never going to happen), I am heartened by the shift in pedagogy toward inquiry-based learning, problem-based learning, 20 Percent Time, and Genius Hour. These instructional shifts provide students opportunities to engage in relevant, real-life learning that may very well introduce them to passions or interests that lie beyond the confines of the traditional classroom.

Students move to digital leadership when they discover these passions and interests. For example, although I've only met sixteen-year-old Gabe Howard, whose vignette you will read in this chapter, via Google Hangouts and Twitter's direct messages, what has struck me most from our conversations is his passion for gaming. When he talks about it, he exudes confidence and conviction.

Similarly, seventeen-year-old Aidan is passionate about STEM and highlighting it in action. Joshua and Braeden are passionate about ending hunger. Hannah's passion for the environment, Michelle's and Olivia's passion for books, and Curran's and Timmy's passion for changing the status quo in schools have led them on their respective paths. Even though most of the kids I've met are exploring their passions outside of school, I have also connected with a number of teachers who are providing their students with time during the school day to explore their interests, create, design, and make, and, as a result, are seeing how incredibly inspired and inspiring they can be.

After all, our job as teachers is to provide our students with opportunities to delve into a variety of subjects and ideas, not just to share content, test, and repeat. We are meant to engage kids in making and creating, to help them discover what they do well, and support them when they aren't quite there yet. If, as each year passes, we look at our curriculum expectations as a way to open up a new world of learning to our students, then I'm confident that, at some point, something will inspire and excite them. Curriculum goals give us guidelines as to what we must teach, but how we teach those goals is up to us and the students in front of us.

These opportunities don't always have to include technology and social media, but embracing a digital leadership stance means we don't preclude this possibility. Remember the story of Stephanie Viveiros' kindergarten class creating a quilt for Monica? In creating that physical keepsake, the students were able to practice communication and critical-thinking skills and build relationships with their classmates. They learned about Monica and shared their creation through technology, but it was secondary to coming up with a purposeful idea and then designing, creating, drafting, and actually producing the quilt. That experience will be one those students always remember.

Project-, Challenge-, and Inquiry-Based Learning

Project- and inquiry-based learning are similar in that both allow students to gain knowledge and skills by "working for an extended period of time to investigate and respond to an authentic, engaging, and complex question, problem, or challenge," says the Buck Institute for Education.[1]

When I worked at the district level, I spent a number of years helping teachers see what inquiry- and project-based learning looks like in the classroom and how technology tools can help students, not just in their research, but also when sharing their learning with authentic audiences. During this time, I saw some amazing examples of this kind of learning, both within my own district and beyond.

One that always comes to mind when I think about what project-based learning could look like is the design-thinking assignment, which Zoe Branigan-Pipe, a teacher of gifted students in Hamilton, Ontario, shared at the Bring IT, Together Conference. She began by asking her students, "How are urban landscapes changing to meet the needs of people and communities of the present and future?"[2] Zoe then challenged them to reimagine their city's harbor area by exploring both global and local examples, as well as engaging in explicit learning around the community, researching the area's history, and finding examples of changing land-scapes. Students then had to draw, sketch, and discuss alternatives to the land before they could finally co-construct their ideas using Minecraft.[3] Zoe said some of her students even had the chance to present their projects at an actual town council meeting.

The success of this project, and the fact that students were so engaged in it, wasn't because they got to play Minecraft; on the contrary, it was because they were dealing with an issue in their own community that mattered to them. Zoe knows that students need to feel compelled and inspired to care.[4] In the end, students learned more about their city, and that they could have a voice in adult matters.

Another great example can be found in Matt Martin's chemistry class at San Diego's High Tech High Media Arts school. His tenth graders learn about saponification, chemical reactions, pH, strong bases, lab skills, and marketing skills, and then apply what they've learned to create high-quality soap, which they sell competitively online and in brick-and-mortar marketplaces.

Matt says:

Never have I seen students more engaged in a project. They have generally been interested in the soap-making process because it is messy, fun, and creates a beautiful, usable product. When we added an entrepreneurial aspect to this project, student excitement and engagement spiked to a level I have not seen before. Creative, social media, logistics, web design, and marketing departments quickly arose out of necessity. There was so much to do and students could pour their energy into an aspect of the project that appealed to them. They created a beautiful and functional website and then successfully ran it. Facebook, Instagram, and Yelp pages helped steer business to our online store and in-person selling events at the Earth Day festival, Vons Store, and various farmers' markets. The logistics team accounted for all of our expenditures and sales, which have topped $20,000 to date (March 2017). These profits have allowed us to give one of our teachers a grant, two scholarships to graduating seniors, and cash to a student at a time of crisis. Paid internships were also created and filled by our class, and we donated thousands of dollars' worth of soap to local San Diegans in need.

And what did Matt's students have to say about their foray into soap-making?

- **Matthew Marshall:** "This project is not just about making soap, but being able to work with others and learn to appreciate others' opinions."
- **Jaci Umpstead:** "I learned how to apply chemistry in the real world."
- **Lucas Santiago:** "Everything in this world, everything that you do, it's all chemistry."
- **Brian Ha:** "This project taught me that there's creativity in all of us."

- **Solomon Stovall-Ceja:** "This project taught me a lot about the real world, especially business."

When we offer our students the chance to engage in authentic learning opportunities, we open up a world of possibilities to them that they otherwise may never have experienced. Technology and social media are a natural part of that because they are how we connect and communicate today.

> "Young people are like goldfish: They can only grow according to the space they have."[5]
>
> —*Ishita Katyal, eleven years old*

Science and Play

You've learned how Karishma Bhagani created a water filter to solve a real-world issue affecting her home country of Kenya for a school project. I was similarly inspired when I read about Kiara Nirghin who created a solution to solve South Africa's drought problem using an "orange-peel mixture" made out of the "waste products from the juice-manufacturing industry."[6]

Karishma and Kiara are just two of the many student-scientists doing amazing things to help their communities and world. For further proof of students' work to help solve global problems, just look at seventeen-year-old Aidan's many inventions, as well as the those of the "STEM Innovators" he features on Developing Innovations' website. Each week, Aidan and his team of Educational Ambassadors go into the community and advocate for young students to receive STEM education. Developing Innovations' STEM Educational Outreach Program has taken Aidan and the teen scientists to countless community centers, libraries, museums, and elementary schools, all in the hopes of inspiring young children to fall in love with STEM.

Aidan says:

There is nothing that makes me prouder than seeing a child with a huge smile on their face and that feeling that I may have inspired the next STEM brilliant child that could make a discovery that would change the world in a positive way!

At this point, you may be thinking these science-oriented students are absolutely exceptional—beyond the norm—and there's no way one of them is sitting in your class full of students who may be reading well below grade level. But here's the thing about tapping into students' passions and interests: It sparks the students' intrinsic motivation to learn and persevere. We never know how the experiences we offer our students will have an impact on them later in life. When we allow them to pursue their love of bugs or rocks or books or film or games, we may very well be setting the stage for future entomologists, geologists, writers, directors, or game designers.

Traci Bond, an EdTech Ambassador from California's Bay Area, shared a video of students at one of her local schools participating in the Imagination Foundation's Global Cardboard Challenge. The students had created arcade games, including whack-a-mole, air hockey, and skee-ball, all out of cardboard. The idea was inspired by the story of Caine Monroy, a nine-year-old boy who used cardboard to recreate an arcade inside his dad's east Los Angeles auto parts shop in summer 2012. The arcade's only customer that summer was filmmaker Nirvan Mullick, who had gone to the shop because he needed a door handle. He saw Caine's arcade and bought a fun pass. He was so impressed with Caine and his arcade that he had the idea to organize a flash mob for him, which led to a short film, which led to founding the Imagination Foundation. The film, *Caine's Arcade*, went viral on the Internet, Twitter, and Reddit and has inspired children all over the world (and many teachers) to create games, robots, and car washes, among other things, all out of cardboard.

The Imagination Foundation is now collaborating with Google on a film series called *Science at Play*,[7] which looks at how creativity, learning, science, and play are redefining what it means to be a scientist. The Imagination Foundation is a wonderful resource for any teacher who may be interested in trying this out in the classroom.

This all goes to show that a small gesture like Nirvan's really can change the life of a child. If we don't provide students with opportunities, at least at some point in their academic year, to make, play, create, and do, we may never help them to tap into their interests. As Josh Shipp, author and youth speaker says, "Every kid is one caring adult away from being a success story."

20 Time, Genius Hour, Innovation Week

The 20 Percent Time concept came from Google, which, as the story goes, offered its top-performing engineers the opportunity to use their passions to create by spending 20 percent of their workday focusing on projects that inspire them and could (and have) become Google products.[8] My cousin, who briefly worked for Google, admits, "Google was (and is) best in class in unlocking the potential of their hires." I love what my cousin said because of its transference to education—our job is to unlock our students' potential.

"Genius Hour" or "20 Time," or another variation of the same name, is the focus of a number of books and resources encouraging teachers to allow their students to explore their passions. In fact, if you search for "#20Time" on Twitter, you'll find teachers engaging in 20 Percent Time projects and sharing their learning and resources. Educators using this model will tell you the rewards far outweigh the obstacles we can sometimes come across while trying to implement this learning experience in our classrooms.

And though there are things our curriculums say we must cover, we can almost always find time if we look hard enough. For instance, when you look at how you are spending your time doing administrative

"The idea is not only to give kids the tools to build the world they can imagine, but imagine the world that they can build."

—*Nirvan Mullick*

tasks—such as taking attendance, waiting for the bell to ring, or assigning ten questions instead of five to test a skill—I think you may just find, as I have in the past, how a self-directed project could actually be doable. It may be for one hour a week or a few weeks at the end of the year.

In my district, intermediate school teachers Brad Blucher and Marisa Benakis dedicate two weeks near the end of the year to what they call "Splice Projects," their iteration of an innovation week. Splice Project can take any form, including construction, culinary arts, music, drama, dance, visual arts, writing, documentary filmmaking, and more. The projects provide students with an opportunity to spend an entire week focused on their self-directed, inquiry-driven projects. Throughout the week, students document and reflect on their process, challenges, and successes. The following week, they present their journeys. Brad and Marisa's administrator, Michele Reaume, supports them wholeheartedly, allowing them to change the students' schedules and eliminate traditional classes for that week so they can focus solely on their Splice Projects.

I had the honor of attending the presentations both years Brad and Marisa implemented this model, and I have to tell you, I was completely blown away—not just by the students' range of projects, but more so by the fact that the Splice Projects concept emphasizes process. Students had to explain their projects in terms of the steps they took, the challenges they faced, the successes they experienced, the role feedback played, and the relationship between their process and the inquiry questions ("Who am I?" "Who do I want to become?" "What is my plan for achieving my goals?" "What are my opportunities?"). The students articulated a rationale for their decisions, as well as how they'd grown from the experience; and they did so in front of a room of 120 of their peers in addition to visitors like me. My favorite thing to do was ask the students about their challenges and successes and then watch as their faces become passionately animated while they explained. As an added bonus, because Marisa and Brad had shared their learning on Twitter and presented the idea to their colleagues at professional learning sessions, the Splices Project concept has now spread to other schools in our district.

Similarly, high school teacher and *The 20Time Project* author Kevin Brookhouser talks about how his students engage in the process of learning through this model. I had the honor of meeting Kevin at the EdTechTeam Toronto Summit, at which I presented. When he shared the learning taking place in his class, I was completely impressed by the extent to which his students were solving authentic problems. His says he believes this generation of kids will likely have to solve "wicked problems," and that we can prepare them for these challenges by helping them develop the skills they'll need while in our classrooms. His students brainstorm ideas for what they want to pursue as their 20Time projects by first coming up with really bad ideas and then settling on the good ones.

Kevin says 20Time, which he models based on Daniel Pink's *Drive*, provides students with three critical ingredients essential to innovation:

1. It gives students **autonomy** because it offers them the opportunity to pursue their own passions and allows them freedom in choosing not only what they learn, but how they learn it.

2. It gives students **mastery** because they can track their own growth and learn and strive to succeed because they want to.

3. It gives students **purpose** because they are meeting their clients', audiences', and customers' needs.[9]

One story, in particular, that Kevin told really inspired me. He said a student in his class traveled in a wheelchair for his project, which led the student to advocate for a paved and accessible road and successfully gain the needed support to have it built. He also shared that one of his students was aware of the isolation that sometimes happens when senior citizens move to a senior home, so she used her 20 Time to teach the residents of a local senior center how to connect with their family members via Facebook. And yet another student showed his local humane society how to market its pets on Instagram.

Kevin's students are incredible testaments to what today's youth can accomplish when we give them the opportunity to change their world and make a positive impact on their communities.

Making and Creating in the Classroom

The shift back to "maker spaces" and "design thinking" in classrooms and libraries is exciting to me, as I see yet another outlet through which students can discover their passions. So when *LAUNCH* authors A.J. Juliani and John Spencer launched the Global Day of Design (GDD)[10] in April 2016 to encourage schools to give their students time to "build, make, and tinker," I rallied our 21C district team and all of our teacher-librarians to participate. My partner, Daniel La Gamba, and I introduced the idea to teachers through a Google Hangout and on Twitter using our district's hashtag.

A.J. and John loaded tons of resources and ideas onto GDD's website, and Daniel and I added a few ideas of our own to the list for our district's teachers to choose from. We even offered a professional learning opportunity: Teachers could sign up and choose from Little Bits (making a robot and obstacle course); Breakout EDU[11] (a critical-thinking game, which they first played and then created their own puzzles); Green Screen Film Creation; and a VR/cardboard design project using *Clouds over Sidra*. We tried to balance making physical items with creating using technology. Many, many schools from our district participated and we modeled the importance of making and creating in the classroom, which combined physical creating with making using technology.

Self-described "maker" and "creator" Yumi Lee, a fourteen-year-old from York Region, Ontario, spoke at a TEDxKitchenerED event about the intersection she sees between digital and analog tools in her talk "How to Be as Awesome as Me":

> You may think of an artist only using paper and paint, but actually, they use digital tools just as much they use analog tools. Digital tools like YouTube, Google, and Pinterest always inspire my creativity. I put them into action with my analog tools and change to my waves. In my opinion, to be an open-minded, creative, and joyous maker, you have to have the right balance of digital and analog tools.[12]

Although I've definitely come to understand the importance of making and creating in the classroom, I had never considered the correlation between making and technology and social media before Yumi's talk, but it makes so much sense for this generation of students. Social media and technology affect everything our kids do, so we need to stop teaching as if they don't exist.

When we give students the opportunity to create, design, and prototype, whether it be physical, virtual, or a combination of both, we may be tapping into passions they didn't know they had. We never know what will inspire a student, so giving them opportunities to create and tinker is essential—even if it just happens a few times a year.

Pop Culture

I haven't always been an advocate for using pop culture references to films, celebrities, books, and games in the classroom, but since taking a course called "Digital Literacies," I have definitely rethought my position. That's because I've learned referencing pop culture gives us an opportunity to tap into and validate our students' interests. It's also a way for us to share our own passions with our students and foster meaningful relationships that transcend academics. Most importantly, it's fun, and laughter and fun are so important for our overall health and well-being.

> The best resources for learning about pop culture are sitting in our classrooms right in front of us.

I love what filmmaker Alexandre O. Philippe said in his 2013 TedxMileHigh Talk, "Why Pop Culture?" He talks about how religion divides us; social issues divide us; cultural beliefs and values divide us; but that, "pop culture is a universal language that manages in all of its seemingly trivial glory to make us dream and smile to connect us across racial, political, and social divides. It is part of our fabric as human beings. It says something about us, about our better nature so, isn't it time for us to respect it, cherish it, and learn to preserve it?"[13]

To find pop culture references, look no further than the social media platforms your kids are using. Before Twitter, I was a pop-culture moron. Now, though, I regularly look at Twitter's "Trends" column to see what people are talking about in the world.

Fortunately, the best resources for learning about pop culture are sitting in our classrooms right in front of us. We are so quick to judge our students' interests as "silly" or "useless," when they could actually lead us to approach our curriculum in new, more interesting ways. I make it a point to pay close attention to and ask my students what they are watching, playing, and talking about.

I had a great conversation about just this a few years ago when a history teacher told me his students had been asking him about the historic moment when President Obama shook Cuban President Raul Castro's hand at the memorial of South African revolutionary and President Nelson Mandela's death in 2013. They had seen it on Instagram, BuzzFeed, and Twitter. He couldn't believe how many questions the kids had been asking about it. He said he entertained a few but steered the conversation back to the "curriculum."

As you can imagine, I was quite "animated" (yes, let's use that word) as I tried to explain how he'd missed an incredible opportunity to use their questions as a starting point for some incredible unpacking of important ideas such as trade agreements, national peace treaties, and racial tension around the world, and their effects. He could have asked his students to show him what the tweets were saying and then had them compare and contrast that language to what more traditional news outlets were reporting. That is the curriculum. And it's our job to teach students in a way that helps them understand and apply ideas and concepts to the world around them, not just regurgitate facts. Current events and pop culture references from social media can provide a vehicle for incredible links to the curriculum, if we look at them as opportunities, not distractions.

Case in point: GIFs and memes (a humorous or interesting captioned video or image that goes viral)[14] are big with teens right now. So I posted an assignment idea for students to use a meme generator, create a meme for a work of literature they are studying, and then upload it to a favorite social media site to share with teachers and their peers. Robert Cannone happened to be teaching eleventh-grade English in summer school and they were studying the play *The Man of La Mancha*. He took the idea and challenged students to create their own memes and share them with one another via Twitter (similar to the way Cara Lodoen used Instagram).

A similar approach could be to have students create GIFs (animations). Simply do a search on Google for "GIF generator," and you can easily find a tool that will create a GIF for you. The students I know can do this well—you need only ask for them to show you.

Then, as an interesting creative writing activity, you could have students take their favorite GIF and create its backstory using their critical- and creative-thinking skills to come up with the setting, plot, and character ideas (all part of the language arts/English curriculum's expectations), which would lead to and explain their selected GIF. Webtoon's "Behind the GIFS" website has some great examples of what these backstories could look like.[15]

I'm not saying we abandon the classics altogether, but noticing what our students are interested in and the apps that they're using can lead to incredible opportunities for discovery and learning the curriculum's expectations, and more importantly, help develop relationships with students.

Gaming

When Robert Cannone's class participated in the "Games We Play" activity for Edcamp Global, (you'll recall the students used Padlet and YouTube to share their favorite games) with his sixth-grade class, something wonderful happened: Classes from five countries simultaneously played a single game of *Kahoot!* (an interactive online game) on the topic of games, and out of all of the students from all of the countries who played, one of Robert's students won. This student had learning difficulties and might not have won had the topic been academic, but because he had a passion for games, he was able to answer all of the questions correctly. The student's mom wrote the most heart-wrenching letter to Robert, thanking him for the opportunity and saying her child's whole demeanor and attitude in the classroom changed. That moment made me rethink the role game-based learning can play in classrooms.

Many young boys play games (as do girls, of course). And while we do need to caution students to be mindful of safety when using their webcam (one friend told her son, "You are inviting these people into our home—be mindful of that") and revealing personal information, the fact is that most of the talk within a game is of strategy and, depending on the game, collaboration. And while we absolutely need to ensure our students moderate the time they spend playing games (think digital health), I think we very much underestimate the skills that students may be developing. Twenty years ago, there likely weren't any jobs in gaming, but today, not only are there careers directly related to gaming, but evidence is suggesting that the skills these kids are practicing during gameplay, including resilience, leadership, risk-taking, and collaboration, will serve them well in the workforce.

A 2010 *Forbes* article titled, "How Playing Videogames Can Boost Your Career," quotes John Hagel III, co-chairman of a tech-oriented strategy center for Deloitte, who says, "We're finding that the younger people coming into the teams who have had experience playing online games are the highest-level performers because they are constantly motivated to seek out the next challenge and grab on to performance metrics."[16] In some cases, gaming can actually be the career: Gabe Howard, whose vignette is featured in this chapter, wants to be a game developer, and is already poised to make money in this career while only in high school.

Full disclosure: I am not and never have been a gamer. When my friends were playing *Pac-Man* and *Space Invaders*, I was listening to my Wham! albums and writing in my journal. I never had the patience or the hand-eye coordination. Even now, although my two teens and my husband play *Flappy Bird*, *Candy Crush Saga*, and *Monster Buster* (their latest obsession), I don't get it and feel myself getting frustrated by how much time they are "wasting."

I recognize we often make assumptions based on our own experiences and values, which has been true for me and game-based learning. Meanwhile, though, some educators whom I admire very much have been swearing for years that using gaming in the classroom is a game-changer (pun intended).

When I was actually forced to play games in my Digital Literacies course at the University of Ontario Institute of Technology, I realized then how little I understood about gaming, game-based learning, and its potential for literacy. Research suggests too that "Game-based learning (GBL), or the use of video games for educational purposes, has been shown to be

> The skills these kids are practicing during gameplay, including resilience, leadership, risk-taking, and collaboration, will serve them well in the workforce.

an effective means of enhancing both learning motivation and academic performance."[17]

By playing some games and speaking to my peers about how they use games like *Forge of Empires*, for example, to examine big ideas in their curriculum,[18] I've learned we can't make assumptions about what will help students learn best based on our own preconceived ideas of learning. Gaming can give students opportunities to differentiate and provide a rich springboard for writing and reading, as well as reinforce critical thinking, problem-solving, and collaboration.

I've also learned I can't expect others to take risks, be open-minded, and stay flexible if I'm not prepared to be. And I can't superficially agree (or disagree) with an idea without first really trying to understand it on a deeper level—after all, I would never want my students or my daughters to do that. I truly understand what it could look like and see the potential for using games to develop digital leadership. (And to the surprise of no one, I've also learned I'm absolutely terrible at all of these games.)

Igniting Passions through Co-Curricular Activities

In my role as a teacher-librarian, I plan and teach with teachers, and I help them look at their lessons with a new set of eyes. This is no different than when I was a literacy consultant. What I've come to learn, however, is that not every teacher is ready to use technology and social media— *yet*—and not everyone believes these tools can lead to transformational learning experiences.

Truthfully, I could get angry and frustrated (and I have), but I also know my personal sphere of influence only goes so far. Teachers feel bound by time, curriculum expectations, and testing mandates, and they must have a smile on their face while doing everything. However, this doesn't mean we stop encouraging them to complement their curriculum with a digital leadership stance or that we stop showing them how giving their students a real, authentic audience increases learning tremendously.

But it does mean that we may have to look for other ways to empower students to leverage technology and social media for digital leadership.

While we wait for those teachers to embrace innovative practices and shift their mindset, students are missing out on opportunities to have their ideas validated and their passions ignited. So, with that in mind, for each club and committee I oversee, I embrace a digital leadership stance, and I encourage you to think about how you could do the same with your school's clubs and councils.

For example, for my school's book club, I encourage members to use Goodreads (a book review site) and create a positive, professional online presence and then to make their thinking visible on Twitter as they read the selected books. I've also shown the students how to use BookSnaps (annotation using the tools in Snapchat) so they can visualize their thinking in a fun, personal way. When students were interested in reading to younger students, I suggested connecting with an organization and contact I knew from Children of Hope because I knew they helped a school in Uganda. Our original idea to create podcasts and visual book talks had to be revisited, and students had to be very creative when we learned that the school didn't have electricity (let alone Wi-Fi). As this book was in its publishing stages, my students were creatively brainstorming how we could add our stories to an iPad and raise funds for solar-powered speakers as well as a lightning rod. They were also inspired to spread awareness of Digital Inequity because they were deeply touched by the experience.

Additionally, I have started my school's first TED-Ed Club. The international program is well-established and offers teachers guided support. During our first meeting, we talked about ourselves, our ideas, and what makes an idea good, then watched and discussed a few TED Talks. It soon became clear to me that this club would provide an amazing opportunity for students to explore their passions and interests. There are organized "connection weeks" in which our group can talk about their ideas and progress, and the culmination of the year's work will be for students to put together their own three- to seven-minute TED Talks to share with our

TED-Ed Club in person, as well as through the school's Twitter account. Although this is our first year and we have a small group, I can't wait to see what the students come up with.

Dan Koch, a Florida technology integration specialist, has created a wonderful model for how students can engage in digital leadership through an extracurricular activity in the form of his middle school's student-run "Genius Squad." Similar to Apple's Genius Bar, the Genius Squad's "Student Geniuses" receive the ultimate real-world learning experience, in that they offer first-level technology support to their entire school community, including their peers, teachers, administrators, staff, and parents, all the while providing their district's IT department critical assistance and strengthening the school's technology program. What's more, Student Geniuses also possess a mastery level of skill and knowledge of foundational apps, including G Suite, Notability, iMovie, Dropbox, and WordPress, thereby allowing them to serve as partners in pedagogy and offer the school's teachers ideas for instructional strategies and project-based learning. Genius Squad students also engage in a variety of learning activities, many of which they share with the world on their blog.

Dan says students:

- Research, review, and recommend the latest applications used in an educational setting
- Create how-to screencast tutorials
- Deliver classroom training and demonstrations
- Host *Genius Squad On-Air*, a live-streaming broadcast
- Consult with app developers
- Present at local, state, and regional conferences
- Moderate Twitter chats
- Pursue their own individual learning endeavors, based on Google's 20 Percent Time project
- Maintain personal blogs that showcase their work and progress toward their learning goals

Since the Genius Squad's inception in 2015, the club has published an iTunes U course with all of the group's how-to videos, which, at the time of writing, has been downloaded more than 150 times by people across the globe. The Club has also conducted Hangouts on Air sessions with educational technology companies, allowing the students to gain insights into the very products they use daily. As this book was in its editing stages, Dan shared that this idea has resulted in an actual course at his school now—proof that time, patience, and good work in the service of our students does not go unnoticed.

The possibilities are endless. How could we engage our school's student council in projects that leverage social media and make a positive difference in people's lives? What opportunities exist for students to connect with others? What could the anime club do? The photography club? All it takes is asking your students, "How can we share our learning with others outside our school?" and I'm sure they will come up with several ideas.

> "If we are going to empower our students, we must help them find what they love and create learning experiences that encourage them to develop their strengths."
>
> —*George Couros,* **The Innovator's Mindset**

Student Vignette 🔊

I think the Twitter chats and gaming chats I participate in have not only given me a voice in my learning—they have given me validation! When I participate in them and others are praising my input and asking me about my experiences, it encourages me to dive deeper into the topic we're talking about. It allows people to see what I am capable of and motivates me to achieve more.

To say Twitter changed me for the better is the biggest understatement of the century. My mother wanted me to join one of her online chats, #MinecraftEdu, which is dedicated to bringing the 2011 indie phenomenon, Minecraft, to the classroom, and so I joined her with mixed feelings. I was legitimately nervous about joining Twitter and all the risks I've been so heavily warned of in the classroom of my school. But when I started meeting everybody in the chat, the anxiety and stress just washed away. Everyone was so nice and supportive of my answers and new ideas; they were excited to hear a student's voice.

We were so successful with the chat, in fact, that my mom and I even hosted one and gave out questions! It truly felt like I was getting somewhere with expressing myself online, both inside and outside of the #MinecraftEdu chat, as I also joined many other chats like #Games4Ed. I felt invigorated and wanted to keep going.

I'm thinking about and concentrating on my future career as an animator, scriptwriter, and video game designer. Whatever I do, I want to be successful. Social media has helped me to focus on not just my career goals, but how I can contribute my talents and gifts to others—how can I help my community, my state, my country, and my world?

Twitter and gaming communities have allowed me to express myself by being open and feeling validated. Not once have my ideas been shot down like I am used to, but, rather, people embrace them and tell me whether this can or cannot work. And if it can't work, they recommend what to do and let me take off trying to fix it. If schools don't change, they may become a thing of the past. Kids are doing so much online and with technology. They are learning from others around the world—so why conform when we don't have to? I don't have to wait for college to pursue my interests and learning—I can take action now, and I am abso-lutely relishing it.

—*Gabe Howard, eleventh grade*

In Summary ⬇

- Students engage in digital leadership practices when their passions are ignited.

- Many of the current trends in education lend themselves to digital leadership.

- It is important to give students opportunities to make, create, investigate, and explore both inside and outside the classroom.

Discussion Questions ✖

1. Do your students consider themselves inventors? If there aren't science fairs in your school district, why not reintroduce the idea of students inventing something to make someone's life better? Check out the resources on the Science Fair's website.

2. Look at the various innovative ways your school is tapping into student passions; can social media be used to celebrate and share beyond the classroom?

3. What is one idea from this section that you will try? Or what is one practice you have used to ignite your students' passion that you would like to share to the #SocialLEADia hashtag on Twitter or the Facebook page?

Chapter 11 Notes

1. "What Is Project Based Learning (PBL)?" *BIE*, bie.org/about/what_pbl.

2. Branigan, Zoe, "Design Thinking–Making Urban Redevelopment a Reality in Minecraft," *Pipedreams*, January 28, 2014, pipedreams-education.ca/2014/01/28/ design-thinking-make-urban-redevelopment-a-reality-in-minecraft/.

3. Ibid.

4. Ibid.

5. Katyal, Ishita, "Before When I Grow Up," *YouTube*, June 9, 2016, youtube.com/watch?v=1JzgJFccUyw&feature=youtu.be.

6. "South African Teen Wins Prize for Orange Peel Innovation," *BBC News*, September 28, 2016, bbc.com/news/world-africa-37497682.

7. "Science at Play, Episode 1: Are You a Scientist?" *Imagination Fdn YouTube*, youtube.com/watch?v=t18bOK-e4rE.

8. This is an oversimplification. If you're interested in learning more, refer to Eric Schmidt and Jonathan Rosenberg's book, *How Google Works*.

9. Brookhouser, Kevin, 20time.org.

10. globaldayofdesign.com

11. breakoutedu.com

12. Lee, Y. "How to Be as Awesome as Me: Yumi Lee," *YouTube*, 2016, youtube.com/watch?v=Cpj8CSpoo_I.

13. Philippe, Alexandre, "Why Pop Culture?" *TEDxMileHigh*, amara.org/en/videos/eqXoW8EkCsCY/info/ why-pop-culture-alexandre-o-philippe-tedxmilehigh/.

14. "Meme," *Merriam Webster*, merriam-webster.com/dictionary/meme.

15. Shared by George Couros on Twitter. webtoons.com/en/comedy/ behind-the-gifs/youre-a-acstuart/viewer?title_no=658&episode _no=21.

16. Chiang, Oliver, "How Playing Videogames Can Boost Your Career," *Forbes*, July 19, 2010, forbes.com/2010/07/19/career-leadership-strategy-technology-videogames.html.

17. Kingsley, T., M. Grabner-Hagen, "Gamification: Questing to Integrate Content Knowledge, Literacy, and 21st Century Learning," *Journal of Adolescent & Adult Literacy*, 59(1), 2015: 51-61.

18. https://us.forgeofempires.com/

MEET THE STUDENTS
YUMI LEE

YumisDozen.com

 yoyoyumi.blogspot.ca

Yumi is a creative middle schooler from York Region, Ontario, Canada. She has her own blog and is an entrepreneur who started and runs an online business called Yumi's Dozen, for which she makes delicious treats and baked goods. Yumi aspires to be a teacher and spends much of her time creating things inspired by her favorite YouTubers.

Use Yumi's Story to Inspire Your Students

▶ Watch Yumi's Kitchener TEDTalk (youtu.be/Cpj8CSpoo_I). What is her main idea about making and creating?

Yumi loves to bake and has created a whole business around her passion for baking. What are the students in your class passionate about? Brainstorm what possible careers or businesses can come from that.

Concluding Thoughts: Forging a New Path

The next time you talk to a young person, instead of asking what they want to do when they grow up, please ask them what they want to do now. Ask them about the real-life problems they are solving. Ask them what they are wishing for a better world. And ask them what they are doing to change this world.

—Ishita Katyal, eleven years old

My good friend, Diana Santos, told me her nine-year-old daughter, Charlotte, had an idea about sharing titles of books that were worth reading with her friends and others. Unlike when my own daughter was nine years old and wanted a YouTube channel, though, Diana helped her daughter create a website, then shared it with me and others through social media.

When I saw Charlotte's beautiful face on Instagram with a note asking to share recommendations for books to read, I was so full of love for her. You see, Charlotte had been struggling to go to school and her parents were at their wit's end trying to figure out how to encourage her. And only until recently was she also a reluctant reader. I shared her website on my own Twitter account and encouraged my network to do the same.

As a result of the encouragement Charlotte had been receiving via social media, Diana said, for the first time in more than a month, her daughter was excited to go to school. She was looking forward to sharing her idea and the people who'd suggested books (which, at that point, ranged from Ontario, to Alberta, to across the States and even Europe) with her teacher and teacher-librarian.

So what happened? One of her peers told her, "Your mom must not love you if she is letting you create a website and put it on the Internet," and her teacher basically said, "That's nice."

I wish this were fiction. Instead of encouraging and celebrating Charlotte, or perhaps even using her website as a place for the class to curate and talk about their favorite books, they disheartened and demoralized her.

I have written this book for the Charlottes of the world. For the students who are being told what they can't do without a guide to what they *can* do. I wrote it so parents can refrain from making the same mistake I made. So that districts, leaders, and teachers might rethink their stance on the role of social media in the classroom. I wrote it to celebrate the students I have met along the journey already modeling digital leadership and the teachers who are leading the way despite obstacles.

It's my hope that these students will soon cease to be the exception and become the norm. In fact, even over the course of writing this book, I have heard from and met many teachers who are thinking differently about the devices in their hands and at their fingertips. And more importantly, I am listening to students who are learning, creating, inventing, and sharing in positive and productive ways which we never acknowledge in "school."

Because of these conversations and because every teacher and student I meet has a story that I wanted to capture, truthfully, I had a difficult time actually finishing this book. But, in the interest of deadlines, I just had to stop.

But the conversation cannot stop with this book. It has to keep going.

What kind of teacher will you choose to be? Will you just say, "That's nice," when a student shares their passion and then move on to your "curriculum"? Or will you look for opportunities to empower your students and encourage them to have a voice and lead the change?

I think it's Albert Einstein who is credited as defining insanity as doing the same thing over and over again and expecting different results. We already know what it's like *not* to embrace social media in school. It's time for a different approach.

So it seems to me that we're standing before two roads diverging in a wood.

Will you stand still and not choose a road, instead opting to shake your head and bemoan the woes of living in a digital age, citing privacy issues and big data, hoping everything will resolve itself or that, miraculously, social media will simply go away?

Will you continue to embark upon the road well traveled? It is where fear and negativity prevail, and the path is so worn that we spend all of our energy trying to fix the potholes. On this path, our lessons cannot include social media because it is blocked and banned, and students are left to navigate digital spaces on their own. It is where the online lives of our students are separate from the curriculum. We know, inevitably, where this road leads because so many of us have been down it before and we are not happy with where this has led us.

And the road less traveled? It is the one that the teachers and students featured in this book have traveled, and continue to travel. It is the one where we think differently and act differently when it comes to leveraging the potential of social media. The next generation of changemakers is leading this road with positivity, creativity, and hope.

Join us.

Acknowledgments

This book is the culmination of my thinking and learning from the past several years. Every learner, scholar, friend, student, writer, and teacher I have encountered in my teaching career is a coauthor.

I have been fortunate to have George Couros as a mentor and friend. You will notice from the many references to his work in this book that I owe much to George for the path upon which I have found myself. I am grateful for the time he has always taken to challenge and support me when he had so many other commitments. I am further indebted to him for writing this book's foreword. George, without you, this book would not exist. Thank you for your inspiration, mentorship and friendship, for your support and critical feedback throughout this journey, and for always pushing me to be a better leader.

I am so grateful to Shelley and Dave Burgess for believing in me and for being the very best publishers and people. Thanks for EMPOWERing me and for your support throughout this process. To Erin Casey and her team, thank you for doing what you do so well, especially in light of the personal obstacles I faced during the editing process.

Thanks to Janette Hughes, PhD, and Robin Kay, PhD, from the University of Ontario Institute of Technology, for offering me the opportunity to pursue my passion for social media in education at the graduate level. I am grateful for your flexibility, mentorship, and support. Thank you, Alec Couros, PhD, for sharing your resources so generously.

I would also like to take this opportunity to thank the York Catholic District School Board (YCDSB), my employer, for allowing me the freedom to pursue my passions and providing opportunities for my own professional learning and development. The points of view in this book, however, are my own and do not necessarily reflect the YCDSB's views or policies.

I am particularly grateful for being a part of a curriculum team and a 21C district team in my role as literacy consultant alongside people who have been instrumental in challenging my thinking, all the while offering support and encouragement. In that role, I had the unique opportunity to work with administrators, superintendents, teacher-librarians, IT personnel, teachers, and students on a variety of initiatives. I am thankful for the leadership and support of Patricia Preston, Diane Murgaski and Darlene Clapham as well as Brian, Scott, Daniel, Carlos, Michelle, Ines, Annette, Angela, and Lori as well as the Curriculum and Pathways teams for being such a great team with whom to work and learn. Thank you to all of the teachers who let me into your classrooms (either physically or virtually) and for taking a risk or two with me. I am grateful for knowing you, working with you, and learning with and from you.

To my personal, or should I say powerful, learning network, both face to face and online, this book is really the result of my learning and growing with you. Thank you especially to my #EduMatch Voxer family, OSSEMOOC leader-friends, #OntEd, #DigiCit crew, #EdTechTeam, and #GlobalEd tribes. Thanks to all of you—too many to list separately—who took this journey with me: This book is a direct result of your influence on me.

Special thanks to Sylvia Duckworth for reading my post about digital leadership almost two years ago and collaborating with me to visualize it. You have been such an amazing cheerleader ever since, and I appreciate your friendship. Thank you, Leigh Cassell, and, Fran Siracusa, for your support, friendship, and advice and for taking the time to help whenever I needed it.

Thanks to Shauna Pollock, Doug Peterson, Katie Martin, Justin Schleider, Brian Costello, and Paul for the many hours you spent providing me with feedback. I am forever grateful! Thanks also to Daniel La Gamba for your time in creating the beautiful sketchquote.

To my parents, Carmela and Sam Casa, who came here from Italy with little formal education but with more intelligence, perseverance, and character than any other people I know. Thanks for your support and for modeling what hard work and family values mean. Everything I am is because of you.

To my in-laws, Judy and Stan Todd, for not only supporting me and treating me like a daughter since you met me, but also for taking the time to be my "critical friends" and cheerleaders for this crazy endeavor. I can't thank you enough. You are the best.

To my family and lifelong friends who patiently waited while I missed so many social engagements because I was busy writing, thanks for your patience, love, and support.

To all of the teachers mentioned and featured in this book, thank you for allowing me to share your stories with the world. I am forever indebted to you for helping to bring authentic classroom experiences to this narrative and for showing other educators what is possible. Thanks especially to Robert Cannone (whom I've featured the most) for always being such a beacon of light for your students and for the rest of us. I may have been your teacher once upon a time, but you have taught me so much in return.

To my family, my husband, Stewart Todd, and daughters, Sydney and Kelsey, who have been there for me even at times when I took on more than I could handle, I could not have done this without your love, encouragement, and support. I am so blessed to be a wife to you, Stewart. You are the most thoughtful, funny, generous, and kind life partner a girl could ask for, as well as the most inspirational leader and administrator I have ever met. Sydney and Kelsey, you are definitely my best creations. I am so proud of you. You are bright, empathetic, kind, thoughtful, and beautiful people. Being your mother is my life's greatest gift. Thank you, Stewart, Sydney, and Kelsey, for assuming the role of scribes and editors during my "dark days," so I didn't have to look at a screen. My heart bursts with love for you.

To the student digital leaders featured in this book, and whom I continue to meet every day, thank you for being positive and inspirational role models for us all and for allowing me to share your narratives. I am a better person and educator for knowing you. I hope that, as a result of this book, more students will find their voices and that more educators will allow those voices to be expressed in the classroom and online.

Bring Jennifer Casa-Todd to Your School!

Jennifer Casa-Todd is a gifted speaker and workshop facilitator who has been described as "engaging," "inspirational," "knowledgeable," and "passionate." She balances her research, stories, and humor with practical takeaways and hands-on learning opportunities. Jennifer brings her unique perspectives as a teacher, consultant, student, and parent to show how technology and social media can transform students' learning experiences.

Her popular topics include:

Social LEADia: Moving Students from Digital Citizenship
to Digital Leadership

The Connected Educator, The Connected Student

Rethink YouTube: From Digital Citizenship to Digital Leadership

Twitter in the Classroom

Fears, Cheers, and Unclears: Parenting in a Modern World

Connecting Students to Each Other and the World
Using Simple Tech Tools

What's Real? What's Fake? Critical Literacy in a Time of Alternative Facts

Reading in the Twenty-First Century

Give Every Student a Voice: Using Technology with Students Accessing
Special Education

She can customize any of these topics to meet your needs.

@JCasaTodd   jencasatodd@gmail.com

JCasaTodd.com • SocialLEADia.org

DaveBurgessConsulting.com/speaking

MORE FROM

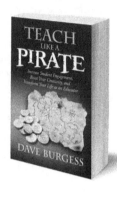

DAVE BURGESS
Consulting, Inc.

Teach Like a PIRATE
Increase Student Engagement, Boost Your Creativity, and Transform Your Life as an Educator
By Dave Burgess (@BurgessDave)

Teach Like a PIRATE is the *New York Times'* best-selling book that has sparked a worldwide educational revolution. It is part inspirational manifesto that ignites passion for the profession, and part practical road map filled with dynamic strategies to dramatically increase student engagement. Translated into multiple languages, its message resonates with educators who want to design outrageously creative lessons and transform school into a life-changing experience for students.

P is for PIRATE
Inspirational ABC's for Educators
By Dave and Shelley Burgess (@Burgess_Shelley)

Teaching is an adventure that stretches the imagination and calls for creativity every day! In *P is for PIRATE*, husband and wife team Dave and Shelley Burgess encourage and inspire educators to make their classrooms fun and exciting places to learn. Tapping into years of personal experience and drawing on the insights of more than seventy educators, the authors offer a wealth of ideas for making learning and teaching more fulfilling than ever before.

Learn Like a PIRATE

*Empower Your Students to
Collaborate, Lead, and Succeed*
By Paul Solarz (@PaulSolarz)

Today's job market demands that students be prepared to take responsibility for their lives and careers. We do them a disservice if we teach them how to earn passing grades without equipping them to take charge of their education. In *Learn Like a PIRATE*, Paul Solarz explains how to design classroom experiences that encourage students to take risks and explore their passions in a stimulating, motivating, and supportive environment where improvement, rather than grades, is the focus. Discover how student-led classrooms help students thrive and develop into self-directed, confident citizens who are capable of making smart, responsible decisions, all on their own.

Play Like a Pirate

Engage Students with Toys, Games, and Comics
By Quinn Rollins (@jedikermit)

Yes! Serious learning can be seriously fun. In *Play Like a Pirate*, Quinn Rollins offers practical, engaging strategies and resources that make it easy to integrate fun into your curriculum. Regardless of the grade level you teach, you'll find inspiration and ideas that will help you engage your students in unforgettable ways.

eXPlore Like a Pirate

Gamification and Game-Inspired Course Design to Engage, Enrich, and Elevate Your Learners
By Michael Matera (@MrMatera)

Are you ready to transform your classroom into an experiential world that flourishes on collaboration and creativity? Then set sail with classroom game designer and educator Michael Matera as he reveals the possibilities and power of game-based learning. In *eXPlore Like a Pirate*, Matera serves as your experienced guide to help you apply the most motivational techniques of game play to your classroom. You'll learn gamification strategies that will work with and enhance (rather than replace) your current curriculum and discover how these engaging methods can be applied to any grade level or subject.

Lead Like a PIRATE

Make School Amazing for Your Students and Staff
By Shelley Burgess and Beth Houf
(@Burgess_Shelley, @BethHouf)

In *Lead Like a PIRATE*, education leaders Shelley Burgess and Beth Houf map out the character traits necessary to captain a school or district. You'll learn where to find the treasure that's already in your classrooms and schools—and how to bring out the very best in your educators. This book will equip and encourage you to be relentless in your quest to make school amazing for your students, staff, parents, and communities.

The Innovator's Mindset

Empower Learning, Unleash Talent, and Lead a Culture of Creativity
By George Couros (@gcouros)

The traditional system of education requires students to hold their questions and compliantly stick to the scheduled curriculum. But our job as educators is to provide new and better opportunities for our students. It's time to recognize that compliance doesn't foster innovation, encourage critical thinking, or inspire creativity—and those are the skills our students need to succeed. In *The Innovator's Mindset*, George Couros encourages teachers and administrators to empower their learners to wonder, to explore—and to become forward-thinking leaders.

Shift This!

How to Implement Gradual Changes for MASSIVE Impact in Your Classroom
By Joy Kirr (@JoyKirr)

Establishing a student-led culture that isn't focused on grades and homework but on individual responsibility and personalized learning, may seem like a daunting task—especially if you think you have to do it all at once. But significant change is possible, sustainable, and even easy when it happens little by little. In *Shift This!* educator and speaker Joy Kirr explains how to make gradual shifts—in your thinking, teaching, and approach to classroom design—that will have a massive impact in your classroom. Make the first shift today!

LAUNCH

*Using Design Thinking to Boost Creativity and
Bring Out the Maker in Every Student*
By John Spencer and A.J. Juliani
(@spencerideas, @ajjuliani)

Something happens in students when they define themselves as makers and inventors and creators. They discover powerful skills—problem-solving, critical thinking, and imagination—that will help them shape the world's future ... our future. In *LAUNCH*, John Spencer and A.J. Juliani provide a process that can be incorporated into every class at every grade level ... even if you don't consider yourself a "creative teacher." And if you dare to innovate and view creativity as an essential skill, you will empower your students to change the world—starting right now.

Pure Genius

*Building a Culture of Innovation and
Taking 20% Time to the Next Level*
By Don Wettrick (@DonWettrick)

For far too long, schools have been bastions of boredom, killers of creativity, and way too comfortable with compliance and conformity. In *Pure Genius*, Don Wettrick explains how collaboration—with experts, students, and other educators—can help you create interesting, and even life-changing, opportunities for learning. Wettrick's book inspires and equips educators with a systematic blueprint for teaching innovation in any school.

Teaching Math with Google Apps

50 G Suite Activities

By Alice Keeler and Diana Herrington

(@AliceKeeler, @mathdiana)

Google Apps give teachers the opportunity to interact with students in a more meaningful way than ever before, while G Suite empowers students to be creative, critical thinkers who collaborate as they explore and learn. In *Teaching Math with Google Apps*, educators Alice Keeler and Diana Herrington demonstrate fifty different ways to bring math classes to the twenty-first century with easy-to-use technology.

Table Talk Math

A Practical Guide for Bringing Math into Everyday Conversations

By John Stevens (@Jstevens009)

Making math part of families' everyday conversations is a powerful way to help children and teens learn to love math. In *Table Talk Math*, John Stevens offers parents (and teachers!) ideas for initiating authentic, math-based conversations that will get kids to notice and be curious about all the numbers, patterns, and equations in the world around them.

The Classroom Chef

Sharpen your lessons. Season your classes. Make math meaningful.

By John Stevens and Matt Vaudrey (@Jstevens009, @MrVaudrey)

In *The Classroom Chef*, math teachers and instructional coaches John Stevens and Matt Vaudrey share their secret recipes, ingredients, and tips for serving up lessons that engage students and help them "get" math. You can use these ideas and methods as-is, or better yet, tweak them and create your own enticing educational meals. The message the authors share is that, with imagination and preparation, every teacher can be a Classroom Chef.

Instant Relevance

Using Today's Experiences to Teach Tomorrow's Lessons

By Denis Sheeran (@MathDenisNJ)

Every day, students in schools around the world ask the question, "When am I ever going to use this in real life?" In *Instant Relevance*, author and keynote speaker Denis Sheeran equips you to create engaging lessons from experiences and events that matter to your students. Learn how to help your students see meaningful connections between the real world and what they learn in the classroom—because that's when learning sticks.

50 Things You Can Do with Google Classroom

By Alice Keeler and Libbi Miller

(@alicekeeler, @MillerLibbi)

It can be challenging to add new technology to the classroom, but it's a must if students are going to be well-equipped for the future. Alice Keeler and Libbi Miller shorten the learning curve by providing a thorough overview of the Google Classroom App. Part of Google Apps for Education (GAfE), Google Classroom was specifically designed to help teachers save time by streamlining the process of going digital. Complete with screenshots, *50 Things You Can Do with Google Classroom* provides ideas and step-by-step instructions to help teachers implement this powerful tool.

50 Things to Go Further with Google Classroom

A Student-Centered Approach

By Alice Keeler and Libbi Miller

(@alicekeeler, @MillerLibbi)

Today's technology empowers educators to move away from the traditional classroom where teachers lead and students work independently—each doing the same thing. In *50 Things to Go Further with Google Classroom: A Student-Centered Approach*, authors and educators Alice Keeler and Libbi Miller offer inspiration and resources to help you create a digitally rich, engaging, student-centered environment. They show you how to tap into the power of individualized learning that is possible with Google Classroom.

140 Twitter Tips for Educators

Get Connected, Grow Your Professional Learning Network, and Reinvigorate Your Career
By Brad Currie, Billy Krakower, and Scott Rocco (@bradmcurrie, @wkrakower, @ScottRRocco)

Whatever questions you have about education or about how you can be even better at your job, you'll find ideas, resources, and a vibrant network of professionals ready to help you on Twitter. In *140 Twitter Tips for Educators*, #Satchat hosts and founders of Evolving Educators, Brad Currie, Billy Krakower, and Scott Rocco offer step-by-step instructions to help you master the basics of Twitter, build an online following, and become a Twitter rock star.

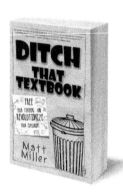

Ditch That Textbook

Free Your Teaching and Revolutionize Your Classroom
By Matt Miller (@jmattmiller)

Textbooks are symbols of centuries of old education. They're often outdated as soon as they hit students' desks. Acting "by the textbook" implies compliance and a lack of creativity. It's time to ditch those textbooks—and those textbook assumptions about learning! In *Ditch That Textbook*, teacher and blogger Matt Miller encourages educators to throw out meaningless, pedestrian teaching and learning practices. He empowers them to evolve and improve on old, standard teaching methods. *Ditch That Textbook* is a support system, toolbox, and manifesto to help educators free their teaching and revolutionize their classrooms.

Your School Rocks … So Tell People!
Passionately Pitch and Promote the Positives Happening on Your Campus
By Ryan McLane and Eric Lowe
(@McLane_Ryan, @EricLowe21)

Great things are happening in your school every day. The problem is, no one beyond your school walls knows about them. School principals Ryan McLane and Eric Lowe want to help you get the word out! In *Your School Rocks … So Tell People!* McLane and Lowe offer more than seventy immediately actionable tips along with easy-to-follow instructions and links to video tutorials. This practical guide will equip you to create an effective and manageable communication strategy using social-media tools. Learn how to keep your students' families and community connected, informed, and excited about what's going on in your school.

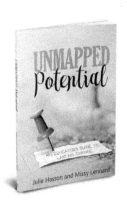

Unmapped Potential
An Educator's Guide to Lasting Change
By Julie Hasson and Missy Lennard
(@PPrincipals)

No matter where you are in your educational career, chances are you have, at times, felt overwhelmed and overworked. Maybe you feel that way right now. If so, you aren't alone. But the more important news is that things can get better! You simply need the right map to guide you from frustrated to fulfilled. *Unmapped Potential* offers advice and practical strategies to help you find your unique path to becoming the kind of educator—the kind of person—you want to be.

The Zen Teacher
Creating FOCUS, SIMPLICITY, and
TRANQUILITY in the Classroom
By Dan Tricarico (@thezenteacher)

Teachers have incredible power to influence, even improve, the future. In *The Zen Teacher,* educator, blogger, and speaker Dan Tricarico provides practical, easy-to-use techniques to help teachers be their best—unrushed and fully focused—so they can maximize their performance and improve their quality of life. In this introductory guide, Dan Tricarico explains what it means to develop a Zen practice—something that has nothing to do with religion and everything to do with your ability to thrive in the classroom.

How Much Water Do We Have?
5 Success Principles for Conquering Any Challenge
and Thriving in Times of Change
By Pete Nunweiler with Kris Nunweiler

In *How Much Water Do We Have?* Pete Nunweiler identifies five key elements that are necessary for the success of any goal, life transition, or challenge: information, planning, motivation, support, and leadership. Referring to these elements as the 5 Waters of Success, Pete explains that, like the water we drink, you need them to thrive in today's rapidly paced world. If you're feeling stressed out, overwhelmed, or uncertain at work or at home, pause and look for the signs of dehydration. Learn how to find, acquire, and use the 5 Waters of Success—so you can share them with your team and family members.

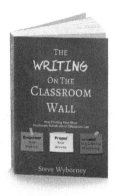

The Writing on the Classroom Wall

How Posting Your Most Passionate Beliefs about Education Can Empower Your Students, Propel Your Growth, and Lead to a Lifetime of Learning

By Steve Wyborney (@SteveWyborney)

In *The Writing on the Classroom Wall*, Steve Wyborney explains how posting and discussing Big Ideas can lead to deeper learning. You'll learn why sharing your ideas will sharpen and refine them. You'll also be encouraged to know that the Big Ideas you share don't have to be profound to make a profound impact on learning. In fact, Steve explains, it's okay if some of your ideas fall off the wall. What matters most is sharing them.

Kids Deserve It!

Pushing Boundaries and Challenging Conventional Thinking

By Todd Nesloney and Adam Welcome (@TechNinjaTodd, @awelcome)

In *Kids Deserve It!*, Todd and Adam encourage you to think big and make learning fun and meaningful for students. Their high-tech, high-touch, and highly engaging practices will inspire you to take risks, shake up the status quo, and be a champion for your students. While you're at it, you just might rediscover why you became an educator in the first place.

Escaping the School Leader's Dunk Tank

How to Prevail When Others Want to See You Drown

By Rebecca Coda and Rick Jetter

(@RebeccaCoda, @RickJetter)

No school leader is immune to the effects of discrimination, bad politics, revenge, or ego-driven coworkers. These kinds of dunk-tank situations can make an educator's life miserable. By sharing real-life stories and insightful research, the authors (who are dunk-tank survivors themselves) equip school leaders with the practical knowledge and emotional tools necessary to survive and, better yet, avoid getting "dunked."

Start. Right. Now.

Teach and Lead for Excellence

By Todd Whitaker, Jeff Zoul, and Jimmy Casas

(@ToddWhitaker, @Jeff_Zoul, @casas_jimmy)

In their work leading up to *Start. Right. Now.* Todd Whitaker, Jeff Zoul, and Jimmy Casas studied educators from across the nation and discovered four key behaviors of excellence: Excellent leaders and teachers Know the Way, Show the Way, Go the Way, and Grow Each Day. If you are ready to take the first step toward excellence, this motivating book will put you on the right path.

Master the Media

How Teaching Media Literacy Can Save Our Plugged-in World

By Julie Smith (@julnilsmith)

Written to help teachers and parents educate the next generation, *Master the Media* explains the history, purpose, and messages behind the media. The point isn't to get kids to unplug; it's to help them make informed choices, understand the difference between truth and lies, and discern perception from reality. Critical thinking leads to smarter decisions—and it's why media literacy can save the world.

About the Author

Jennifer Casa-Todd is a teacher-librarian at Cardinal Carter Catholic High School in Aurora, Ontario, Canada. Before this, she spent six years at the York Catholic District School Board as a program resource teacher for literacy, as well as a literacy consultant, respectively. In her district-level role, through the Journey 2020 21C initiative, she had the honor of working with teachers from kindergarten through twelfth grade to integrate technology in the classroom; support literacy, assessment, and differentiation; and promote twenty-first-century competencies. Jennifer has written curriculum for the Ontario Ministry of Education's 21st Century Learning office as well as the Catholic Curriculum Corporation. She is a lifelong learner currently studying at the University of Ontario's Institute of Technology, with a focus on social media in education and digital citizenship.

Jennifer has been the co-chair and an active member of her daughters' school's parent council for more than a decade, working to bring the school's parent and school communities together for a variety of issues. She has also worked closely with the Bully Free Alliance of York Region and is an associate for the Digital Citizenship Institute.

She's passionate about bringing students' voices into conversations around education and hopes this book will help her do just that.

 @JCasaTodd   ✉ jencasatodd@gmail.com

 JCasaTodd.com • SocialLEADia.org

CPSIA information can be obtained
at www.ICGtesting.com
Printed in the USA
BVHW010339190820
586749BV00021B/310